Clearing the Air

To Linda and Wendy:

Who not only listen to—but hear—the noises of humanity

Clearing the Air

EDWARD P. MORGAN

ROBERT B. LUCE, INC.
Washington, D.C.

CLEARING THE AIR

*The author wishes to acknowledge his
appreciation to the American Broadcasting
Company for its gracious permission to use
the broadcast material which appears in
this book.*

 Library of Congress Catalog Card Number: 63-9332

MANUFACTURED IN THE UNITED STATES OF AMERICA

VAN REES PRESS • NEW YORK

Table of Contents

THE OPENING COMMERCIAL

I—THE AMERICAN SCENE

The Senator and the Squirrels   1
The Literary Bug Doesn't Bite   2
A Plug for Piety   4
It's the High-Octane Gypsy in Me   6
Nix Deus Ex Machina   7
Where Is Slap-Happy Week?   9
We Are Cooking with Gastronomy   10
Candy Bars for the Refugees   12
Billboard and Beer-Bottle Scenery   13
The Miracle of Queens Village   14
A Bomb Fell on Carolina   16
It's a Small World   18
Soliloquy on a Sack   20
Cherry Blossoms, Orchids, and Poison Ivy   22
The Power of Negative Thinking   24
Jefferson and the Foot-Long Hot Dog   26
Be Sure to Sterilize Your Christmas Cards   28
Truth or Consequences   30
A Powerful, Lovely Lobby   32
The American Gospel   34
Don't Just Call Me Al   36
Through Blaze and Blizzard, the Bets Must Get
    Through   38
The Vicious Virtues of Varsity Sport   41
Wrong Number   43
Move Over, Lysistrata   46
Where Are the True Disbelievers?   48

Something for Nothing, Incorporated   50
Johnny's Parents Can't Read, Either   52
How to Build a Monstrosity   55
Uglifying America the Beautiful   57
We'd Better Pray for the Pious Hypocrites   60

II–POLITICS
Diapers, Demagogues, and the District of Columbia   63
Quaking with Security   65
Politics Begins at Home   67
Knighthood Never Flowered like This   68
How to Win Elections   70
Those Subversive Harvard Republicans   72
Flaps Down on the Flighty Right Wing   75

III–PRESS, RADIO AND TELEVISION
The Voice Thrower   79
Which Toni Is the Phony?   80
Listen to the Listeners   82
Forgive Us Our Press Passes   84
That's a Silly Question   86
We Pause for a Message to the Sponsor   88
Who Will Be Left to Print What's Fit?   90
Through Murky Channels and Wavering Wave
    Lengths   92
Pique-a-Boo at the White House   95

IV–PEOPLE
The Met Makes the Grade   97
Death of a Salesman–of Fear   99
Salute to the Salty Twang of Truth   101
A Towering Man   103
Salute to a Socialist   105
The Loss of a Man   107
The Curious Impact of Ike   109
Death in the Morning   111
Long Live Walter Mitty   114
On a Beauty and Beastliness   116
Darkness in July   118
Disquieting Developments Along the Potomac   121

V—LABOR AND MANAGEMENT

Collier's Christmas Present	125
Dave, the Goliath	127
The Case of the Bouncing Charter	129
Teamsters off the Team	131
Ghost Town	133
Where Does Culture Come Off Here?	135
Business as Usual?	137
I Didn't Raise My Boy to Be a Miner	140
A Simple Man	142
A Futile Family Feud	145
Who Wants to Join a Union?	147
Improve Those Shining Hours	149
Confidence Men	152

VI—CENSORSHIP

Through the Brass, Darkly	155
Horseman on Foot	157
Freedom Is More than Academic	159

VII—HOLIDAYS AND HEROES

Do We Know the Next Unknown Soldier?	163
Sane Fourth in Mad World	165
A Tower for Taft	167
A Certain Fabulous Fellow	169
Commemorating a Cataclysm	171
And Now, Back to Jesus Christ	173

VIII—CIVIL RIGHTS

The Missiles of Hate	177
A Matter of Understanding	179
SMU Survives Subversion	181
Contact Through a Storm	182
A Scenario of Paramount Importance	185
The Blue Yonder of the Cosmos	187
Democracy Is More than a Gag	189
Christ and George Singlemann	192

IX—A REPORTER ABROAD

Journalist Lost in the Jungle 195
Storm Signal in Siberia 197
Marble and The Masses 200
With Socrates at the Summit 202
"Lafayette, We Are—er—Here!" 204
Blue Reflections on the Danube 205

X—INTERNATIONAL AFFAIRS

Happy Birthday, Everybody! 209
An Oily Arabian Knight 211
Light for the Dark Continent 213
Is the Free World a Bargain? 215
But What Echoes from the Satellite? 217
Wanted: Some National Self-Respect 219
Yes, Virginia, There Is a World 221
The Peace Corps Scores 224
And How Guiltless Are We? 226

XI—STRICTLY PERSONAL

Check the Baggage, or Carry It? 229
Ode to a Watermelon 230
On Tulips and Test Tubes 232
Mother Nature Deserves an Item 234
Savor That Flavor, Man 236
The "Andrea Doria" 238
Don't Smile, Damn You 249
A Toast to Anger 251
We Haven't Come Far from the Fish 253
The Cause of the Human Spirit 255
Something Keeps Bothering Me 257
Call the Doctor, Roll Out the Couch 258
Tyranny Starts Small 259
Never Mind How My Garden Grows 262
Have We Really Got Rhythm? 264
Think—with Supple Minds 266

Foreword

THE OPENING COMMERCIAL

I AM WRITING from memory now, trying to retrace the long ravines and hummocks of experience that led me here. I am not sure I know; there was no travel plan. I don't remember ever having proclaimed that I was going to grow up to be a reporter in Washington. "A train engineer" was my stock answer when people asked me what I wanted to be. I must have meant it, because going somewhere seemed so important. It still does.

Thirty years—a bare twinkle in time—I have plied a reporter's restless trade, through most of the alleys and the avenues of it. Yet I boggle at the sweep of events caught in it: those years from the Great Depression to the questionably Affluent Society, from radio's cat-whisker crystal set to Telstar, from popgun defenses to Polaris, from a world the League of Nations couldn't hold together to a world the United Nations is trying to keep from being blown apart.

For the last third of those three decades, I have had the instructive, rewarding assignment of reporting the daily news from Washington—mostly by radio—and adding a ramble of comment upon it. This book is a selection of these comments. There are no scoops, no "exclusives" here. They are, rather, one reporter's daily reactions to events and the people who made them. Every now and then, I find, I have made a pilgrimage to the premises of fantasy or to the reassuring acreages of Nature—whereto every man must flee, from time to time, a fugitive from the madness of civilized affairs.

When I originally composed these essays, I was not conscious of cutting them to fit any particular pattern. Now that I look back at them, I am somewhat surprised to find that perhaps the most persistent themes are anger and impatience; humans have a way of being their own worst enemies, and in their cussedness they too often manage to do things *to* each other instead of *for* each other. But my indignation is intertwined with a stubborn hope that somehow we are learning from our struggles. If we can remember not to take our pompous selves too seriously or too self-righteously, we may still muddle through. This is a gamble, but we must risk it.

There seemed nothing particularly risky about my private world when I started off to college in the late twenties. I don't remember having had very clear, determined thoughts about anything. By this time I did carry with me a vague, transitory idea of becoming a doctor; Warwick Deeping's *Sorrell and Son* had laid a mood of dedication mistily upon me. Then I all but flunked freshman chemistry, and that was the end of that. In the rocky bottom of the depression, I got a job as a cub reporter on the sports staff of the *Seattle Star*—now defunct. It was not exactly a job. It was more an apprenticeship emeritus. I received a press card and later a precious byline, but no wages. This went on for six months. Finally, in a heroic manipulation of the *Star*'s budget, I was put on the payroll at $15.00 a week.

I think I have always loved and hated writing with almost equal ardor. There can be music in the cadence of words. The clean brush of a sentence can color an idea with bold, articulate power or reproduce a panorama of events with depth and meaning. But this never came easily for me. Writing is still a cruel exercise, the hardest work I know. The look, the feel, and the mood of things have always seemed as important to me as the hard facts. In Honolulu, as a United Press correspondent in the mid-thirties, I covered the pioneering of commercial air service across the Pacific. The day Pan American flew its first clipper ship from California to Pearl Harbor, I was less interested in the fuel consumption and the welcoming festivities than in a queenly old Hawaiian woman who moved majestically up to the flying boat, as it was being hauled up the ramp, and patted its silver side with incredulity and affection.

In Honolulu I got my first taste of broadcasting—a two-minute description for NBC of a major eruption of Mauna Loa after I had flown around the volcano on the island of Hawaii aboard a Navy PBY patrol plane. It was amazing to me how much could be told about an event in 120 seconds and how far the words could carry, moving strangers on the mainland to report that they had heard the story. I still find something rather magical in the intimacy radio produces between an unseen voice and an anonymous listener. Radio then was the medium of excitement and glamor, but I did not manage to get back to it—except for a few BBC broadcasts from London to North America during the war—until the summer of 1946, when I did some reporting for CBS from Germany.

In the United Press the emphasis was more on speed than on depth. I remember the messages of praise (but no raise) that came my way when I was lucky enough to beat the opposition services by two minutes on the assassination of Leon Trotsky in Mexico. This seems a meager margin to crow about, but such narrow differences often determine which news service gets the play in the papers. How envious I was of the authority and easy importance with which celebrities like H. V. Kaltenborn, John Gunther, and Eric Sevareid dispatched their broadcasts as they moved through Mexico to more active fronts.

I eventually got to the combat areas myself. As a war correspondent for the *Chicago Daily News* Foreign Service, I was scared to death most of the time—whether in an air raid in London or with the troops toiling up the leg of Italy below Rome. What absorbed me most were not the vast panoramas of war, but the little dramas of chaos and courage, of tragedy and numb but preposterous perseverance which the civilians were caught up in. Many of my colleagues reported the war in terms of high adventure and won Pulitzer prizes for their brave dispatches, but I was overwhelmed by the enormity of it and could only grapple with the little things, clutching at them as if to keep them from being swept away from my senses.

In peace or war, life is harsh, with long stretches of dullness, with fleeting respites of richness and beauty, a struggle tangled with joys and sorrows, with small triumphs and personal tragedies that may be unidentifiable in the mass, but are the very skeins of individual existence. Where is this not so? I have come to think that this is an important point of departure for a reporter trying to relate the world's events and trying to engage people's interest in them.

The world is a package of common experience. Yet its hates and fears, loves and hopes are compartmentalized first by continents and then by national boundaries, again by sections and states, tribes and families, separated from each other by the prejudices of ignorance. I have a theory that ignorance is a deeper root of evil than money. But ignorance, irony of ironies, is the platform for almost everybody's education. Rare is the citizen who was brought up free of the narrow, confining brand of his tribe, familial or political, religious or racial, a kind of introspective imprint in which history is refracted through a prism of prideful defensiveness or self-justifying ambitions.

Somewhere along the line, I seem to have developed an impatience with this narrowness and a conviction that it is needless and troublesome. I cannot detach myself from the angry feeling that social injustice (whether springing from it or from other causes) is a personal affront. Some, no doubt, will object that this is a crusading, missionary approach to journalism and not an objective one. There is some truth to this. While I vigorously (and successfully) rebelled against my mother's ambition for me to become a preacher as her father, Edward Anson Paddock, was, I admired him vastly. It is not impossible that I inherited some of the zeal of that hearty man from the Wisconsin woods, who, at the turn of the century, invaded the mining-boom saloons of Leadville and Cripple Creek with hymn books and who built seven Congregational churches with his own hands in various parts of the West before he died at the age of ninety-four. I am quite sure that it was my grandfather who awakened in me an admiration for Lincoln. Granddad, as a raw and inexperienced soldier in the Union Army, had seen him once, and was fired by the figure of that tall, craggy man and his lonely trial with the presidency.

As for objectivity, I have long believed that we aggressive occupiers of the Fourth Estate have stretched that virtue into unrecognizable shape by our strenuous claims for it. There is probably no such thing as pure objectivity. It would be more accurate (if not more objective) to measure our balance by the

xii

degrees to which we are able to control our subjectivity in this business of dealing so intimately with human conflict. In any case, I think the cynical posture of aloofness we reporters often develop is really a false front to hide our personal involvement with the story, and that we and journalism would both be better off if we shed it.

I won't say that it was the siren wail of a Union Pacific freight train that pulled me beyond the Weiser Valley of the Snake River in southwestern Idaho, but it helped. At least, before the train slid from sight around the base of Indian Head and across the river into Oregon, it left a trail of haunting sound and beckoning white smoke for a boy to dream about. Otherwise, the chores of mowing the lawn, weeding the peonies, and picking the currants would have been unbearable.

And, when my journeys did begin, the train was the long black cartridge of adventure, shooting along a steel trajectory to far and wonderful targets. I haven't been able to sleep on a train for years, but in those earlier days a Pullman berth was a moving snuggery. Between the buttoned green curtains (hushing more the soft pad of the porter in the aisle) and the fleeting glimpse of the darkened landscape through the window (the small string hammock stuffed with shirt and underwear swaying gently across the glass), between those wonderful walls a stream of consciousness rushed along happily with the train. Then the hypnotic rhythm of the rails took over and drew the eager traveler down into a soft tunnel of slumber. At daylight (on a train, a boy never awoke later than daylight), a clanging stop to load milk cans, and the sleeper, aroused, brushed the cinders off the pillow, rubbed the steam off the window, and looked out with a pounding heart at new country. The train window was an explorer's periscope to a boy struggling to surface on larger, stranger seas.

Then came the piston planes, and now the jets, shrinking oceans to puddles and allowing a reporter to absorb the look, the feel, the smell, and the taste of whole countries in a week's time.

The planet has already been shrunk to a neighborhood, whose inhabitants are obliged to rub shoulders with increasing intimacy; but too often their contacts are more hostile than perceptive—like a subway crowd at the rush hour. New people and new places, strange new sights and sounds are being flashed on our consciousness so fast that frequently we do not see what we are looking at and do not listen to what we hear. To me there is a growing urgency to understand our world. The facts themselves are not enough. They must be swung into focus so that their dimensions engage people and enable them to see—as they spin through their private orbits—that their personal spheres *are* related.

Somehow radio seems peculiarly tuned to this mission. It is, on the whole, far less confining and far less distracting than television (except for "live" coverage of major events, in which TV can be superb). Regular TV news programs—at least those B. C. S. (Before Communcations Satellite)—are too often limited to film strips of fires and bathing beauties and shots of dignitaries arriving at and departing from airports with vapid remarks.

Radio, on the other hand, allows the listener not only mobility of physical movement—from the kitchen to the car, from the bedroom to the ball park—but mobility of mind as well. A kind of magnetic field is set up, in which ideas move fluidly and word pictures, clearly drawn, can mean more than photograph or film. Radio can alert the inner ear and the mind's eye to broad horizons in a twinkling. Given this wonderful flexibility, it seems downright criminal to me that it is not more meaningfully exploited. Instead, the air waves are saturated with musical junk, the flotsam and jetsam of jellied love songs, deadening drum beats and wailing horns, punctuated every hour on the hour with capsuled headlines wrapped in the tone of doom, and sliced with impassioned sales pitches for nostrums to control body odor and regularize the bowels.

News should be reported "live." It doesn't keep well when "canned" or prerecorded. I have had to improvise exceptions to this in order to meet deadlines while traveling. The formula is a simple one and has served me well from Walla Walla to New Delhi. A broadcast circuit is leased from, say, Vienna, site of the Kennedy-Khrushchev meeting, to New York and Washington. I use it to report my lead story and commentary in advance of actual air time, but leave a "hole" of several minutes in the middle, so that, when the tape is actually broadcast, an ABC colleague reports from Washington "live" to fill the hole with headline stories I didn't have. Only three times out of seven major journeys to Africa, Europe, and Asia did I fail to get my part of the program through—once from Khartoum, once from Leningrad and once from Novosibirsk in Siberia. The failures were due to a combination of political and technical problems.

John Crosby once said I had "one of the most enviable jobs around." I marvel at and revel in the freedom with which my network, the American Broadcasting Company, and my sponsor, the AFL-CIO, allow me to report and comment on the news—even to the extent of biting the hands that feed me if an unfavorable opinion of the company or broadcasting or organized labor seems necessary. The only unenviable thing about the assignment is its uniqueness. I wish other networks and other sponsors would give more of my colleagues equal freedom.

I realize that such freedom carries heavy responsibility with it. This involves the exercise of the fairest judgment possible and a constant alertness against the ever-present danger of becoming enchanted with the sound of one's own voice. Where I have fallen down on both counts, I have tried to balance the errors with corrections and have punctured my own pomposity by laughing at myself on the air.

I hope this shows up in the pieces that follow in this book. I do believe that everybody would feel better if we adopted as a national calisthenic the practice of deflating stuffiness with good humor, of penetrating pretense with honest fact, and curling back prejudice with the patient strength of reason.

One of the things that bothers me most about my job as a correspondent in Washington is how little I know about matters of vast importance and how my knowledge continues to shrink as these matters become more and more technical and complicated. A leading Washington journalist once asked Mr. Justice Felix Frankfurter how a reporter should go about picking his way through the labyrinth of the Pentagon, how he could apply his uninformed judgment to the arguments about military services, missile systems, weapons testing, and disarmament—just to name a handful of items. His answer was, in effect, that a layman couldn't be expected to follow all the esoteric data of the scientist or the technician, that therefore he had to seek out somebody in the field whom he could trust and then be guided by his counsel and common sense.

I know of no better approach to the problem, but it means a lot of inconclusive conclusions on my part. I would love to be the pundit who expertly culls the blacks from the white, the right from the wrong, the hero from the villain, and the wheat from the chaff, but I am not so decisively equipped. This is by way of warning that in the pages ahead will be found no ringing pronunciamento about the line our foreign policy must take, what went wrong at Valley Forge, or how the farm problem should be handled. I do not even hold any deep convictions on the selection of our national flower, although Senator Paul Douglas' nomination of the corn tassel attracts me for more reasons than one.

What follows, rather, is a collection of one man's wonderment about our soft lives and hard times, of alternating complaints and cheers over the behavior and behaviorisms of people. On occasion, I am impelled to conclude that we Americans are living in and recklessly contributing to a kind of modern decline and fall of the Roman Empire. I am shocked at our wastefulness and selfish lust for things. I am pained by both our thoughtless and conscious cruelties. I am outraged by the arrogant hypocrisy of bigots and professional patriots, and I grieve over the staggering damage they so needlessly wreak.

Then—almost in the next breath—I thrill to the power and richness of this lovely land and the capacity for goodness of its people. I am awed by our generosity to struggling new nations while we attempt to adjust ourselves to the awful uncertainties of the age. Perhaps most of all, I am humbled by and grateful for the brave, determined battle which the American Negro is fighting for all of us, to enhance the dignity and advance the liberty of man. Nowhere, it seems to me, does the struggle for human freedom mean more to us than in the one taking place right here at home, within our fifty states and before our very eyes.

A man is a mosaic of influences, the fragments lifted from the knowledge and experience of other men. In reflection, I discover, unsurprisingly, that those who taught me most about what to put into a microphone shared two striking traits: discontent and anger. But it was enlightened (did some poet say divine?) discontent and purposeful anger by which such tireless goaders of the public conscience as Edward R. Murrow, Howard K. Smith,

Eric Sevareid, and the late Elmer Davis have registered their impacts. I owe them and others much. John Gunther, who probably has done more than any other man to take the stuffiness out of current history, showed me the value of the odd fact, the little splash of color, to bring the warmth of human interest to important but otherwise dull political accounts. I never knew an editor with more empathy for his proud charges and their problems than Carroll Binder, who directed the *Chicago Daily News* Foreign Service when it was at the height of its prestige and influence. And long before I enjoyed—too briefly—his friendship, I had drawn from the rich and ridiculous lore of James Thurber the invaluable lesson that one of the best ways to penetrate the jungles of civilization is to go armed with the lance of sardonic humor, tracking down the ubiquitous humbug, running through the stuff-shirted wild bore and bagging the puff-breasted piffle bird along the way.

There is an added premium of inspiration and wisdom (and sometimes madness) in electronic journalism that is less accessible to newspaper and magazine writers: letters from listeners. Perhaps it is because the voice is a more personal instrument than the linotype, but people seem to respond more copiously and vividly to broadcasts than to matter spread before them in print. My mail is modest in volume, but utterly fascinating in content. A man from Colorado once sent me a package which looked alarmingly as if it housed a bomb. The contents turned out to be a round, rare (and delicious) type of watermelon, in tribute to an essay (included in this book) which I had done on that incomparable fruit. Not long ago a lady in New Jersey sent me a cake of home-made, nondetergent soap, in gratitude for a broadcast in which I had described the plight of Long Island residents whose drinking-water supply was being invaded by the sudsy surplus of detergent waste seeping through the ground.

There have been requests from high-school girls to help them write their English themes, appeals from invalids to notify somebody of their plight, telegrams from armchair strategists dictating what move President Kennedy should make next in the cold war, and now and then (usually after a broadcast about racists or the radical right) a telephoned invitation to drop dead.

But the great preponderance of these messages is in sober,

xvii

serious vein from citizens of all ages in all parts of the country who are demonstrably concerned about the fate of the republic and the fate of the world. I would be starved for ideas without the vital nourishment of these moving and voluntary communications. They have comprised the most rewarding part of this bountiful assignment. I never cease to get excited over what a letter from a listener represents: the establishment of a circuit of communication, one way by microphone, one way by mail. I get fidgety with guilt if these messages are not individually answered.

For they represent, to me at least, not just lonely souls longing for somebody to talk to (and who from time to time does not share that longing?); they represent the hidden strength of America, the quiet, durable, thoughtful people—a minority themselves, but an influential minority—who face their own personal crises and still have time to look farther down the street, across town, and over more distant boundaries at the problems of society as a whole. These are the people the politicians and the pundits and the preachers should talk—and listen—to. For they—not the crackpots, the calamity howlers, the demagogues, or the sycophants—they are the custodians of the American revolutionary tradition, which can make us great, but has not yet done so.

At the risk of being indicted for the serious double crime of pomposity and presumptuousness, I would suggest to a budding journalist that he address himself to this audience. Surely there is something more to the big business of mass communications than superficial fact and bland opinion, purveyed synthetically by a personality with a pear-shaped voice, something more than colorless columns of newspaper monopolies, whose publishers run them like supermarkets, whose profits are vastly more important than information or the intelligent provocation of honest controversy. Surely it is an insult to the intelligence of a thoughtful people to settle for this.

The power of an idea can generate more energy, if given a chance, than a hydrogen bomb. I can think of no more maddening—or inspiring—dilemma than the one we face in the second half of the twentieth century: For the first time in history, civilization has at hand the means and wherewithal to feed and clothe and shelter and mature the population of the world peaceably—and it

xviii

insists on fiddling recklessly with utter destruction. Are my anger and impatience misplaced regarding this monstrous paradox?

What is our message to the world in this age of instant image by satellite? Television commercials? Westerns that bushmen in Nigeria come into the clearings to see on community TV? Headlines on the latest revelations of that lay evangelist of the fertilizer circuit, Billie Sol Estes? News of some business complex's newest perversion of the profit motive or Jimmy Hoffa's latest corruption of the ideals of trade unionism? The recurrent outrages of the white supremacists against civil rights, or the house-haunting, witch-burning antics of that sad little group of superpatriots huddled on the creaking edge of the radical right?

The message of America is not this tawdry stuff (which *Pravda* and Radio Moscow gleefully and profitably traffic in), but a message of revolution that no Communist transmitter can successfully jam: the revolutionary example of a democratic society of free men recognizing its problems and solving them openly, with enough courage and wisdom to spare to inspire others, and enough generosity to help that inspiration along.

We have all the ingredients to do this, and shoot the moon, too, but it gains us little to pierce the envelope of the earth's atmosphere in search of new worlds to conquer if we allow the operation to divert us from the fact that we still have so much to master and set right in our own back yard.

This, in the aggregate, I guess, is what the pieces in this book are all about.

EDWARD P. MORGAN

Washington, D.C.
1962

The American Scene

THE SENATOR AND
THE SQUIRRELS

March 22, 1955

IN THE SENATE this afternoon, Oregon's Senator Richard Neuberger noted that this is National Wild Life Week and launched a "save-the-White-House-squirrels-fund." He quoted news reports that President Eisenhower was having the squirrels caught and carted away because they scratch up the presidential putting green.*

"I strenuously protest this undertaking," the Senator said in a carefully researched fifteen-minute speech. According to the Library of Congress biologist, he said, "Few mammals are better loved than the gray squirrel." Neuberger announced that the fund, to which he personally donated $25.00 as a starter, would finance an aluminum fence to protect the President's golf green from any ravages by these furry little fellows. There was one catch. The fund would operate only if the trapping and deportation of White House squirrels ceased immediately.

A bit of a duffer himself, the Senator sympathized with Mr. Eisenhower's fondness for golf. He conceded that the exacting White House job calls for relaxation. "But surely," he commented, "a few squirrels on the White House lawn need not spoil the

* The putting green is still there (though President Kennedy prefers the swimming pool), and the squirrels are back, which would please Dick Neuberger. The Senator, who died of cancer in 1960, was a true liberal and a passionate conservationist. As he told me before his speech, he knew, rightly, that he would be accused of headline-hunting, but he thought it would do no harm and, besides, he really did feel for the squirrels.

1

President's practice putts and pitch shots." Neuberger said that he understood such golfers as Hogan, Nelson, and Snead played tolerably well without requiring the mass eviction of squirrel populations from their respective fairways.

"The American people love animals because animals love us," said the Senator—giving people the benefit of the doubt. He noted that the White House squirrels were neither Republicans nor Democrats and that their ancestry stretched back to the days of John Quincy Adams, maybe earlier.

But now the line is broken. No longer do the squirrels scamper down the trunks of White House trees and across the lawn to take a peanut thrust by a child's hand through the iron fence. Not only are squirrels being captured, Neuberger said, but their homes are being removed from the trees. He pictured whole families of squirrels being torn apart, mothers and fathers separated from their offspring, brothers and sisters banished to parts unknown.

Neuberger resented this, not as a senator, he said, but as an everyday, run-of-the-mill citizen. A little piece of the White House belongs to every American, he told the Senate, adding, "I don't want my piece of the White House to be without squirrels."

There were chuckles from the gallery as Senator Neuberger spoke, and at one point Senator Barkley broke in to quote the Bible: "The birds have nests and the foxes have holes," the ex-Veep said deliciously, paraphrasing his Matthew, "but the son of man hath not where to putt."

THE LITERARY BUG
DOESN'T BITE

August 15, 1955

PERHAPS you remember the gag about the fellow who wanted to buy his friend a book for a present, and the friend said, "No thanks, I've read a book." Well, it seems they're going to have to revise that joke, downward, and it becomes more ironic than funny. According to a recent Gallup poll, the so-called typical

American has not read a book—any book—save the Bible—in a year or more.*

Seventy-three per cent of the adults Dr. Gallup polled had not read a book in the last month. Sixty-one per cent had not read a book in the last year. Presumably, this did not include comic books.

This, of course, is wonderful news. It removes the bothersome necessity of book-burning or of book-branding. Since nobody reads anything anyway, these safeguards against allegedly subversive literature can be abandoned, and the time and effort and money saved can be diverted to something even more useful, like research in thought control. This research will come in the nick of time, because, if a job prospect hasn't read anything, the investigators checking him as a possible security risk will consider it more important than ever to find out whether he has thought anything. Naturally, if he hasn't thought anything or read anything, he will be the perfect, risk-proof employee.

But we mustn't let cynical contemplation of this monstrous readership statistic carry us too far afield. Liberals may be tempted to conclude, with a certain vindictive pleasure, that the late unlamented scourge called McCarthyism withered people's reading habits, too. There is no comprehensive proof of this. Bookworms may blame television, but figures indicate neither TV nor other diversions are guilty. Seven times more books were sold in the United States in 1954 than in 1929.

Even so, the Gallup poll reveals a chronic condition, rather than a suddenly acquired quirk in the often cockeyed way we Americans do things. For instance, another survey shows that in Great Britain, where the typical citizen has far less formal schooling than the typical citizen here, three times as many people read books as do in the United States.

Why? The managing director of the American Book Publishers Council, Dan Lacy, has a partial answer. Books in this country, he says, are a good deal harder to get at than they are in Britain and elsewhere. How many bookstores would you guess there are in this country, that is, not counting drugstores or gift shops, but bookstores with a reasonably adequate stock and equipped to

* These figures were only slightly improved in 1962.

order your book if they haven't got it? In the entire nation, according to Lacy, there are a mere fifteen hundred such book-shops.

How many Americans would you guess had no access to a library? Thirty million, says the Publishers Council—mostly in rural areas. This is a fifth of the country's total population. Another two-fifths, Lacy estimates, have woefully inadequate library service. Three-fifths of the population of the most powerful nation in the world without adequate access to a book! A bill to finance library-service programs in rural areas has been kicking around in Congress for years without decision.

Admittedly, we do consume millions of magazines and news-papers and, presumably, listen occasionally to news and comment on the air. This is good, as far as it goes, but it doesn't go far enough.

A book is the only place I know in which you can examine a fragile thought without breaking it, or explore an explosive idea without fear it will go off in your face. It is one of the few sources of information left that is served up without the silent black noise of a headline, the doomy hullabaloo of a commercial. It is one of the few havens remaining where a man's mind can get both provocation and privacy.

We're a great nation. We've come a long way as we are. But who knows what would happen if we read a book?

A PLUG FOR PIETY

September 12, 1955

LIKE MOST other things in America, religion has grown big, or at least the outward manifestations of it have. But how solid is this expansion in an intrinsic sense? How real is it? If we are getting more churches and more people are joining them, why are such things as crime and juvenile delinquency on the increase? Why is there a drop in so-called morality? In England, church-going is said to have declined drastically, but morals are not perilously crumbling. Are Americans guilty of some hypocrisy? According to the Gallup poll, only forty-six per cent of the adult

4

population attended church "regularly" in 1954. Why did they attend? Thirty per cent said the main reason was fear—unrest, uncertainty of the future.

This thirsty quest for what has come to be labeled as "peace of soul" or "peace of mind" has produced some highly controversial results. From his pulpit in the All Souls' Unitarian Church in Washington yesterday, Dr. A. Powell Davies ° preached a sermon sharply barbed with satire. "Try God, folks," he said, "He will clear away your troubles in a twinkling. Works for you while you sleep. . . . Cures your worries instantly. Nothing for you to do and so inexpensive. Remember the name, folks! God—G-O-D, easy to pronounce, easy to remember, easy for you in every way."

Thus, this Unitarian leader ridiculed the growing tendency to swallow religion like a vitamin pill and deplored what he implied were the superficial ministrations of such ministers as Dr. Norman Vincent Peale, who has been described as the most successful Protestant clergyman of our time. After his sermon, Dr. Davies explained he was not making a personal attack on Dr. Peale, but on what might be called religion-by-slogan and the public's inclination toward it. "What people want," he said, "is to feel good without being good. . . . Peace of mind should only properly come when you are doing right."

Dr. Peale's message of the "power of positive thinking" has been proliferated by virtually every known medium, including radio, television, books, magazines, and phonograph records, many of which can be bought conveniently in his own church in New York City. His followers may take exception to Dr. Davies' remarks. Others may take exception to the remarks of at least three clergymen in New York City yesterday. They were skeptical about the quality of the apparent revival of religious "faith," and questioned the effectiveness of evangelism, such as that of Billy Graham.

Such questioning is bound to produce discussion, even argument. If conducted on a respectable plane, debate can only invigorate and clarify the subject of religion at a time when people, including preachers and politicians, are inclined to be falsely pious or piously false about it.

° Dr. Davies, a gentleman of great militance, died in 1957. His provocative sermons became so popular that additional rooms in his church were wired for sound to take care of the crowds.

5

IT'S THE HIGH-OCTANE
GYPSY IN ME

October 6, 1955

THIS IS AN astounding country. We seem to be a combined nation of nomads and stay-at-homes—of motorized gypsies who tour from coast to coast and people who have never budged beyond the county seat.

A new superhighway slashes through the hinterland; quickly there begins an unending parade of giant trucks, trailers, and private cars from everywhere, leaving the acrid perfume of rolling rubber, carbon-monoxide-laden air, and the winding black path of oil drip along the right of way. Not everybody has been caught up in this vortex of motion, yet. In a less than two hours' drive from the national capital, for example, you can find families along the Blue Ridge who have never been out of sight of the farm, and they may or may not be able to read and write. Yet just down the road a piece from them may be a supermodern motel, advertising individual television, private ceramic bathrooms, and wall-to-wall carpeting. I will leave it to the sociologists and the historians to assess the permanent changes these swollen veins of travel are going to make on our folkways and mores. But even the passing motorist is staggered by the size of this movement of octane-propelled traffic and the general growth and change it seems to reflect.

When I was younger and toured overnight in a Model T, we slept by the side of the road or in a tourist camp. Now, every twenty-four hours, motorists spend three million dollars in motels —that is an annual gross to this amazing new industry of more than a billion a year. According to the American Automobile Association, four billion dollars have already have invested in fifty-two thousand motels across the face of the United States, and fifteen hundred new ones, on the average, are springing up every year.*

* Although many have folded, motels are still multiplying, and the trend is toward bigger ones. By the end of 1961, the U.S. counted sixty-three thousand motels, thirty-five per cent of which contained fifty to one hundred units; total investment—nine billion, fifty-eight million dollars.

6

I stayed in one of these plush digs the other night, down in the vicinity of Richmond, Virginia. It was confusing. I could not make up my mind whether I was fleeing from the metropolis for a little rustic living or being given the V.I.P. treatment in the Waldorf Towers. I soon found it was impossible to rough it, unless you count breaking a fingernail trying to tear the jacket off a sterilized drinking glass. I might as well have been at the Statler, except that my personalized motel guest room was about half the price.

Here is a partial inventory of what southern hospitality, motel style, has come to. I have already mentioned TV and wall-to-wall carpets. I also got a complimentary bucket of ice cubes, delivered by the manager himself. A sign printed in Old English script, which I first mistook for the Ten Commandments, advised that I could get two cents a gallon off on my gasoline at the adjoining pump. I could have cards, card tables, irons, ironing boards, and sewing kits for my pleasure and convenience. If still able to navigate, I could try croquet, shuffleboard, and swings for the children. If I collapsed, the motel house physician was on call. A reliable baby-sitting service was offered, as well as a glassine stationery bag containing, not only writing paper and colored postcards, but also a mileage chart to principal cities. If I wanted to abandon myself to the seductive atmosphere of my surroundings and overstay my leave, I could forestall guilt feelings and a call from the home office by utilizing a telephone dictation service operated by a stenographer downtown—immediate delivery guaranteed.

Come to think of it, I don't know quite how I managed to make it back to work at the end of my vacation.

NIX DEUS EX MACHINA

November 24, 1955

I NOTE THAT a contestant made a mistake on a quiz show the other night, but won the money anyway because the M.C. did not know the difference. Where else but here can you pick up $32,000 with the wrong answer? This poses the companion questions: Whither are we drifting?—and what are we going to do with our 32,000 bucks in the additional spare time promised us in the mechanized, labor-saving near future?

The Nobel Prize-winning British physicist Sir George Thompson thinks men's brains "will be released from a tangle of hindrances" tomorrow or the next day. He suggests that, if the complexities of civilization seem too much for present-day brains, we can produce bigger and better brains by mutations, man-made changes in our skull department, to cope with the problems of the future.

I submit that there comes a time when you should just leave problems alone and not try to cope. The trouble is, we Americans simply cannot sit still. We have developed a sort of national twitch, ranging from the grim-jawed way we chew gum to the hyperthyroid activities with which we fill our free time.

In an essay on our leisure, the warmly human American philosopher Dr. Irwin Edman wrote before he died that "there is probably no other country in the world where idleness is one of the deadly sins." If we explore leisure, he said, "we may learn still to be at peace long enough to think and dream after our own fashion. We may learn to be expert in some little territory of art or thought or science without losing the amateur touch. We may still find time to live rather than time to kill. If we do, we shall have learned what the spiritual life really means. For it means nothing more than those moments in experience when we have some free glint of life for its own sake, some lovely unforced glimmer of laughter or reason or love."

I suggest we all go out and sin in the Edman manner and be thankful that our minds and spirits are still unmechanized enough to be capable of it.

WHERE IS SLAP-HAPPY WEEK?

December 21, 1955

Do LOOK what the Chamber of Commerce has done for us with a special calendar: We start right out on New Year's Day, plodding our way through the no man's land of hangovers and irresolute resolutions to observe Odorless Decoration Week. This presumes that the Christmas tree will have lost its pungent smell and most of its needles by then, and the house will be due for an airing anyway. During January you can also sink your teeth into the Louisiana yam supper season, Take Tea and See Week, and the glorification of the potato chip.

February and March have been designated as Good Breakfast Months, but, possibly in deference to newlyweds and respect for that household law that practice makes perfect, September has been set aside as Better Breakfast Month. February is loaded with other goodies and occasions, including the interesting cluster of: Groundhog Day; Kraut and Frankfurter Week; Pimento Week; Beauty Parlor, Crime Prevention, and National Defense Weeks simultaneously, followed by National Canned Salmon Week, National Cherry Week, and World Day of Prayer, with Mardi Gras and Valentine's Day tucked in between. After National Peanut Week in March, National Smile Week and National Television Servicemen's Week are celebrated at the same time, if that is possible.

I do not know what wry humorist in the Chamber of Commerce was responsible for placing Mother-in-Law Day, National Noise Abatement Week, and American Comedy Week all on overlapping dates in April. These come during a two-month Spring Festival of Gas Ranges and before Clean Oil Month and Do-It-Yourself Week.

There is a happier juxtaposition of dates in May, with Correct Posture Week, American Camp Week, and Better Bedding Time —all sharing the spotlight together. There might be some quarrel between Foot Health and Let's Go Fishing Weeks, both in mid-

9

May, but American Fresh-Water-Pearl Month stands out glistening and alone in June, like an oyster out of season.

July, August, and September offer such pleasures as Picnic Month, Relaxation Week, Old Stove Roundup Time, and National Sweater Week.

October is the month of conflict. Anti-Freeze Week and Fire Prevention Week come at the same time, tending to cancel each other out. Worse yet, Temperance Sunday comes during National Wine Week, and the United Nations must share observance with the Pretzel and Pass the Laugh Week—whatever that is!

In November, Ice Cream's Chocolate Revue begins, followed by Cat Week, Cranberry Week, Election Day, and, soon after, Optimist Week, just ahead of seven days set aside to pay tribute to caged birds.

During December you can gorge yourself dangerously if you choose, because Holiday Butter Cookie Time and Holiday Eggnog Time have been booked solid for the whole month. You are given only a week to pay tribute to National Prosperity; whether that has any projected post-election significance, I cannot say. I looked desperately for a week the Chamber of Commerce might have set aside as Observe-Nothing-in-Particular Week, but I could not find it.

WE ARE COOKING
WITH GASTRONOMY

November 9, 1956

AN ENTERPRISING *Wall Street Journal* reporter named Victor J. Hillery has scouted a grocery list that is mouth-watering in its way, but certainly a far cry from the grub we sagebrush gourmets used to pick up at the country store. What the housewife is ordering at the corner food mart currently makes a Chinese menu read like supper in a monastery. As you know, Americans have been traveling abroad in record numbers, and this, the *Wall Street Journal* dispatch says, accounts for the whetted national

10

appetite, not only for paté de foie gras and snails, but also for such other tidbits as fried grasshoppers, kangaroo-tail soup, bees in soy sauce, quail eggs, skewered octopus, shark-fin soup, canned wild boar, and, if possible, kissproof garlic.

This newly cutivated palate embraces much bigger groups than just the patrician element of our society. The middle class, the *Journal* reports, is buying more fancy food—from rattlesnake meat to Roquefort cheese—and embellishing its recipes further with rosemary, tarragon, and all manner of other herbs and spices. The demand for fancy foodstuffs has prompted the markets to set up special "party counters," sort of built-in delicatessens, to cater to the trade.

What all this may lead to in a change of national taste is frightening to contemplate, but what is even more disturbing is how these and other more common comestibles are likely to be served to us in the future. No sooner had I finished the *Wall Street Journal* piece, my appetite aching for kangaroo soup and a quail egg, than I came upon a rash of data describing, among other things, the American kitchen of 1976. In the first place, there will be no more standing in line at the checker's counter in the super-market. The lady of the house will simply pick up her television-telephone, look at the things she wants for her larder, and order them sent, according to an article in *Parade*. As for the actual preparation of the meal, it seems to me the cook is going to have to be a combination of Betty Crocker and a graduate of Oak Ridge. Dinner, allegedly, will be prepared in disposable sheet-aluminum receptacles on a marble stove that does not get hot because it utilizes radiant heat conducted by a daub of current-carrying paint. I am frank to say I do not understand any of this, and my heart goes out to the bride of the next generation who flunks electronics. What if she forgets to peel the aluminum off the casserole, or boils her highball instead of the stew?

Still, we stick-in-the-muds must not stand in the way of change. I maintain, nevertheless, that the most delectable meal I ever had consisted of one Idaho potato baked in a jacket of clay under an open bed of glowing coals in a field outside our house, when I was ten. I got smoke in my eyes and I burned my fingers, but it was worth it.

11

CANDY BARS FOR
THE REFUGEES

November 22, 1956

IMAGINE THAT YOU are a Hungarian refugee. Not many days ago, you were beyond the borders of Austria. After having felt the heavy heel first of the Nazis and then of the Communists, you were the more saddened, but not too surprised, when the rebellion that had at last bravely caught fire was smothered. So, with only the clothes you wore and the miserable packet of belongings you could carry, you fled. Somehow, you reached Vienna; and then, marvel of marvels, a plane lifted you across the Atlantic and landed you in the United States of America on the very eve of Thanksgiving. Your feeling of freedom could hardly have had a more poignant thrust into the fullest meaning of the word. Perhaps the whole almost unbearable drama of the occasion was best caught by a single sentence in which one reporter noted that there was no baggage in the cargo compartment of the plane which brought the first sixty refugees to American shores.

And yet how uncomfortably self-conscious our welcome seemed to be. Here were people who had escaped the caldron of tyranny, leaving other brave ones behind. We heaped upon them the standard bounty of candy bars and other packaged merchandise, as if they had just won a television quiz show. And then, as if reflecting our own forgetfulness over the bitter price of freedom, Army Secretary Brucker saw fit to lecture the newcomers on the virtues of good citizenship in our society, and requested them to applaud the American flag and the assembled U. S. officials, while other bureaucrats—for reasons not immediately clear—waited to fingerprint them.

What a shriveled thing this touching occasion could become if we merely roused ourselves to lick its sentiments like a lollipop, and then sank back into the complacency of our comforts. How worthy are we, anyway, as hosts, as custodians of the torch of

12

liberty for which Hungarians have just risked (and thousands lost) their lives?

In the darkness which the Hungarian refugees have fled, the human mind exists in a cubicle of conformity assailed by a religion of terror. They and the others still trapped behind might not have had to risk their lives to burst out of that cell if free men everywhere had thought it worth the effort to guard liberty every time it was threatened.*

BILLBOARD AND
BEER-BOTTLE SCENERY

September 3, 1957

THERE IS plenty to see in this fabulous land. New England, which I accidentally but lamentably had bypassed during my previous travels, is no exception. Indeed, besides its tidy and supremely satisfying Grandma Moses landscapes, New England has something that many other parts of the country do not have— a certain mellowness in age and tradition. The combination of this gentle, quiet, verdant scenic beauty and almost palpable history is a fulfilling experience; you feel somehow that your own private roots in the American heritage are being specially nourished.

And yet this beauty and this heritage are being menaced, partly by shortsightedness, largely by the explosive expansion of the American population. We still have vast areas of wonderful wilderness in the U.S.A., but as the population rockets toward two hundred million, it takes less time for coke bottles and beer cans to litter what we do have left, and there is more opportunity for more carelessly tossed matches and cigarette butts to char more virgin forests. The severe, straight white lines of a New Hampshire village church are being threatened with obscurity in all their sweet, simple grace behind the garish sign of the Bide-

* Since 1956, approximately sixty thousand Hungarian refugees have come to the United States.

a-Wee Motel. The rich scrub-oak, bayberry, and beach-plum wilderness of Martha's Vineyard is being bulldozed because the swollen tourist traffic to this lovely island requires better roads.

I wish the careless congressmen who neglected to ban billboard advertising on the federal-highway complex could have driven with me through Vermont, which has doggedly (though not faultlessly) managed to limit these monstrosities, and then compared with me the uncluttered beauty there with the commercial vulgarities along so many roadsides of, say, Maine.* And so many of New England's once-sparkling streams have been befouled by the wanton dumping of factory refuse.

All of this represents more than a problem of aesthetics. It reflects the bigger problem of American physical growth and the foolhardiness, if not criminal negligence, in not planning for it adequately.

THE MIRACLE OF
QUEENS VILLAGE

January 24, 1958

Tow-HEADED, SIX-YEAR-OLD David Fleming, Jr., of Queens Village, New York, almost died, but he didn't. His was a drama rare in the annals of medicine. Behind it lies the dedication of a little band of skilled, purposeful people who made the impossible happen.

David had a defect in his aorta. At a point where this big vessel descends through the chest to carry the heart's blood to the lower body, the aorta was puckered to a narrow channel. This caused a dangerous swelling, as if from a crimp in a thin garden hose. The problem: to replace the diseased section with a piece of healthy tissue taken from the aorta of a dead man—an extremely delicate and risky operation even if everything went perfectly.

* Federal law says that on new interstate superhighway systems, billboards must be 660 feet from the edge of the right of way. States don't lose money if they don't conform. If they do conform, they get a sweetener in additional federal funds. There are numerous technicalities.

14

Things did not go perfectly. Surgeons at St. Francis Hospital in Roslyn, Long Island, found the aorta had already sprung a leak and the blood had clotted outside it. After David had been on the operating table two hours, the leak burst. The boy began bleeding to death; his heart stopped. Instantly, the chief resident surgeon took the heart in his two hands and began massaging it in an effort to keep the blood flowing to David's upper body, especially the brain.

For nearly three hours, doctors took turns at this tense, tender exercise, while the operating team worked with desperate efficiency on the broken aorta. The six-pint supply of David's type O Rh-negative blood was used up in transfusions. An urgent call had been broadcast for more. It arrived just in time. Fourteen pints were needed in all. Finally, the last stitch was made.

The resident surgeon, Dr. Raj Mahajan, stared at the still heart he was pressing between his hands. "One moment," he recalled, "it was a flabby, dead organ. Suddenly it swelled alive—strong, firm, and pumping steadily."

Today, David Fleming is alive and convalescing, thanks not only to rare good fortune and brilliant surgery, but also to an unmeasurable kind of power generated by co-operation that can, when mobilized, cut through human obstacles to demonstrate that man is still a more marvelous mechanism than any machine or missile he has yet invented.

Dr. Mahajan is a thirty-year-old Hindu from India, who came here in 1951 on a Fulbright fellowship. The surgical director of St. Francis, Dr. Edgar P. Mannis, who was in charge of the operation, and Dr. Edward Braunstein, the chief cardiac surgeon, are Catholics. The assistant cardiologist, Dr. Dorothy Finken, is Jewish. The rest of the medical staff—there were fifteen persons directly involved in the operation—included Dr. Rocco Andriello, lately of Naples; Dr. Oliver French, lately of Oxford, England; and Dr. Thomas Economopoulos, recently of Athens.

St. Francis Hospital, which specializes in cardiac services, has an interesting history itself. Its land was donated by a Quaker; it was planned by a Jew; its present medical director is a Protestant; and its head of surgery, a Catholic.

The public, too, starred in the cast of David's drama. More than 125 persons responded to radio appeals for blood. They were, said

15

Dr. Mahajan, of virtually every possible religion and ethnic origin. This may or may not be an item of interest to a senator from Georgia who is pressing a bill in the state legislature to segregate blood banks.* But the deeply wonderful fact about this story, it seems to me, is that, underneath their many skins, men are capable of pooling their efforts in vast achievement. And if they can revive a heartbeat, what is there, really, that they cannot do, if they are moved to?

A BOMB FELL ON CAROLINA

March 12, 1958

AN ATOMIC BOMB fell on South Carolina yesterday. The warhead didn't explode, but politicians did. Today, Congressman L. Mendel Rivers of Charleston demanded immediate restitution for the damage caused by the TNT trigger of the bomb which shook the whole Mars Bluff community, just east of the city of Florence, demolished one house, and damaged six others and a church. If compensation for such nuclear-age accidents is not already provided for, Rivers wants a law passed to cover it.

Of course, yesterday's damage must be made right by the government, and, of course, Representative Rivers is correct when he says a bomb down on South Carolina is everybody's business; it could happen to almost any hamlet in the land. And certainly we need to be made aware of the hazards of the times in which we live. If that atomic bomb had exploded, Florence and its thirty thousand souls would have been another Hiroshima this morning.

But haven't we, perchance, insisted on fabricating for ourselves a kind of fool's paradise? On this business of defense, haven't we, in effect, been saying to our friends abroad, "Look, we're putting up the money; we're making the financial sacrifice; all we ask you to do is risk your lives." The pressure of our policies has created

* Louisiana and Arkansas make no bones about having segregated blood banks. Practices vary in other southern states, sometimes within counties. Accurate information is hard to obtain.

16

that image of us in the eyes of our allies. Before the bomb dropped on Florence, how many citizens of South Carolina, or any other state, gave a second thought to our English cousins' persisting fears about U.S. Air Force planes constantly patrolling with hydrogen bombs in British skies? *

Two points of major importance emerge from this incident. One is the precariousness of our existence at this nuclearized juncture of history. The second is the incontrovertible fact that we cannot delegate to others the sacrificial uncertainties of this trembling era—we Americans have got to share in the risks ourselves.

Even a military secret cannot be totally insured against a theft by Dame Fortune. An accident happens; souvenir hunters scurry off with classified bomb fragments; and the Air Force may or may not be able to preserve the secret sanctity of this lethal bauble. Accidents are always happening. A similar one, at a missile-launching site or aboard a submarine, could catapult the world into the hydrogen holocaust the scientists have warned us about.

What if Florence, South Carolina, had been Florence, Italy, or East Berlin?

The utter wine-glass fragility of a defense which one mistake, one mishap, could blow up—and most of civilization with it— behooves us to seek a sounder one. If this kind of defense is the best we can devise, Heaven help us. And yet, in looking for a better one, it might be well to keep in mind that security is not an end in itself. Life continues to be a risky business. There is always that banana peel on the sidewalk. If we are prepared to live dangerously, though not recklessly, and accept our share of the risks, we may be able to worm our way out of this explosive dead end that the nuclear-armaments race has reached. But nothing, as the people of Florence, South Carolina, must realize tonight, is certain.

* It is reliably reported that such patrols have been retired since the South Carolina incident, due partly, no doubt, to the increased reliance on Polaris and ICBMs.

IT'S A SMALL WORLD

March 14, 1958

AT DINNER the other evening, a man of some standing in this not completely unworldly town of Washington, D.C., observed that the trouble with us Americans is that we know too much. He pointed an accusing finger at me and said, "You fellows are to blame. If you reporters would quit raking up crises in every corner of the globe and throwing them at us in the paper, on television and the radio, we'd all be better off. Why should we worry about troubles in a lot of unimportant places? We've got problems of our own."

Ignorance, in other words, is not only bliss; it is a way of life. It is a path to mental health and emotional stability. This is an intriguing theory and deserves some thought, but not much. The way to solve the quavering crisis in North Africa is to disengage ourselves and forget about it. The way to end the cold war is to tell the postman we are not at home to any more letters from Bulganin and turn on the Walt Disney show. The way to—but why go on? You get the hang of it: Ostriches of the world, unite! We have nothing to lose but our necks.

Still, there is a factor in this process of nearly instantaneous communication which we must not overlook. Now that our aural and optic senses are exposed almost constantly, not only to international crises, but also to political pratfalls, pestilence, or infinite additional disorders in the remotest corners of the planet, we may become so overwhelmed by the cumulative enormity of the world's problems that we render ourselves incapable of facing up to the simplest of them. The trick is not to deny their existence, but to realize we may not be able to solve them all by breakfast-time tomorrow morning. In fact—a fact tending to nettle the impatient American temperament—it is quite possible we may never be able to solve all the world's problems. This realization could give us heart to tackle more purposefully the ones most imminently at hand, without tripping blindly over the others.

We have color television and satellites and the chemise—or is it the sad sack? What else could we wish for? Well, one of the things we seem to yearn for most is a kind of reverse Aladdin's lamp with which we could wish things away. The *Baltimore Sun* laments editorially that it is being circularized by businessmen, individually and in groups, from many parts of the country, urging it and other papers to publish less about the recession. The theme: "Prosperity depends on confidence. . . . Print just the good news. . . ."

"The course of the present recession," the *Sun* concludes, "will undoubtedly add to the general body of knowledge about such things, but only insofar as the developing facts are recorded for all to see. You can't cure a depression by sweeping it under the rug and pretending it isn't there."

That shatteringly simple truth applies to all the facts of life, and the uglier and more unpleasant they are or the stranger they look, the more it is likely to apply. It is only human nature, I suppose, to prefer the company of the agreeable and the familiar.

There was another aspect of my dinner associate's remark which bothered me. He spoke of "unimportant places." An Ecuadorian head-shrinker could hardly have done a better job in reducing the size of the world than the airplane, the wireless, and now the missile have done. Given its present golf-ball dimension by the measure of modern communications, friendly and unfriendly, who dares to say what acreage of the globe, however backwoodsy, is unimportant? Indeed, henceforth we cannot even gaze upon the moon and the stars as simply shining and twinkling adornments of the heavens. They are potential real estate and, as such, are arenas of new challenge and contention. Returning to our own terrestrial surface, a harassed but perceptive bureaucrat has remarked that, as the world's navigable size has shrunk and its problems grown, there is just no place left where we can afford to send second-rate officials any more. It's a small world, all right, but let us keep tenderly in mind that, for the time being at least, it's the only one we've got.

SOLILOQUY ON A SACK

March 28, 1958

I HAPPEN TO HAVE a habit of looking at girls. This may symptomize some deep psychological disturbance, but the fact is I enjoy it—or did until recently. Now I am caught up in a crisis of confusion. I cannot tell whether the girls who wear the current fashions are coming or going. A colleague of mine recently observed that these devotees of the chemise and the sheath are like the new cars: The front is indistinguishable from the rear. In some instances under my observation, the camouflage becomes absolutely dizzying. For those ladies who have chosen maternity clothes in the mode, the effect is one of carrying a pregnancy backwards, like a papoose.

Victor Hugo was content with creating only one Hunchback of Notre Dame. Now the "hautest" priests of the *haute couture* decree that all our dames become hunchbacks, or that they emerge from the salons as vertical blanket rolls or packaged as parachutes that have failed to open. I encountered one full-page photograph in a style magazine of what appeared to be a tea towel wrapped around a stilt. Actually, the stilt was a model, dying of hunger, bandaged in what the text insisted was a prize from one of the Paris collections—and a prize it was indeed.

For a while, I reasoned that the cause of all this sackcloth and cigarette ashes was the callow carelessness and inexperience of that twenty-two-year-old squirt, St. Laurent, I believe his name is, who now—when he isn't cutting out paper dolls—dominates the house of the late Christian Dior.* But last night, while thumbing through a recent copy of *Vogue*, I stumbled upon the truth. It is all a carefully drawn conspiracy, hatched, I can hardly bear to report, by the current equivalent of the gold digger. With almost arrogant candor, Miss Anita Loos, who immortalized the flapper

---

* After unhappy bouts with both Dior and the French Army, Yves St. Laurent has been making headlines since January, 1962, with a dress line of his own. At last reports, he had taken the female out of the sack and placed her in a tube.

of the twenties by writing about the blondes whom gentlemen prefer, bares the whole plot in a one-page article entitled "The New Vamp."

Miss Loos defines a vamp as "a girl who is intrigued by a member of the opposite sex to a point where she will make an effort to please him." But for these pleasures, gentlemen, she expects something in return, and obviously something containing more carats than compassion. Indeed, Miss Loos seems to underline the callous axiom that diamonds are a girl's best friend. She even states blandly that "girls now prefer jobs to gentlemen," because today "the gifts that gentlemen can afford have degenerated into mere tokens of sentiment, in which there is nothing to gain except the spirit in which they are given. . . .

"I believe it will be delightfully nostalgic," she muses sacrificially, "if girls can forget that the pleasing of gentlemen has become a nonpaying occupation. And that, with the return of the chemise, we may be able to take our minds off jobs and become sentimental over gentlemen once again."

The intrigue here is as plain as the safety belt on a sheath. What Anita Loos is saying is that the girls who left us for careers because we failed to enhance our romantic advances with Van Cleef and Arpels' necklaces are now bored with their jobs and ready to play with us again. But they still have their price—it may well be inflationary despite the recession—and they are simply trying to hide it in what they fancy to be the beguiling folds of the new fashion.

"A chemise," reports Miss Loos, "has the advantage of quite often concealing the female form, and, as a consequence, it supplies girls with an added dimension of mystery." This may well be true, but I find myself sufficiently confused by damsels in nothing bulkier than bikinis.

Still, it is plain that this new crop is going to be ruthless to the extreme. "It should be noted," notes Miss Loos diabolically, "that a girl who is loosely garbed in a chemise can overlook the fact that she is all dressed up, and be herself to a much greater extent."

Run for your lives, men, before we are all sacked by a vamp, or vice versa.

CHERRY BLOSSOMS, ORCHIDS,
AND POISON IVY

April 18, 1958

THIS HAS BEEN an ecstatic but bewildering week for nature-lovers in Washington. Almost overnight, the Japanese cherry trees around the tidal basin have exploded into pink pop-corn balls of blossom. Daffodils are buttering the flowerbeds of Georgetown, and magnolias are gorgeously waxing the yards and parks of the whole capital with opulent tapers of white and pink-ish mauve. But something extra-special has been added to this bower of blooms. Vast hedges of orchids are sweeping through the town in mobile units, converging on the hothouse of Constitution Hall. They are, of course, a special genus of this exotic flora, which springs up annually in Washington at this time of year, its lavish petals of high-blood-pressure purple delicately affixed to the tender stalk of a DAR.

Behind this clever camouflage of the orchid corsage, the vigilant Daughters of the American Revolution, like a commando unit in the Cambodian jungle, move relentlessly against the enemy. In fact, the image is even more apt than first appears. As the trained warrior knows that death may lurk behind every seductive frond of the tropics, so the stealthy shock troops of the DAR know that treason is concealed under every garlanded cherry branch, and they will stamp it out if they have to fell the whole tree of liberty in the process.

If they have been fearless in the past, they have been downright foolhardy with bravery this year on the battlefield of their sixty-seventh Continental Congress. There is almost nothing they have not dared take on in their campaign to preserve the "fruits of freedom," which is the theme of their gathering. They have mounted such a massive offensive that it is difficult to see what they will have left to defend next year. Their achievements make an American Legion convention look like Lenin's hotel room before the October revolution.

Here are some of the sharpest spears of their condemning resolutions. They demand not only that the United States get out of

22

the United Nations, but also that the UN get out of the United States. Foreign aid and reciprocal trade—alien operations that they are—must go. Fluoridation of community drinking water probably should go too; one delegate called it an international plot to weaken America with drugs.

The Supreme Court, of course, must be curbed. Teachers should be forced to take loyalty oaths, and "true American history" should be a required subject in schools; whether there were enough unsubversive true Americans to teach it was not made clear. Amazonian opposition to UNESCO, the World Health Organization, Communist China, and the federal income tax is so traditional for the darling Daughters that it is hardly worth mention.

But they struck out in new fields. They condemned subliminal advertising on television and attacked the National Council of Churches of Christ in America because, among other things, it was for federal aid to education and against the McCarran-Walter immigration act. They are still for the Bricker amendment to curb the President's treaty-making powers, but they oppose the Eisenhower plan to reorganize the Pentagon, and any change in the east front of the national Capitol.

One of their stands would surely bring a benign smile to the ghost of that martyred hero of racial purity, Adolf Hitler. "Racial integrity is a fundamental Christian principle," the descendants of revolutionary purebreds vowed, condemning mixture of races by marriage.

But Republican Congresswoman Katharine St. George of New York was shocked, as am I, that the DAR had recently hired a press agent to improve its relations with the public.* We do not want a thing about these ladies to change, I maintain. We want them for just the anachronistic lovelies that they are. They represent something which is lost. For a moment I couldn't remember what, and then the lines of Elizabeth Akers Allen's poem came to me:

> Backward, turn backward, O Time, in your flight,
> Make me a child again just for tonight.

The name of the poem, of course, is "Rock Me to Sleep." **

* The Daughters still engage a press agent, part-time—a Mr. Dinwiddie.
** First published in the *Saturday Evening Post,* June 9, 1860, and written under the pen name "Florence Percy."

THE POWER OF
NEGATIVE THINKING

April 30, 1958

MAYBE I SHOULD WAIT for Winchell or Hedda Hopper to give you this, but I've got a piece of gossip that just won't keep: The DAR and the United States Chamber of Commerce are going steady. When you stop to think about it, they make a lovely couple. Those Chamber fellows perhaps are not so pretty as the girls of the DAR, but what they lack in sex appeal they make up in fossilized thinking, and that gives the romance a common ground of interest that promises them a long and happy life together.

Pondering this love match a little more, I suppose you'd have to say it really was inevitable. Both the DAR and the Chamber of Commerce meet in Washington every spring just as the birds and the bees and the flowers are at the height of their seductive dirty work. This year the DAR was here with the cherry blossoms. Now the Chamber conclave is in town with the lilacs and the dogwood. Even without this fragrant continuity of floral wonders, the billing and cooing between them would be indubitably sustained, for they speak the same language. Not with the voice of the turtle but with the squeak of the dinosaur, they are happily engaged in trying to frighten each other and the country to death. The hobgoblin of the DAR is really the whole wide world, through which spies and subversionists are chewing like mice through cheese. The spook haunting Chamber businessmen are a little less global, maybe, but no less sinister and take the shape of a socialistic labor movement, lusting for power.

A New York labor-management specialist, Theodore R. Iserman, warned the U.S. Chamber, that the actual power of union leaders today "constitutes a more immediate threat to our way of life than does the military might of Soviet Russia." At roughly the same time he was uttering those words, General Motors somehow managed to wiggle out of Walter Reuther's pocket long enough

24

to announce it was canceling its contract with the United Auto Workers.

Another Chamber speaker, Arizona's Senator Barry Goldwater, boldly called his business audience a bunch of cowards for sitting by and letting labor "socialize" the United States. I had always identified the Senator with what some pundit has labeled the "radical right." Radical, my foot. This man is a veritable anarchist. Listen.

"I don't care where power is," Senator Goldwater said, "whether it is in government or in business or in labor—power is wrong."

As soon as I recovered from the crushing blow of that sentence I staggered to Webster's; I relay to you his definition of anarchy: "the state of society where there is no law or supreme power; a state of political disorder." Synonym: chaos.

But we should be grateful to the Senator and Attorney Iserman for giving us such a candid glimpse of the dream world in which they and their friends of the radical right would like to live. In that world there would be no more big government, no more big taxes, and especially no more big, wicked labor leaders to kick people around. Everybody would virtuously enjoy all the best things in life for free, especially enterprise. Indeed, in his speech Iserman rather projected the Little Lord Fauntleroy behavior the public could expect from businessmen in this Utopia. While labor publications now drench their columns with political bias, he said, he hardly knew of a business house organ that breathed anything more controversial than company softball scores, weddings, deaths, and quarter-century clubs. He bitterly resented the interest of "labor politicians," not only in labor legislation, but also in housing, taxes, education, atomic energy, disarmament, the farm problem, and even foreign affairs—all with a socialized bias, of course.

The trouble with this thinking is that it belongs in another century, say the eighteenth. The free enterprise that Senator Goldwater longs for predates the industrial revolution or at least the conquest of the American frontier. The problem is not to abolish power, but to make the power centers of our society more responsible and responsive to public needs. With all the distance organized labor still must travel in this direction, and the distance is admittedly a long one, I cannot help wondering if it is not making

better and more realistic headway than the U.S. Chamber of
Commerce.

JEFFERSON AND THE
FOOT-LONG HOT DOG

July 28, 1958

CRISIS OR NO CRISIS, recession or no recession, thousands
of Americans are grimly pursuing the exhausting pleasures of
midsummer vacations. Many of them turn to the historic sights
of Virginia, as did this reporter over the week end. There is, of
course, old dependable "Mt. Vernon." "Monticello," the home of
Thomas Jefferson, is even more rewarding in many respects,
although it involves a deeper invasion of the Old Dominion to
Charlottesville.

Complete with nervous dogs and bottle-hungry babies, an endless stream of tourists treks to this lovely place atop its little green
mountain overlooking James Monroe's "Ash Lawn" on one side
and the University of Virginia on the other—both of which Jefferson planned. In shorts and sack dresses, in loud shirts and sun
suits, they brave the sticky heat to snap Polaroid and color shots
of the grand sweep of the lawn and garden. They shuffle patiently
through the rooms of the magnificent mansion, faithfully gathering informational tidbits from the lady guide who dispenses facts
with the tolerant ennui of a retiring history teacher. They gape
and ponder and move along the corridors and pathways once
trodden by Jefferson.

The lively spirit of this extraordinary man permeates "Monticello." Gadget-minded boys of all ages are fascinated with the
clock that runs by cannon-ball weights and ticks off the days of
the week as well as the hours. The females admire Jefferson's
painstaking talent for design, down to the very window curtains.
The well-worn, hardwood writing desk and the ingenious red-
leather swivel chair and leg rest quickly conjure up a picture of
Jefferson sitting there in his study-bedroom attending to his

26

voluminous correspondence, which he did so meticulously and with such grace and interest.

One dares to wonder what this democratic da Vinci of the Western Hemisphere would have thought if he could have peered one hundred and fifty years ahead to our time. In a next-day postscript to a letter he wrote John Adams on August 10, 1815, Jefferson said he had just received news of Napoleon's second abdication, which had occurred some six weeks before. Now, as a visitor retreats from "Monticello" and heads for an air-conditioned motel on the Skyline Drive of the Blue Ridge Mountains, he tunes in on his dashboard to the voice of an American reporter in Moscow. Within the same broadcast, he hears about the latest spite letter in the chain of Kremlin-White House correspondence and about the friendly atmosphere of the U.S.-Russian track meet. Are we better equipped or more inclined to measure the impact of these instantaneous events than Jefferson was to digest a fact that had taken almost two months to reach him?

There are other puzzling questions that separate the Jeffersonian world from ours. The former President surely would have applauded the spectacle of hordes of Americans of almost every economic level exercising their democratic right to travel, to move around. But, without challenging our right, would he not have marveled, with some horror, at our capacity to consume with relish or at least without protest the most execrable food at the most synthetically atmospheric of roadside taverns and chain restaurants? Would not this fastidious revolutionary have been aghast and depressed by our tasteless appetite for the monstrosities in the swarming curio stores and "gifte shoppes" littering the crossroads?

Piffling points, you may say. I do not think so. This tawdriness of taste, this propensity for the foot-long hot dog and the plaster-of-Paris ash tray all reflect a jumbled carelessness of mind about other values—a failure to distinguish between claptrap and quality. Certain aristocrats and diehards argue that mediocrity is the price we pay for the dubious luxury of democracy. Jefferson undoubtedly would refute that, maintaining that we need not lose quality in the midst of quantity if we would only educate the public to be more discerning. Of course, it would quicken the process for the rest of us if there were a few more public figures around with a Jeffersonian sense of values to encourage the educating.

BE SURE TO STERILIZE
YOUR CHRISTMAS CARDS

April 23, 1959

FOR A WHILE THERE I thought the DAR was going to let us down. But O me of little faith! I should have known better. Today these grandmotherly Daughters of the American Revolution, amply manning the breastworks of freedom as usual, reaffirmed their determination to secede from the world and hospitably take the rest of us with them into the safety of their bomb shelters of the past.

Last year, the DAR demanded that the United States withdraw from the United Nations and—to demonstrate that their fairness featured a two-way stretch—they resolved vice versa, too: that the UN withdraw from the U.S. It may have been that the country did not have its hearing aid turned on at the time; at any rate, nothing much happened to indicate that the ladies were being heeded. And since hell's fury cannot match that of a woman scorned, it is unsurprising that the DAR's Sixty-eighth Continental Congress has just trumpeted these demands again in more strident tones.

There was, however, a troubling overtone to the action, hinting that somebody must have been boring from within the very bosom of the DAR. While the secession motion carried with gusto, fairly setting the host of corsages in Constitution Hall aquiver, there was opposition—more of it than on any similar action before. Of the 3,000 voting delegates, more than a hundred rose in the teeth of the gale and voted "no."

As if to purge themselves of subversive elements, the ladies of the majority came out, in a manner of speaking, against children and Christmas. They objected that Christmas cards sold by the United Nations Children's Fund were "devoid of the spirit of

28

Christmas," as interpreted by the DAR. The assemblage criticized UNICEF even more pointedly, alleging that "a very substantial part of its total funds goes to Communist and Communist-controlled countries." That this did not square with the truth did not seem to matter, despite the telegraphed protest of UNICEF Director Maurice Pate. Pate pointed out that 105 countries and territories now receive Children's Fund aid, only two of which—Poland and Yugoslavia—have Communist governments.* He also stressed that, during the last eight years, UNICEF has allocated less than three per cent of its funds to countries with Communist governments. He hardly could have expected to cut any ice with the reminder that Poland and Yugoslavia receive direct American aid, as well; the DAR is stoutly opposed to all those arrangements, too.**

I wonder, however, if both the DAR and UNICEF did not muff a point in this exchange. Are children political activists? Does hunger or rickets or the tuberculosis of a child in a Communist country rate a lower priority in the world scheme of things than a similar malady suffered by a child fortunate enough to live outside the Iron Curtain? These points present challenging possibilities. Here, within the framework of UNICEF, is just about the nearest approach to a functioning, all-inclusive world organization that we have yet achieved, touching more governments than are actually represented at the UN. Its common denominator is just about as nonpolitical as could possibly be conceived: the health and welfare of children. Yet the distribution of this aid, according to the DAR, should be determined by what ticket the youngsters vote, or at least by the political coloration of their home atmospheres. No machine politician, surely, could have drawn up a more efficient pressure system or one, I might add, more likely to explode in the faces of its benign inventors, so insensitive to the realities of human nature and human needs.

But you have to hand it to the good Daughters for their consistency. When they stand for chauvinism, they will not stand

* By 1962, UNICEF aid was going to ninety-eight countries, still including only two with Communist governments, Poland and Yugoslavia.
** But *somebody* listens to the DAR. The Senate banned aid to the Marxist governments in 1962—then Congress eliminated that broad category but put restrictions on both aid and trade with Poland and Yugoslavia.

for anything else. I'm not even sure that they recognize Rotary International. And it just occurs to me that their militant opposition to the Children's Fund clarifies, more than they realize, perhaps, what the DAR interpretation of the Christmas spirit really is.

TRUTH OR CONSEQUENCES

November 2, 1959

IT WAS INEVITABLE, of course, that there would be drama in the staging in the old House office building of that tragic scenario called "The Decline and Fall of Charles Van Doren." There was suspense. Would he demand a closed hearing? He would not, and that guaranteed the excitement of a personal appearance of a celebrity. The plot was sure-fire: a brilliant, personable, promising member of one of America's most distinguished literary families caught in a trap of circumstance, struggling with a moral issue. The climax was moving, even though recent events had telegraphed the outcome. Before a standing-room-only crowd in the cavernous isolation chamber of the ivory-walled caucus room, Charles Van Doren, impeccably dressed in a tailored gray suit, white, button-down, Oxford-cloth shirt and a dark, figured, narrow tie, confessed that he had cheated and lied, and said he was sorry.

There were some unexpected, incidental horrors added to the plot. Instead of crumbling somewhere midway in the program before the temptation of great riches, it turned out that Charles knew the quiz show "21" was fixed before he ever went on it the first time. He didn't like the idea, but he was told nobody was going to get hurt. Little did he know. And not until a fortnight ago, according to his twelve-and-a-half-page prepared statement, did he come to a "full understanding" of what he had done nearly three years ago, and how he must try to undo it, by finally telling the truth.

Some of the investigating congressmen seemed so carried away with relief by this exercise that they invoked their and God's

30

blessings on the handsome witness. But when it came to the turn of Steven B. Derounian, a Republican of Long Island, to question him, Derounian said sternly, "I don't think an adult of your intelligence ought to be commended for telling the truth." Then the gentleman from Arkansas, Chairman Oren Harris, had to gavel for silence in the ensuing applause, while Van Doren sat at the table below him, his head of brown, wavy hair bowed, his blue eyes puffed with emotion and fatigue.

Oh, there was drama, all right, but to this observer the scene was not the kind seen in a theater, but rather in a hospital ward, and it was society, not just the witness, who was sick. Society, in fact, already had the disease before Charles caught it, and one of the most troubling questions about this whole spectacle is how much, if at all, the public leeching of Charles Van Doren's conscience will purify the blood stream of the body politic. I do not know what the medical terms are for the malady, but they must involve inflammation of the perspective and a general swelling of the glands of greed. With its cynical exploitation of the big-money quiz shows and its parallel insistence that even truth has to be fictionalized to be interesting—and, above all, salable—television has both intensified and spread the areas of infection; but it did not invent the disease.

"What you did, you did for money," Congressman Derounian persisted in his brief grilling of the witness, and he flung it out more like an accusation than a question. Van Doren protested there were other reasons, too.

It would be a blindly silly denial of human nature to contend that our objective here is suddenly a kind of national selflessness. But we have allowed our lives to become saturated with merchandising that appeals more to human weakness than to human strength. One of the most piercing ironies of the Van Doren story is this: While he rationalized that, in their innocence to his deception, thousands of his fans were being encouraged to admire and respect intelligence, he was being used by the program not because he was educated, but because it was profitable to exploit his transitory pull on audiences. This may or may not be a shattering revelation of the softness of the American intellectual, but should it be any more shattering than the fact that we've voted ourselves billions for a federal highway program without any plan for education? Should it be any more shattering than the cloth-coat and vicuna-coat morality that has gone before it?

The decline and fall of Charles Van Doren is a tortured personal tragedy, but it will be a much larger one for all of us if we don't see our own implication in it and do something more than talk about it.*

A POWERFUL, LOVELY LOBBY

April 28, 1960

SOME SAY a woman doesn't reach the peak of her irresistible charm until she is at least forty. Well, this week in St. Louis, the League of Women Voters has been celebrating its fortieth anniversary, and I find myself in a long queue of admirers wishing these dynamic ladies well. I use the word "dynamic" advisedly. The ladies of the League have got their wagon in forward gear and are steady on the climb.

The League of Women Voters sprang from the suffragette movement. It is a little dizzying to contemplate that it was scarcely more than two generations ago, in November, 1920, that American women voted in a national election for the first time. The fact that their judgment did not seem to be any better than their men's, and that we got Harding anyway, is beside the point. The League has probably done more than any single nonpartisan organization to provide political education to all hands. In contributing to the growth of the citizen by producing antitoxins to the poisons of prejudice, chauvinism, chicanery, and sheer political cussedness, these females of the species have surely proved more deadly than the male.

While the DAR was turning its orchid-purple passions loose in the petrified forest of the past, the League with dispassionate purpose was plowing the fields of change, in order to cultivate a crop of realism and common sense with which to face the present and

* At a trial growing out of the investigations, Van Doren pleaded guilty to perjury, changing his earlier not-guilty plea. He received a suspended sentence on January 17, 1962.

the future. Almost invariably, they have tackled the toughest issues of the times. They helped get better food and drug laws. They supported the Tennessee Valley Authority when foes of public power tried even more frenziedly than today to cripple it with the tag of creeping socialism. They backed Lend Lease against the America Firsters in World War II. They have consistently defended the United Nations, reciprocal trade, and civil liberties, although I wish they could have been a little more resolute on racial issues. On the local level, they have fought City Hall and won better urban zoning, charters, schools, health services, and tax reforms. How they have been able to do all these things without tearing themselves apart, in the frightening image of the contentious American clubwoman, is beyond me, but they have.

While they have been scrupulously nonpartisan in their approach to issues—Democrats and Republicans working side by side—this has not destroyed their individual loyalties; indeed, the major parties have found the League a valuable training ground for party activity. Perhaps the League's greatest single contribution to good government has been its sustained campaigns to get out the vote. Some of these have verged on the extreme. In restaurants in Toledo, Ohio, in 1924, the waiter brought, not only the menu, but information on the date of the primaries. The day after the primaries, the waiter would inquire whether the diner had voted. The League of Women Voters has the quaint idea that the people, who are the government, should actively participate in it. "Voters of America, arise," the ladies seem to be saying, "you have nothing to lose but your franchise." No small loss, that. Ask a Korean.*

* Voting frauds were a main grievance of those who toppled the Synghman Rhee government, but, under subsequent military coups, voting rights were completely suspended. The government says it plans to restore them in the spring of 1963.

THE AMERICAN GOSPEL

September 16, 1960

I<small>T IS HEARTENING</small> to note that Dr. Norman Vincent Peale, presumably by invoking—albeit belatedly—his own powers of positive thinking, has disassociated himself from a Protestant group which last week declared that Senator Kennedy's religion had to be an issue in the presidential campaign, because the Pope would pressure him in the White House. How deeply, and in how many directions, the issue still will cut remains to be seen. This latest development, however, may or may not impel Adlai Stevenson to edit a recent observation he made contrasting Dr. Peale with the apostle Paul. He found St. Paul appealing and Peale appalling.

Unquestionably appalling has been the golden success of this lively clergyman in merchandising the country with what might be called piously packaged religiosity. Long before bigotry bruised its way to prominence in the 1960 race, long before Dr. Peale himself became publicly involved with the issue, he had prospered the concept of applied Christianity with sermons, lectures, radio programs, syndicated columns, magazine articles, and best-selling books. I have just bought a copy of perhaps his most famous work, *The Power of Positive Thinking*, the jacket of which announced I was getting the two-million-copy anniversary edition of a practical guide to mastering the problems of everyday living. There was not, and I did not expect there would be, a vestige of religious prejudice in it. Instead, even more than I had imagined possible, it was loaded—and the verb is used advisedly—with the rich, sun-drenched wisdom of rectitude and the bright promise of virtuous success. For a moment, I thought the bookshop clerk had mistakenly handed me that other best-selling tract by an acrobatic dancer on how to make several million dollars in the stock market, or the success story of an insurance salesman.

Then, suddenly, I realized the source of my confusion. What I held throbbing in my hand was the American gospel. Pulsating

34

under the covers of Dr. Peale's Sunday punch was the power preached, not only from the pulpit, but from the podium of every chamber of commerce across the land. It energized the public-relations pitch emanating from leading corporation board rooms. It spun the buxom wheels of women's clubs into a swivet of civic duty. It motivated many politicians, in a fearlessly nonpartisan way, to quote chapter and verse of its simple message: Work hard, down doubts, conquer fears, believe in God; and, *ergo,* in this greatest of all possible lands, enjoy new life the American way —new power, increased efficiency, greater happiness—and suspect anybody who says it is not so.

In a chapter headed "A Peaceful Mind Generates Power," Peale writes: "It is important to eliminate from conversations all negative ideas, for they tend to produce tension and annoyance inwardly. For example, when you are with a group of people at luncheon, do not comment that 'the Communists are going to take over the country.'"

Like a butterfly hovering over a rose, the doctor glories in the beauty of the word "tranquillity," exhorts his readers to turn a deaf ear to bad news, to fill their minds with all peaceful experiences possible, and to revel in the "healing, soothing, healthy practice" of observing silence. He is a great hand at pulling the plug and washing trouble down the drain, or heaving it over the side.

At one point, he recalled how, on a cruise to Hawaii, he successfully exhorted passengers with worries in their baggage to go to the stern of the vessel, imaginatively take out each anxious thought, drop it overboard, and watch it disappear in the wake.

In another chapter, entitled "Relax for Easy Power," the author produced the following recipe: "Collapse physically. Practice this several times a day. Let go every muscle in the body. Conceive of yourself as a jellyfish, getting your body into complete looseness. Form a mental picture of a huge burlap bag of potatoes. Then mentally cut the bag, allowing the potatoes to roll out. Think of yourself as the bag."

While the reader is still collapsed on the floor, a hole in his side, Peale asks him to "drain the mind" and then refill it with peace by thinking spiritually.

The more I read of this powerful stuff, the more I wondered

35

why the two major parties had bothered to write platforms—especially the Republicans. As far as I can make out, they are basing virtually their whole campaign on Peale's philosophy, without giving the pastor credit: Think big, dash doubts, and wish your troubles away. When you go to lunch, do not mention that Khrushchev has opened a branch in Cuba. Fill your mind with sweet serenity, enjoy the life you have never had so good, and do not listen to disloyal talk about gains in Soviet economic power. As for defense, the administration is probably unwilling to drop air power and "Try Prayer Power," as another of the doctor's chapters is headed, but one can only guess how far Peale's positivism will carry the campaign. Already Vice-President Nixon has accused the Democrats of negative thinking.

As for me, my mind is a jellyfish entangled in a surplus bag of potatoes, yearning for the tranquillity which Senator Kennedy, on his new frontier, stubbornly refuses to guarantee.

DON'T JUST CALL ME AL

January 13, 1961

WITHOUT PIQUE, indeed with a certain dignified diffidence, the president-elect has let it be known that he does not think it befits the august dimensions of his office for the headline writers to call him "Jack." He prefers "Kennedy." If that will not fit over the impending White House dispatches, then "JFK" will do.

This fastidiousness, however discreetly proclaimed, may produce only smirks from the men on the copy desks—with or without the encouragement of their predominantly Republican publishers —on the ground that what was good enough for "Ike" ought to suffice for a man twenty-seven years his junior. The outgoing president says, with obvious pride in simple things, that he has always answered to that handle. Certainly, that three-letter label has become so universally recognized that even the stuffiest historian will have to include the nickname "Ike" in his accounts of the Eisenhower years.

But, for all the endearment attached to the references to the chief executive and first lady as "Ike" and "Mamie," I submit there is a limit to the back-slapping American pastime of indulging in folksiness. Perhaps the 1960 Republican presidential candidate found political mileage in using the ticket of "Pat and Dick" as a psychological ploy of unpretentiousness for easy identification with the multitude. But I maintain that it is neither dignified nor proper to refer to the President of the United States as Tom, Dick, Harry, or Jack. Oddly enough, during even the stormiest intervals of the Truman regime, it was almost invariably "HST" and not "Harry" in the headlines. If the Vice-President had made it, as he almost did, the issue might not have come up, because the name "Nixon" fits almost as handily inside a column as "Dick."

An AP poll indicates that there are only a few journalistic holdouts for "Jack"; that in practice most papers intend to bill the next president as "Kennedy" or "JFK." I suspect, however, that the temptation will be too much for the society editors; "Jack and Jackie" is too neat and logical a following line to "Ike and Mamie" for the women's pages to resist.*

I sometimes wonder how history would have read if historians had followed the American penchant for first names. "Cleo and I are having a little binge on her barge," Julius Caesar might have written one of his trusted legionaries, "and we would be happy to have you join us, but let's leave Tony out of it." The official Paris gazette of Napoleon's day could have taken care of the Russian debacle with this simple headline: "BONY BEATS IT BACK FROM MOSCOW."

As for current events, the opportunities for intimate brevity are endless. I can see this Buckingham Palace bulletin in the *London Times*: "Her Majesty Queen Liz tells sister Peg that keeping up with the Joneses doesn't necessarily mean staying out all night in a Mayfair club." And sooner or later the society section of *Pravda* would report that "Nicky and his little dumpling, Ninita Khrushchev, poured the vodka and spread the caviar at a top-secret supper at their country *dacha* last night." I will have to skip an example from India because I do not know how to provide a nickname for Jawaharlal Nehru. As for Castro, what

---

* I was wrong, however. The White House says it has almost never spotted such a combo, though "Jackie" is an inevitable label for the First Lady.

they're calling him around the State Department isn't fit for a family-type broadcast.

I can't really explain how or why we Americans have developed such an overriding compulsion to dispense with the formality of the family name. If there are any professors left at Harvard, they might suggest it as a doctor's thesis. Even in the days of the hospitable Old Frontier it was not "Hi, Jack," but "Howdy, stranger," at least until they could tell which hip you carried your holster on.

Today you meet a corporation executive, and it's "Jimmy" and "Si" and "Bobby" and "Al" before you're through your first business-lunch martini. And at Kiwanis, Rotary, or the Lions Club, you wear a huge, inescapable nickname-plate on your lapel.

Are we so in need of togetherness that we have to advertise for informality? Are we so unsure of ourselves individually that we must get lost in a communal pot of given names? Years ago, somebody founded a society to oppose calling all sleeping-car porters "George." I like to think it thrived. At any rate, I think it's time we restored some dignity to personal identity—from Pullman porters to the presidency.

THROUGH BLAZE AND
BLIZZARD, THE BETS
MUST GET THROUGH

February 3, 1961

YESTERDAY, the coldest day in eighteen years, an accident happened on the very edge of the nation's capital. Its ramifications may be of some use in reading the direction of our national purpose and in evaluating those American pioneer qualities of fortitude and perseverance needed to carry us forward to a new frontier.

A Pennsylvania Railroad special, carrying three hundred dedicated citizens bent on the serious business of placing bets on the horses at Bowie, Maryland—despite near-zero weather—met disaster as it was rounding a curve too fast into the race-track spur. Six people were killed, and more than a hundred were injured as the train left the rails and tumbled down an embankment. With a singleness of intent reminiscent of men courageously committed to an offensive in battle, many of those unhurt left the dead and the dying behind; without the slightest hesitation, they forged ahead on foot the remaining three icy miles to the pari-mutuel windows. Even some of the wounded made this forced march, but suffered heroically in silence. One middle-aged man, his face blackened with dirt, his clothes torn, limped up to the admission gate. "Hey buddy," the attendant said, "you're hurt. You better go to the infirmary."

"I'll get straightened out later," the man replied gamely. "I got to get a bet on the fourth race. I came all the way from Philadelphia to play this horse."

There were other heart-warming examples of self-discipline and control in the face of hardship and tragedy. One man described his experience this way: "People were thrown all around, and glass was flying everywhere. Two or three seats back of me, a man was hanging out of the window, and I think he was dead. I climbed out the window and headed toward the race track in the snow. I was very fortunate." Modestly, the man told a reporter that he did not want his name used in the story.

For the hardy survivors who reached the Bowie track, the train wreck was only part of their misfortune. Willing as they were to continue to brave the elements and donate their earnings to the sport of kings, they were forced to retreat homeward when the ninth race was canceled after an extra betting room at the track caught fire. This particular facility is not used except when the crowds are large. Yesterday, 6,313 loyal customers volunteered to bet their money at Bowie, and, though that crowd was below the daily average in 1960 of 11,304, the frostbitten fans were liberal with their savings. The gross receipts at the betting windows came to $847 more than half a million.

This is indeed a modest sum, however, when compared with the total net receipts from pari-mutuel betting for 1959, which, according to Commerce Department figures, hit four hundred and seventy-three million dollars. According to the National Association of State Racing Commissions, the total pari-mutuel turnover for 1959 was $3,246,154,581.

There has been a lot of loose bureaucratic and liberal-lobby talk lately about faulty distribution of our wealth and unproductive uses of our income. One of these alarmists, Harvard professor emeritus of political economy Alvin Hansen, has just published a book entitled *Economic Issues of the 1960's*. In it, he argues (to borrow a summation from columnist TRB in the *New Republic*) that "we have reached the point where enormous, uninhibited private spending, plus necessary federal outlays for defense, are starving public investment in research, education, housing, resource development, and the like." Hansen alleges that "an optimum rate of growth cannot be reached without a change in social values which will permit a better use of our productive resources."

That is pretty revolutionary talk, when you stop to think about it. Changing our social values means, if anything, altering the very fabric of American life, in which we exercise the privilege of spending more for cosmetics than cancer research, more for soft drinks than scholarships. Why, assuming a public school-teacher's salary averages $4,500 a year, it would take more than 700,000 of them contributing their entire annual income to equal the three-and-a-quarter billion poured into the economy through the pari-mutuel machines year before last.

Bowie race track was closed today by a blizzard. That reversal was partly counterbalanced by the fact that most schools in the Washington area were closed, too, dramatizing how much the taxpayers saved by not buying adequate snow-clearing equipment to keep the schools open. And, to keep the children out from underfoot while daddy is perusing the *Daily Racing Form*, they might be assigned to study for inspiration and guidance the triumph over tragedy at the rail and race tracks at Bowie yesterday.

THE VICIOUS VIRTUES
OF VARSITY SPORTS

April 27, 1961

MORE DISCOURAGING NEWS, even downright disgusting news, emerges about the second major college-basketball scandal in a decade. A gambler named Aaron Wagman has been indicted in New York on multiple charges of corrupting ten players from six schools.* Apparently it was the same old story: bribing athletes to throw games or shave points, so betting syndicates could clean up on the fixes.

Varsity football may have escaped this particular kind of tincture, but it is hardly a noble pastime, either. The hard fact is that intercollegiate spectator sports, notably football and basketball, have become crassly commercialized ventures dispensing payola to sustain star players. This emphasis on showmanship over scholarship has had an impact clear down to grade school. It is an impact with jagged edges reflecting rank hypocrisy in our supposed concern over education. We do not really care about mining and refining our most precious natural resource—the mental capacities of our younger generation. All we really want is a winning ball team. If that sounds too cynical, who would dare put it to an honest vote?

The attitude, admittedly, is not unanimous. I once commented on the move of Marquette University in Milwaukee to abandon football and track because the setup involved, in effect, a $230,000 bite in the University's budget to sustain muscular free-loaders in one way or another. After that broadcast, listeners in various parts of the country volunteered added testimony on the subject.

* Wagman's corrupting days may be over—for a while, at least. Already convicted and jailed on the basketball fix, he was indicted again on February 14, 1962, and he pleaded guilty to thirty-eight counts of conspiracy and bribery in New York. According to the Justice Department, he has also been indicted in North Carolina on thirty-four counts of bribery: offering money to shave basketball scores. *And* he is under sentence in Florida for bribery in a football conspiracy.

41

What we have here, it seems increasingly clear, is a national scandal corrupting our sense of values. Under these circumstances, bribery and cheating are incidental and unsurprising.

A boy in a well-known prep school on the edge of New York City wrote that the problem was not restricted to higher education. Private secondary schools, he said, can spend lots of money, comparatively, on such luxuries as a winning football team. As a result, the whole student body suffers because of deficient attention given to the development of the individual.

A mother in Austin, Texas, reported, "Just recently, over the objections of medical experts, educators, and [other] responsible citizens, football has been added to the curriculum of the lower grades of the Austin junior high schools. We need public kindergartens, more school rooms, and so many other related things. But we got football."

And from the University of Iowa came a long and bitterly devastating lament by an assistant professor of philosophy, Harry M. Bracken. "Not only is football financially more expensive than it seems at first sight..." he wrote; "it is educationally more expensive....

"American colleges and universities spend a lot more time and money recruiting a team than they do students, and, in many cases, than they do recruiting a faculty. The bright high-school student is entitled to some cynicism about the lofty ideals of institutions of higher learning.... His high-school coaches were probably his best-paid and least competent teachers. [Recent surveys firmly support at least the first part of the professor's statement.] ...

"Not long ago," Bracken continued, "I checked our figures for scholarship and fellowship and gift aid [at Iowa] and discovered that in the year 1957-58 we gave the athletes and members of the band one-third of the total aid awarded in all colleges of the university!

"As at Marquette, there are the hidden expenses: the impact of this distorted view on the students themselves.... Tutors are needed for the players, and, at least at Iowa, cash bonuses for helping get a star through a final are not unheard of. If the recent price-fixing conspiracy in the electrical industry represents the new American way, the American university deserves a fair

42

share of the credit." He went on to quote a charge in *Sports Illustrated* that payola is now dispensed in the Big Ten conference by cash in the mail on Monday morning from alumni through the university to the players.

Certain TV and newspaper interests in the midwest, Professor Bracken said, have been "extremely hostile" to various faculty attempts in the Big Ten to gain some share of control of athletic programs. Given this vested interest in the *status quo,* he argued, the public is not ever likely to be well informed about the problem. "I like to think," he concluded almost wistfully, "that if people appreciated that a pleasant afternoon's game involves universities in all sorts of chicanery, from pressures on faculties and retention of low admissions ... requirements, to payola for high school coaches (the suppliers of talent) and star players, they would call a halt to it all."

Who is looking for an answer to the question inspired by President Kennedy: "What can you do for your country?"

WRONG NUMBER

November 10, 1961

I THINK the phone company has got the wrong number. What I mean is: This drive to load all our dials with nothing but digits is going to reduce us to a nation of ciphers. Not to say that this is not going along with the trend. At the present rate of escalation of thermonuclear madness, we are all going to be reduced to smoking ciphers anyway, and it might be a step toward grim reality, if not convenience, if everybody changed the letter prefix of his phone number now to, say ARmageddon 6, INferno 7, or just plain GRound Zero.

I do not deny that the telephone people have an argument, and they are pushing it impressively. They have even got out a clever little booklet to support their numbers game, although they did not dare abandon the alphabet in their title. In fact the initials "ANC"—standing for "All-Number Calling"—sound ironically like an addition to the letter-prefix exchange which they have set their hearts on eliminating.

They claim that ANC is a necessary switch because the bursting population growth of the country has so increased the need for new telephones and new telephone exchanges that by 1970 they will have exhausted all possible letter combinations. They insist that ANC will improve both local and long-distance service and minimize the incidence of wrong numbers dialed. ANC, they vow, will be adequate to carry us at least through the year 2000.

I admire their boldness in looking and planning that far ahead, but in my slow-footed way I maintain they are pressing the change with foolhardy haste. Research indicates that some subscribers have already rebelled against being listed as a seven-digit number instead of a number of five digits following two letters (a prefix to some memorable exchange like HYacinth or BUbbling Rock). In the national capital recently, *Washington Post* reporter Thomas Wolfe tracked down a newly arrived couple who had told some friends that their phone number was FUllbloom 7, et cetera; others, that it was EUthanasia 7; and still others, that it was EVolution 7. All the beginning letters are in the same holes on the dial, which also make up the couple's real exchange, 387. "But that's so impersonal," they explained. "So we think up our own exchanges.... If you have any ideas, call us at EThereal 7...."

The fact is that telephone exchanges have become important status symbols. Imagine the traumatic experience of having to trade BUtterfield 8, HIckory 4, or GRanite 2 for a flock of faceless numbers. Furthermore, we are a nation of name-droppers and name-labelers, including our own. Stenographers and receptionists put their names (but not, of course, their phone numbers) on desk tops; convention delegates pin them to their lapels; members of the armed forces have their "John Hancocks" sewn on their uniforms over the heart; chauffeurs, elevator operators, airplane pilots, and truck drivers have their identities prominently and proudly displayed in their respective conveyances, so their monikers will stand out in the multitude and give them a personalized contact, or something, with the public. Do you think for a minute that a third assistant vice-president with his name in gold letters on the door is going to settle for a phone number that sounds as if it were straight out of the penitentiary?

Then there is this matter of memory. I have enough trouble as it is carrying in my head from the directory to the dial tone the present combo which is, say XErxes 9-9999. Give me two more digits to remember and I will be forced to revert to the wigwag system of the Boy Scouts of America—assuming they have not junked it in favor of electronic smoke signals. The telephone company, however, stoutly maintains that business firms and even housewives are mad for All-Number Calling, causing others to queue up impatiently for the change-over. The ANC booklet, in a silent admission, I suspect, that there is a problem, suggests that a helpful memory tip is to group numbers into two parts such as 555 (pause) 2368. O.K., maybe so. But I am going to come right back at the company with the contention that that is a figurative quibble. This is only part of the equation it proposes to feed into that overworked IBM machine called the human brain. We have just recently added three extra digits in the "area code number" which enables you to dial long distance direct. Suppose you are trying to reach your cousin in Wellington, Kansas, whose area code number is 316. Suppose he is staying in room 1123 at the Waterloo Hotel, whose telephone number is 186 (pause) 5249. You have fourteen digits there; try and get your cousin!

I know, of course, that the phone company has already won this battle with inexorable reasons of the electronic age, but before my HOneysuckle exchange is struck down I have one favor to ask.* When they install that direct line between the Kremlin and the White House to forestall holocaust by mistake, will they please make the prefix Seven Come Eleven? We need all the luck we can get.

---

* Perhaps I shouldn't have been so hasty. In July, 1962, in San Francisco, a group of citizens formed the Anti-Digit Dialing League to "oppose creeping numeralism." They all wear ADDL buttons. The *San Francisco Chronicle* ran a poll of readers, and nearly two-thirds of the ballots returned were opposed to all-number dialing. Sister or similar leagues have been quickly formed in other areas, including Los Angeles, Indiana University, and Washington, D.C.

MOVE OVER, LYSISTRATA

November 22, 1961

THERE IS A CRACK in my ivory tower.

I am being picketed and pelted by angry citizens, most of them lady citizens, from coast to coast. The common denominator of their complaints, hitting me like a battering ram, is that I am so preoccupied with my own fuzzy thoughts on Washington's lofty plain that I do not recognize a genuine public uprising when I see one. I plead partially guilty. I have detected more than one public outcry against the world's insane drift, but, manifestly, I have not given them the attention they increasingly deserve. One of the many troubles with pundits, including those wired for sound, is that we are quick to tell the public what it ought to think and do, and then, when its thoughts lead to action, we either run in alarm or ignore the results as unworthy of note.

The day Khrushchev let go his lovely fifty-megaton globe-buster, I noted that the Women Strike for Peace movement was planning a nation-wide demonstration, which I called a "touching but sadly impotent" gesture in view of Mr. K.'s generous Halloween contribution to fall-out. Impotent indeed. Little did I know. I quickly heard from one listener in Los Angeles who wrote, in part:

"We know that the label 'appeaser' is an effective one in American political life. Why then is it a necessarily impotent act for citizens to let elected officials know that there are many who do not term negotiation and strengthening the United Nations appeasement?"

Another lady described the peace-movement demonstration in Los Angeles, which drew two thousand participants. "No beatniks, these women," she wrote. "There might have been one or two, but most of the women were well-dressed, middle-class women from professions and homes, who have never done anything like this in their lives, but feel that the time has come when something must be done. [Reporters] looked long and hard for some underlying group behind this strike, and they found none. Is it so unbelievable that ordinary people can become so sick of this mad world that they must do something, even though some consider it 'ineffective'?"

Warning that she hoped to organize women all over the country into small correspondence groups to fire off letters on issues of importance to politicians, editors, and even commentators, this listener added: "I refuse to let a vocal right-wing minority in this country rule me by default, and that is what the right wingers do—they write and write and write."

Two mothers on Long Island have written of plans to circulate petitions to be signed only by children who are willing to declare they do not want to be the "last generation." Hard-bitten politicians, harassed diplomats, overburdened heads of state may throw up their hands at these gestures as inept impediments to their own efforts. The trouble is, their own efforts are not doing very well. It might not be a bad idea to pay more attention to the people. They are what Washington is supposed to be a government of.

A mother of four wrote to me from San Diego that she was disturbed by a remark she heard recently: "The Americans are not afraid to die; they're just afraid to negotiate."

"Fear of being afraid," she said, "or of being considered cowardly, is, to me, the most tragic kind of fear."

The women of Greece, who hated war, too, may pale before their aroused American counterparts. Lysistrata, move over. You have competition, and the competition is a fast, determined company.*

* Indeed it is. Started by seven Washington, D.C., housewives in September, 1961, the Women Strike for Peace movement now claims five hundred thousand supporters in the U.S., plus representation in twenty foreign countries. They pay no dues, have no formal membership, but work in their own communities (including 120 U.S. cities) "for a peaceful world." They have committees on radiation problems, peace research, and monitoring. The last scans newspapers and comic strips, listens to radio and TV; if they detect "warmongering," they write letters of protest. In April, 1962, a delegation, including Mrs. Martin Luther King, told their peace story to all seventeen members of the Disarmament Conference in Geneva. In the summer of 1962, another delegation went to Moscow and exchanged views with Russian women.

WHERE ARE THE TRUE
DISBELIEVERS?

New York City
January 30, 1962

WHEN I WAS very young, I suffered a vast indignity. In that far juncture of history, Levis—blue jeans, I believe they are called today—led the mode of male fashion at the Snake River West Side School. Their jauntiness perilously hung from the hipbones—a style, I take it from TV westerns and junior-high pacesetters, which endures to this day. At any rate, they were the vital status symbols of the time, and I coveted a pair, copper rivets and all. My parents would have none of it. To mow the lawn and pick the gooseberries in, yes; for sixth-grade garb, absolutely no. Oh, the burning humiliation of it!

Looking back now, I suppose I should be grateful to them for not permitting me to run with the herd. I finally did get a pair, but I was a mighty reluctant nonconformist in the interim. Regardless of age, I suppose we all are children in this respect and demand to have what the Joneses have. To borrow FCC Chairman Newton Minow's TV term, the individualist truly lives in a wasteland today. Consciously or unconsciously, big industries, labor unions, and government encourage a kind of "group-think."

So, to a small-bore iconoclast like me, it was a delight to read in the *New York Times* that the independent thinker has been the hero of an international symposium at the University of California Medical Center in San Francisco. However, Lawrence E. Davies reported that the nonconformist was warned, principally by Dr. Carl R. Rogers of the University of Wisconsin, that "conformity is a powerful and growing attribute of modern society," and that in practice the exponent of neither the Western nor the Communist culture wants persons to be free.

For the most part, society, Dr. Rogers said, is extremely fearful of and ambivalent toward any process which leads to inner free-

48

dom. "Nevertheless," he went on, "it is my conviction that rigidity and constriction are the surest road to world catastrophe, and that one of the major hopes for the future is that, through education, we might utilize our knowledge to develop flexible, adaptive, creative individuals who are in the process of learning to be free."

University of California psychologist Richard S. Crutchfield submitted experimental data indicating that women are greater conformists than men. He did not say, or at least the dispatch did not reveal, whether this basically involved the female's slavish dedication to the whims of fashion. Crutchfield found that young people conformed more than old people and that military officers, on the average, conformed more than research scientists or architects.

I don't know whether the San Francisco symposium specifically explored conformity and nonconformity in the regions of religion, but the participants would probably agree that this is a field in which the threshold of tolerance is dangerously low, not between one denomination and another as much as between believers and nonbelievers.

In a provocatively thoughtful tract recently published in the *Harvard Alumni Bulletin,* the eminent psychoanalyst Dr. Lawrence S. Kubie raises the painful but necessary question: "Who is to defend the basic right not to believe?

"Much is made in this country," Dr. Kubie wrote, "of the right to believe and worship in any way that man may please. To that basic freedom no one who supports the democratic process can object. But what has happened to the equally basic right not to believe? Belief must be weak indeed if it needs buttressing and sanction by social pressures, by congressional action, and by university prestige. Man's weak-kneed impulse to hide himself in the crowd by intolerance of disbelief is hardly worthy of our once-courageous country. Therefore," the psychoanalyst argued, "in an effort to strengthen faith itself, the ministers of every faith should be the first to champion man's right to disbelieve." But he found few doing it.

His recommended corrective: ". . . a tough, objective critical study of the history of religion and of religious error" as a vital ingredient of university scholarship. ". . . . An important first step," he said, "in the breakdown of the clear and necessary separation between church and state occurs when there is any breakdown in the separation between faith and education." Injury has already been suffered, he charged, in our higher education, and it must be reversed.

"One great preacher," Kubie concluded, "said ... that a true religion is a search for truth, but that the moment any religion thinks it has found the truth, it has ceased to be a religion.... On the basis of that sound platform, but on no other—our universities can defend our liberties from both the internal and external threats to their destruction."

Whether you and I agree with that thesis or not, how urgently important it is that we be exposed to it and our beliefs tested by it.

SOMETHING FOR NOTHING, INCORPORATED

April 3, 1962

BEFORE A WAVE of national self-righteousness washes our seven dauntless astronauts out of house and home, let us get a few things straight. We Americans are a nation of pot-of-gold-at-the-end-of-the-rainbow chasers. We do not have a national lottery, but we really do not need one. There is an opportunity to get something for nothing on every hand. Or at least there seemed to be until the TV-quiz scandals broke. But the giveaway is not dead yet. Name the country John F. Kennedy is the president of, and win a thousand dollars. Fly around the world in a space capsule and win security for life, including a brand-new home, fully furnished, absolutely free, no strings attached.

There is a difference between these sets of circumstances, but not much. Where so many of us get mixed up is in expecting our heroes to behave differently from the rest of us; in assuming they will suddenly display the taste and moral strength the rest of us lack, and rise like the gods above the temptations of our society.

50

This can happen, but it does not often. The astronauts seemed well on their clean-cut, exhilarating way to bring it off; now they have stubbed their collective toe, or some eager agent has stubbed it for them. Not since Lindbergh's flight have the heart and imagination of the country been so completely captured as John Glenn captured it with his glorious, perilous orbit in triplicate. His glowing image was only slightly tarnished when it dawned on the country that he and his six colleagues would share half a million dollars for writing of their exploits exclusively for Henry Luce's *Life* magazine. After all, presidents and prime ministers had similarly profited. But somehow the blemishes became more noticeable when it developed that the astronauts were investing their publication checks, not in scholarships or some other public field, but in real estate—in an apartment complex in Washington, D.C., and in luxury motels at Cape Canaveral and in the Grand Bahamas. At these locations, the associations of their fame are not likely to detract from their fortunes.

Even though, after a day of soul-searching in Washington, the spacemen turned down the offer of free living space in Texas near the new ninety-million-dollar manned-space-flight center, the damage had already been done—intangibly at least—because earlier they had accepted the offer, rejecting it only when the government had a twinge of conscience in their behalf.

Interestingly enough, they had a precedent to follow which they ignored until the White House, the Pentagon, and the National Aeronautics and Space Administration all restudied the affair today. Months earlier, the *Washington Post* revealed that Representative Frank Boykin of Alabama had tried without success to bring the prestige of President Kennedy and the first American astronaut, Commander Alan Shepard, to bear on a Maryland real-estate promotion in which Boykin and an ex-convict were financially interested—by giving Shepard a twenty-five-thousand-dollar home in the development. The effort failed, for obvious reasons.

But there was nothing so gross or clumsy in the approach of the Houston Homebuilders Association in offering each astronaut a twenty-four-thousand-dollar home "as a gift from the community by the industry." Everything was magnanimity with a capital Mmm-mmm; there would not be any vulgar promotion;

51

it was just a heart-warming gesture to get these families a roof over their heads. If some salesman enlivened his pitch to another prospect by pointing to the status symbol involved in living along Astronaut Alley, well, that was small risk for the high stakes of togetherness involved.

Who is fooling whom? We are fooling each other, and we love it. This, thank Heaven, is not creeping socialism; it is cantering capitalism, and if an ethic bounces off here and there, who cares? Our handling of national heroes is always linked, one way or another, to commercial crassness, whether it is the pictures of baseball idols on bubble-gum postcards or Lindbergh's own flight beginning as a publicity stunt for a couple of New York hotels.

It is surprising under the circumstances that citizens feel inclined in our society to make sacrifices, but they do. Not enough, but several distinguished men in business and industry have foregone fortunes to serve their government; labor leaders, scientists, and others have made similar sacrifices. The astronauts themselves have dedicated their lives to the exploration of space, and if some fellow citizens object to the extra emoluments en route, let it be remembered that these fringe benefits have been created by the society in which we live and, seemingly, with our approval. We appear glad to support a system in which the Yanks' Roger Maris, at $65,000 a year, gets five times as much base pay as the astronauts; and their base, in turn, is double that of many college professors. We may change this dizzy sense of values, but, at the rate we are going, we are not likely to do it quickly.

JOHNNY'S PARENTS
CAN'T READ, EITHER

April 9, 1962

ONE OF THE heroines of my western boyhood on the Snake River was a gentlewoman named Miss Olive Locey, who wore amber combs in her auburn hair—but that was only an incidental reason for her attraction. She was the town librarian and, if not quite so comely as Marian the librarian in that Broadway delight *The Music Man,* she was very special. She reigned over a quiet cove only half as big as the Metropole Billiard Parlor and not nearly so well-populated, but to move into her shaded realm was a journey of high adventure. The modest stacks anchored to the linseed-oiled floor were like strange ships waiting to share their cargoes of books with the curious traveler.

There was great dignity to this, the Idaho dry-farming community's cultural waterfront, where nobody ever spoke above a whisper, but Miss Locey's advice and counsel seemed to be more authoritative in subdued tones. Perhaps it was the sense she gave of wanting to share an intellectual conspiracy that got me onto the high seas with Melville and Conrad and into some of the inviting intricacies of Balzac. Otherwise, I might have been permanently drydocked with Ralph Henry Barbour or tooling along inanely, but, oh so happily, with *The Motor Boys Across the Plains* and "Old Doc Yak," who, as I fuzzily remember it, was the funny-paper precursor of "Andy Gump."

Recalling these early tentative samplings of serious reading only serves to emphasize the promised excitement of a new, unread book, and I boggle incredulously at the thought that there are still areas in this so-called civilized country of ours that have not shared that experience, because neither books nor libraries are available. During National Library Week, this is a thought to ponder along with the equally, if not more, shocking intelligence that the House Rules Committee is sitting on a bill to provide federal aid to combat adult illiteracy. Of course, that pillar of eighteenth-century enlightenment, Rules Committee Chairman Howard Smith of old Virginia, may figure that the taxpayers cannot stand the cultural spurt that would be involved in bringing book-learning to the more than eleven million citizens over eighteen who cannot read or write, especially since the taxpayers have not even provided adequate libraries for the literate to use.

If you doubt this latter fact, here is some proof furnished by the American Library Association: Two-thirds of all the elementary schools in the country are without libraries; one out of five college libraries has less than 25,000 volumes, and there are some American junior colleges with enrollments of as high as a thousand students which have no library facilities. Less than fifty per cent of all the college libraries in the country can meet the modest standard of a 50,000-volume library recommended by the Association.

These and other worse situations in some rural areas are undoubtedly happy ones for those voluntary guardians of the public morals, the would-be book-burners and book-banners. On second thought, of course, their work is never done. The self-appointed superpatriot or community paragon can nearly always find some passage in some volume, usually out of context, as actually or potentially capable, in his righteous eyes, of subverting or perverting some segment of the population.

I concede the need for certain restrictive rules in the selection of books for elementary- and high-school libraries, but, almost without exception, the librarians themselves are far better equipped to draw and apply these rules than a protesting citizen. And what an exercise in ignorant arrogance it is; what indignity to, and feverish distrust of, a so-called free society it is to allow zealots or pressure groups to dictate what the public can or cannot read.

There is some dreadful drivel and no lack of garbage in Henry Miller's *Tropic of Cancer,* and it is perfectly possible that Western culture would not have missed it if it had not been written—but who can really say? There are some moving and purgatively literary passages in it, too. With what special moral judgments have the county authorities in Maryland, Virginia, and elsewhere been endowed to justify their action in banning the book and prosecuting the booksellers? There is risk, admittedly, in the printed word, but where the risk is highest is in the closed, not the open society. This should be our rule, of which only the rarest exception is sufficient proof.

This being so, it is heartening to note a slight improvement in American reading habits. The circulation of so-called adult books has increased about thirty per cent in the last five years. Emphasis has shifted from westerns and mysteries—not necessarily useless in themselves—toward the more culturally dimensional veins of art, music, science, and even political affairs.

An apt motto for our celebration of National Library Week might go something like this: Read a book; the mind you aid may be your own.

54

HOW TO BUILD A
MONSTROSITY

April 17, 1962

ONE OF THE more eloquent testimonials to the stable, long-suffering qualities of the *genus Americanus* is the fact that, after the ordeal of April 15th, we don't all flock in droves or gaggles to join one of those right-wing societies that so alluringly advocate the abolition of the income tax. But let not the public servant toy or dawdle with our patience indefinitely, for it is not unlimited. One of the areas in which it is, or should be, reaching the breaking point has to do with the construction of government buildings in Washington, D.C.

It is not that the federal structure does not have a place on the horizon of the nation's capital. But, at the rate at which this massive art form is multiplying on every avenue, Pierre L'Enfant's fair city is fast becoming a grand canyon of stricken stone, a petrified forest of concrete colossi. As if this solid affront to aesthetics and simple good taste were not enough, these new buildings inevitably cost millions more than the government, on behalf of the taxpayer, bargained for. To crown the outrage, they unfailingly develop construction bugs that cost vast additional funds to eradicate.

Take, for example, the new Senate Office Building. This marble monstrosity, a happy marriage of the neo-fascist architecture of Mussolini's time and the graceful lines of a dockside warehouse, was supposed to cost modestly upwards of twenty and a half million dollars. Final cost: more than thirty million. That word "final," however, is misleading. Alteration bills have hardly ceased coming in. First, there was the item of the fancy rubber-tile floors. Capitol Architect J. George Stewart and his fellow planners had failed to calculate the resonance with which the floors would echo countless electric typewriters, or the danger their slick surfaces presented to high-heeled secretaries. So they asked for $150,000 for wall-to-wall carpeting to deaden the noise and to protect the

55

nyloned limbs of senatorial help. But then all the massive hardwood doors had to be unhinged and planed down to clear the carpets.

Senators found they could not commandeer the automatic elevators, and special button arrangements were installed. The ornate electric clocks in the hearings rooms would not work because the fancy, heavy hands were too much for the motors to lift. Bugs developed in the hearing-room public-address systems which persist to this day.

And, of course, everybody is familiar with the story of the subway connecting the New Senate Office Building with the Capitol. Perhaps the world's most expensive railroad, above- or underground, it covers a distance of little more than four well-hit home runs. The cost: more than six million dollars. Original estimate: two million plus. The original steel wheels of the subway cars made too much noise. They were replaced not once but twice, the final solution borrowing the idea of the hard-rubber wheels of the Paris *Metro*.

These items are not new, but they unfortunately seem to reflect the trend of planning and building on Capitol Hill. The controversial projection of the east front of the Capitol, which many leading architects condemned, cost twenty-four million instead of the expected seventeen. Now Stewart proposes to build a 1,900-car garage under it at a cost above $41,000,000, which the Senate's leading economist, Paul Douglas of Illinois, estimates will work out to more than $22,000 per car.

A new gleam in Stewart's eye is the possibility of extending the west- or downtown-side front of the Capitol. In an editorial pointedly entitled "Let Bad Enough Alone," the *New York Times* denounced the idea, described the east-front extension as a "hard, grotesque vulgarity."

But if this is grotesquerie now, it may look enchanting beside the gigantic, fortresslike third House Office Building, now being completed on a slope of Independence Avenue southwest of the Capitol. Original cost estimates: sixty-five million. Current estimates: almost, but not quite, double that.

Today, residents of a choice and lovely two-block area back of the Capitol are in an uproar over plans to build a Library of

Congress annex there.* On an adjoining site already acquired by the government, it is planned to erect a memorial to James Madison.

The question is whether to raise a monument to shortsighted, graceless, and expensive planning on Capitol Hill, as well. As its inspiration some critics blame Stewart, who, at seventy-one, is only the eighth man to hold the job of Capitol architect since it was created in 1793. With a new preoccupation toward culture and beauty, the White House reportedly is reviewing the prospects for a successor. Stewart, who is not officially an architect, but a construction man and a former Republican congressman from Delaware, seems singularly uninterested in resigning. Nor can he justly be made the exclusive villain. He cannot do anything that Congress, that arbiter of federal taste, does not go along with, subways and all.

UGLIFYING AMERICA
THE BEAUTIFUL

April 25, 1962

Sometimes when i let my imagination run lugubriously wild, but not very wild, I wonder how long it will take us, at the greedy rate we are going, to befoul, deface, or destroy most of the fantastic beauty and fabulous natural resources of this fair land. This is not just a silly aesthetic question, either. Our health and welfare, our lives and livelihood are directly involved. How many crimes do we commit against the public interest in the sacred name of private enterprise, which, all too often, serves as a legalized front for private piracy and selfish or wanton destruction?

Off Christmas Island, somewhere over the Pacific this morning, we fired a nuclear test device. Men and women of good will deplore it, or at least deplore the lawlessness among nations that obliged us to shoot it off in anticipatory self-defense. We grieve,

* Estimated cost, including purchase of land: seventy million dollars.

with a twinge of collective guilt, that, in the distance of time, the debris of this explosion may deform just one baby or induce cancer in just one parent.

But if our feelings are logical, as well as sincere, why do we mill around doing so little while our rivers are being polluted, the air we breathe is being choked with monoxide fumes and other toxic stuff, and the very earth itself is being poisoned with factory refuse and other waste? The human lives placed in jeopardy by this state of affairs are far more numerous than those affected or affectable by fall-out from nuclear test explosions, sinister as this unwelcome new ingredient is. The public, you and I, cannot do very much directly to affect the drift or surge of the cold war. But are we as voters and taxpayers impotent to prevent the rape of our resources, the spread of urban sprawl, the hideous structural scars on town and country horizons, and the avaricious appetites of promoters and venal, petty politicians who are so largely to blame for this mess and waste?

The answer is that we are not impotent, but we are mighty slow to anger and to action. There are exceptions which should inspire us. The other day in Washington, a militant lady from Texas, Katharyn Duff, was given the Thomas L. Stokes Award for a 1961 series of articles in the Abilene, Texas, *Reporter-News*, exposing the scandalous salt-water problem in West Texas, in which rivers, streams, and wells have been polluted with salt seepage, a good deal of it caused by careless or unscrupulous oil prospecting. Second prize went to Helene Monberg of Congressional Quarterly Service, one of the richest gold mines of significant facts in the whole business of journalism, for her syndicated reports on the public-private power struggle, land reclamation, and other related subjects. A special salute was given to the Grand Junction, Colorado, *Sentinel* for its many-fronted fight for conservation.

Tom Stokes, who died an untimely death of cancer in 1958, was a crusading reporter in the best and fullest sense of the term, and these awards were for work in the best Stokes tradition of public service. But there is hardly a community in the land, with or without the impetus of a prize, which does not need a cleansing exposé of its resources problems.

Perhaps the greatest problem of all is water. Western states are fighting each other over it. Despite the beginnings of a solution, northern and southern California are still bitterly rowing about it. The United States and Mexico are recurrently at odds on it. The U.S. population continues to burst, and the nation's water table continues to fall as if by some gigantic leak. The supplies that we have are misused. The Potomac River is virtually an open sewer as it runs past Washington, D.C., yet massive construction is permitted on its banks with arrogant disregard of intelligent civic planning, under shockingly shortsighted commercial and political pressure, scarring the beauty of the nation's capital in the questionable bargain.

Now a new threat is coming, literally, to the surface. Synthetic detergents, which, according to those magnetic TV commercials, wash all household cares away, are now regurgitating in drains, cesspools, and septic tanks, contaminating water supplies. A page-one story in the *New York Times* vividly described how countless thousands of families in New York, New Jersey, and Connecticut are threatened. In sections of Long Island, suds pour out with the tap water, and it is not beer.

As one geologist explained it, "First, certain wells near the shoreline were overpumped, and salt water was drawn into the supplies from the ocean and Long Island Sound. Now there is this inexcusable pollution by synthetic detergents, with the officials, detergent manufacturers, and most of the people [involved] being fully aware of what they are doing to themselves."

"Health officials and water experts," the *Times* story said, "attribute Suffolk [County's] over-all inability to meet the water-supply and sewage-disposal needs of its burgeoning population to a combination of greed, indifference, petty politics, ignorance, and apathy at several levels."

"God bless America," as Kate Smith used to sing. But do we really deserve it?

59

WE'D BETTER PRAY FOR
THE PIOUS HYPOCRITES

June 27, 1962

WHAT AN EMOTIONAL BUNCH of hypocrites we Americans are capable of being! How obviously, but how flimsily, we wear our religious beliefs on our sleeves, as if we wanted to make sure everybody sees them, no matter how thinly held they are.

The Supreme Court decision declaring unconstitutional a government-composed and -sponsored prayer in New York public schools does not threaten to turn the country over to atheists and nonbelievers. It does, however, threaten the pretentious religiosity that too many Americans have accepted in place of devout belief. This, I suggest, is a main reason for the sanctimonious furor over the Court's action.

There is richness in America's spiritual tradition. But too often we do no more than pay lip service to it. Too many parents are inclined to leave the character formation of their children to the schools, as if God-fearing patriots and all-round good citizens can be produced on an assembly-line basis, merely by exposing children to the pledge of allegiance to the flag and the Lord's Prayer.

But this is not government's business. As Justice Black, speaking for the six-to-one majority of the Court, said so clearly in his opinion: "Under the [First] amendment's prohibition against governmental establishment of religion, as reinforced by the provisions of the Fourteenth Amendment, government in this country, be it state or federal, is without power to prescribe by law any particular form of prayer which is to be used as an official prayer in carrying on any program of governmentally sponsored religious activity."

The Court was simply doing its job of upholding the Constitution. No—it was doing something more. It was reaffirming the principle, which should be welcomed by most thoughtful citizens, that religion is a private affair between man and his Maker. Or, as Justice Black put it: "Religion is too personal, too sacred, too

holy, to permit its 'unhallowed perversion' by a civil magistrate."
The point is not that the twenty-two-word prayer conceived by
the New York State Board of Regents was brief, bland, and, therefore, presumably innocuous. The point is, as Justice Douglas made
it in quoting a dissent in a prior case, that "if a religious leaven
is to be worked into the affairs of our people, it is to be done by
individuals and groups, not by the government."

How interesting it would be if the Supreme Court's harshest
critics practiced what they preached. "They put the Negroes in
the schools," cried Congressman George Andrews of Alabama,
"and now they've driven God out." What kind of God, Congressman, is it that would condemn twenty million Americans to
second-class citizenship? Is this Christianity in action?

Representative John Bell Williams of Mississippi branded the
decisions as part of "a deliberate and carefully planned conspiracy
to substitute materialism for spiritual values." And Congress in
its wisdom has taken care to keep the material and the spiritual
separate in District of Columbia schools, where it encouraged
religious services, but has refused sufficient funds for textbooks.
Senator Hubert Humphrey of Minnesota exposed a scandal in the
heart of Washington when he revealed the capital's schools were
using science, arithmetic, and geography books printed before the
dawn of the atomic age. Some of them were so tattered and torn,
they looked as if they were relics from the nineteenth century.

"There is enough money in this city," Humphrey told the Senate
angrily, "to build new hotels, cocktail bars, racetracks, and a
stadium . . . [and] to give it one of the highest per capita income
ratings in the world. But there is not enough money in this city
to buy even simple arithmetic books for ten-year-old children."

And, it might be added, there seems to be enough of the
Pharisee in many of us to argue, in effect, that our educational
system will collapse without prayer. But is there not enough candor and common sense among us to make us see that no prayer,
however fervid, can correct the monstrous and growing inade-
quacies of our educational system if we continue to insist on short-
changing it?

As an erudite Frenchman observed to me, this situation could
not come up in Catholic France, where the nonreligious character
of public schools is so jealously guarded. Why, in a country set

on keeping government out of business, do we get so upset when the Constitution is applied to keep it out of religion? I suspect one reason is that we have victimized ourselves in a tyranny of conformity. Where were the voices of prominent public servants and of the multitude hailing the Court's decision as another victory for the constitutional separation of church and state? They were muffled, I suggest, in the fear that, however deep and private your own convictions, you must pay lip service to a kind of public piety.

Supporting the Court's unpopular decision, the President said we had a ready remedy—to pray a good deal more at home. We can start by asking for help in improving our synthetic spiritual values.

Politics

DIAPERS, DEMAGOGUES, AND THE DISTRICT OF COLUMBIA

May 2, 1956

This is a little essay about diapers and demagogues. It shows how democracy works in the District of Columbia.

A few weeks ago, Congress was asked to address itself to diapers. The companies that supply and haul these vital items around to the babies of the nation's capital asked a Senate committee to kill a two per cent local D.C. sales tax affecting them. If you think the legislators have no time for such matters as the laundering of infants' loincloths, you are wrong. They have to *take* time. That is the way things are in Washington.

Last January, while the nation debated Secretary Dulles' "brink-of-war" analysis of our foreign policy, a contingent of congressmen was hearing appeals from the PTA to raise teachers' salaries in the District of Columbia.

While British Prime Minister Eden was here discussing the Middle East crisis with President Eisenhower, a group of senators and representatives toiled with legislation on the question of whether the capital should have street cars or buses,* and how they should be run.

While Washington buzzed with excitement over the gas-lobby scandal, a Congressional committee solemnly concerned itself with the problem of a new bridge across the Potomac.

This all sounds ridiculous, and it is. All these matters are impor-

* It got buses, some of them air-conditioned, but the rapid-transit system is still a mess.

tant in their place, but their place is before a city government, not cluttering up Congress. But Washington does not have a city government. With a population of nearly a million, the District of Columbia is the only community in the country, indeed the only major city in the democratic world, that cannot elect its own government. It is house-mothered by Congress, which acts as its city council. Nobody wants it that way; nobody, that is, except a demagogic minority in Congress and some business interests that must be called "vested."

What the District needs is home rule. The most shopworn argument against home rule is that the capital's large Negro population would exercise "undue influence" if District citizens could vote. Congressman James C. Davis,* Democrat of Georgia, a member of the House District Committee, and a passionate advocate of white supremacy, sees the most sinister consequences in enfranchising Washington. "It would offer too fine an opportunity," he says, "for subversive elements to come in and take over the city government.... There's a lot of riffraff ... not interested in good government ... [that] could be pulled around by schemers." So far, such statesmanlike logic has helped roadblock the Bill of Rights in this seat of democracy.

But it may well be that the thin camouflage of racial prejudice has been used to try to disguise more powerful obstacles to home rule. Commercial interests comprising Washington's Board of Trade argue that "things are all right as they are." Meaning (suggests a citizens' home-rule committee) that the board does not want to disturb its cozy and influential relationship with the District commissioners; and meaning, perhaps, that the board fears an elected city government might do something about a revised workman's compensation act for the District, as requested by the White House, and might do something to regulate the destructive volume of commercial trucks choking city traffic.

There may be a portent of change in the air. Yesterday Washington had an election. Not a full-blown one, only a primary to select D.C. representation to the Republican and Democratic national conventions. But it was the first "official" election of any kind the capital had had in eighty-two years; a proposal favoring

* In one of the most significant victories for political sanity in years, Davis was beaten in a primary run-off in the summer of 1962.

home rule was overwhelmingly approved. Congressman Davis may well be alarmed afresh tonight. Given the right to vote, citizens of Washington, D.C., may take the issues of diapers and demagogues in their stride.*

QUAKING WITH SECURITY

July 9, 1956

I AM NOT an overly demonstrative fellow, and the Fourth of July is already past, but I feel like raising three cheers tonight for nine lawyers who have come up with one of the most admirable documents in the whole twitching decade of the cold war. People who favor what might be called the "cops-and-robbers school of government" may be outraged by what these men have done, but the dissenters will find it hard to dismiss the lawyers' conclusions as careless or wishful or partisan.

Acting as a committee, these lawyers, some Republicans, some Democrats, all distinguished practicing attorneys in their communities, from New York to Los Angeles, unanimously decided that a sharp simplification of the federal loyalty-security-risk program is urgently necessary. Their findings, financed by a $100,000 grant from the Fund for the Republic, took more than a year of research under the sedate and responsible guidance of the Association of the Bar of the City of New York.

Their report, available to the public in a trenchantly written 300-page book, comes not a moment too soon. A government commission which has been tippy-toeing up to the same subject, without much visible activity, should embrace it as its basic text and guide. The administration itself should commit it to memory, preferably before it does any more equivocating on the subject of

* District of Columbia citizens finally won the right to vote in *presidential* elections on March 29, 1961, when Kansas became the thirty-eighth state to ratify the Twenty-third Amendment to the Constitution. This amendment fairly whizzed through state legislatures in a total of 286 days, two days faster than the Twenty-first Amendment, repealing prohibition. But Congress still governs the District of Columbia; home-rule legislation continues bottled up in committee.

"risk" employees. You will remember that the Supreme Court recently, in the so-called Cole case, held that the federal security program, and firings under same, could apply only to "sensitive" jobs.* This provoked a spate of legislation to derail the court decision and extend the security program to *all* government jobs, whether janitorial or atomic. The administration endorsed these efforts, but with confusing variations of warmth, ranging from tepid in Attorney General Brownell's office to red-hot on the part of Civil Service Commission Chairman Philip Young.

The lawyers, whose findings went to the printer before the Cole opinion was handed down, agree with the court (for different reasons) that the security program should be shrunk, not stretched. They would reduce the number of persons covered (in civilian positions) from six million to less than a million and a half, confining the program to sensitive areas only—that is, areas involving secret material. They also urge sharply improved screening and processing of suspected individuals, to protect their constitutional rights.

Do these lawyers believe, then, that the danger is past, that we can let down our guard? Listen to the opening words of their report: "Our enemy," Chapter One begins, "is a new kind of imperialism. It seeks to destroy not only our nation, but the ideals of liberty for which our country stands. The battlefield is the world, and it encompasses every field of human endeavor and aspiration, whether spiritual or material. . . .

"For the United States to depart from its ideals to the end of *supposed* greater security," the lawyers warn, "would be to shift the contest to a level on which we cannot win. We can never equal the Communist countries in enforced internal conformity."

And because, they reason, security "is gained through liberty rather than in opposition to it," it follows that a more tightly and humanely organized system, concentrating on clearance for sensi-

* There have been no further major Supreme Court decisions on security since the Cole case. The federal security program still operates under Executive Order Number 10450, issued in 1953. However, the Justice Department apparently is operating on the theory that, in view of the Court's decisions, the government would meet with no success with a security case in the courts unless the individual in question had been afforded full confrontation of accusing witnesses. This is something, at least.

tive jobs alone, "would enhance rather than lessen the national security."

One of the most simple, penetrating truths that I have come across in a long time in this tortuous subject of security is a sentence I just quoted a moment ago. Here it is again: "We can never equal the Communist countries in enforced internal conformity." This will spoil the fun of the Dick Tracy comic-strip minds of both parties that are bent on trying to police a citizen's spirit, but to have these lawyers so dispassionately declare it, is a reassuring tribute to the high ethics and good sense of the American bar.

Why, these intelligent men are asking us, why try to beat the Communists at their own game, particularly when, as recent events so vividly show, they are having such an awful time trying to play it themselves?

POLITICS BEGINS AT HOME

October 26, 1956

An eleven-year-old friend of mine who recently pulled a ten-inch trout out of Lake Washington has just got himself elected to public office. He proved he could angle for votes as artfully as for fish, and he is now president of the student body of his Seattle grade school.

But disillusionment has already begun to set in. He ran on a platform of high principles, but he is grieved to find the ricochet of innuendo rampant among his constituents. His experience is all the more shattering because the bitterness seems to center among the lady voters of the fourth grade.

One of the planks of his platform read as follows: "I cannot promise rashly gum machines in every classroom, Coke dispensers in the halls, lollipops given out at recess, or snacks when someone is hungry, but I would like you to know that I *am* in favor of them."

Surely, this plank has a shrewd mixture of appeal and candor that would arouse the admiration and incite the envy of every Frank Skeffington on the professional circuit. But what raised havoc instead of a hurrah was not *that* pledge, but the following one: "Already," the candidate said, "I feel that the fourth grade should have a regular gym period, as the fifth and sixth grades do."

Some of the females of the fourth did not share his feeling for calisthenics, preferring, perhaps, their equivalent of Elvis Presley or Proust. One of the president-elect's own one-time supporters, disappointed, maybe, at not getting a cabinet post as secretary of lollipop distribution, has turned on him and exploited this distaff discontent. Things have reached that point of crisis at which my eleven-year-old angler is wondering why he ever forsook his fishing pole for politics.

If he asked my advice, which he has not, I would urge him to stick it out, not just for the grade school's, but the country's sake. We need more principled politicians like him.

KNIGHTHOOD NEVER FLOWERED LIKE THIS

March 13, 1959

GETTING THE JUMP on spring, the Senate recently burst into full flower. The crucial question was not Khrushchev or Western rights in Berlin, but selection of a proper national floral emblem for the United States. The lawmakers were, understandably, unable to reach a floral settlement in their florid floor debate, and the argument has been postponed until the first week in May. Then, under the questionable auspices of the Falls Church, Virginia, Garden Club, four senators and one lobbyist will have at it again. Perhaps "questionable" is the wrong adjective for the club's auspices, especially since Washington's cherry blossoms will be gone by May, so the capital area will not be able to exert any undue atmospheric advantage over the discussion; but I do wonder whether the Garden Club will be aggressively objective enough to insist that the protagonists check their stamens and their pistils at the door.

At any rate, adversaries in the war of the roses versus the field daisy will let the petals fall where they may, with Pennsylvania's Senator Hugh Scott, a Republican, championing the rose. His opposition comes from: GOP Senator Gordon Allott of Colorado, who is advocating, not the columbine, but the carnation; Senator Paul Douglas, Democrat of Illinois, pushing the corn tassel; a Philadelphia seedsman named David Burpee, who is a registered lobbyist for the marigold; and still another Republican, Senator Thruston Morton of Kentucky, whose choice is grass.

A hint of how the tide of battle may flow, or perhaps fertilize, in May, comes from the *Congressional Record*'s verbatim account of the recent debate on the Senate floor. Senator Allott opened by extolling the carnation as a posey which "grew wild in the hills of Greece before the birth of Christ," has become the official flower of Mother's Day, and is suitable for both sexes to wear, particularly men, with "confidence in its ruggedness, its fertility, its virility."

"I think any flower," gallantly interrupted Senator Keating, "looks better when worn by a woman." Though a rose man himself, he was wearing a carnation given him by Senator Allott.

Iowa's Senator Hickenlooper, a corn-tassel constituent, damned the carnation with dubious praise, noting it was a wonderful flower, "seen in profusion at funerals."

It was Kentucky's Morton who brought sex into the argument. The corn tassel, he explained, "is not a full flower. It is merely the male flower. The ear of corn is the female flower." Adopting the tassel without the ear, he feared, would lose the woman's vote and possibly mobilize the Anti-Saloon League as well, because of the intoxicating aspect of certain corn products. Without ever saying it had to be blue, Morton made an impassioned plea for grass. "Let us look at the cow," he said, "the foster mother of mankind. Where would the cow be . . . where would mankind be, but for grass?"

Whereupon Senator Douglas bitterly accused his Kentucky colleague of heaping scorn on corn. "Nothing could be more beautiful than a field of corn in full flower," he rhapsodized. ". . . It was corn which kept the Pilgrims alive during the first hard winter at Plymouth. . . . Corn went with pioneers across this nation."

Not necessarily conceding victory, Senator Keating had already said he could not really be against corn. Incidentally, in what may be a bald attempt to influence Congress, a vote at the Capital Flower Show today put the rose away ahead as choice for the national flower. Dogwood was a poor second. In the recent Senate session, nobody defended the marigold, but that may have been because seedsman Burpee, being a lobbyist, is not allowed to speak from the floor. He will be given his head at the Garden Club forum in May.

There may even be some added starters by that time.* Apart from a late entry of Hawaii's night-blooming cereus, how, for instance, about the cowslip or that hardy political perennial, the purple poppycock?

HOW TO WIN ELECTIONS

September 30, 1960

CANDIDATES FOR public office make pretty much the same kind of speech all the time. In a squirrel cage of repetition, they leave themselves, the hapless reporters assigned to hang significance on their every word, and the public in a dizzy swivet of boredom. I am waiting for the day when the law of average political speeches breaks down as the nominee addresses his fawning, gape-mouthed flock as follows:

"Ladies and gentlemen:

"My wife and I can't find it in our hearts to thank you for this measly welcome. We had a better turnout at the last stop in Square Corners in a cloudburst. What happened? Didn't our advance men get the message across that those special buses from Round Circle had to be filled so the photographers could shoot better crowd pictures than my opponent had yesterday? And never mind all this propaganda about the Russians being ahead of us in education; where are all those screaming schoolchildren the other party rounded up? I am very much afraid Square Corners' next appropriation for flood control may suffer from this.

---

* Proposed legislation on the national flower is a hardy perennial, too. The Senate bills have gone to committee, but never have had hearings. In the House, there were some hearings but no action.

70

"Actually, I am glad to be here this morning because it gives me a chance to speak my mind. Who are the nogginheads responsible for picking these Jukeses and Kallikaks on the state ticket? It would be suicide for me to endorse these political lepers. And as for the congressman from this district, get him off my back; I was supposed to be running on *his* coattails.

"That brings me to my running mate. We haven't seen eye to eye since we were watching a chorus line at the Copacabana, and I can't think why the convention picked him. Something about a winning smile on television, but if the national committee thinks it can get away without giving me equal time, it's got another think coming.

"And another thing. I've got a religious issue of my own. If anybody had told me that I was supposed to go to church every Sunday so I could have my picture taken with the minister, I never would have accepted the nomination. I play croquet on Sunday, and when it rains I like to lie in bed late, just like the rest of you.

"Nobody asked me why we didn't bring the children with us, but I'll tell you anyway. They're juvenile delinquents, and I can't stand the sight of them.

"Well, I guess that just about does it. I don't have to say anything about the issues, because you complacent, self-seeking pressure groups we laughingly call voters wouldn't understand it anyway. As for the headlines, those sex-mad alcoholics representing that great American tradition of the free press have already written them from the canned handouts my ghost writers provide. Still, I suppose the least I could do, now that I'm here, is to drop a few clichés.

"I am for progress. What we need to get going is to move. To rise, we must get our feet off the ground. And I am for peace and freedom and all that other radical nonsense a candidate has to be for in order to be elected. We must do more and spend less. Let me give you an example: If my administration is confronted with two programs, one that will do the job more efficiently and economically, and another that is more expensive and won't work so well, do you know which one I will pick? Don't be silly. It's your money. I haven't got any.

"One more point. In order to be strong we must have strength, and that means the greatest military establishment on the face of the earth, administered, of course—as Lincoln Steffens told me only the other day—by good, clean local government, true to our ideals of freedom and a fair percentage of the defense contracts.

"It was grand of you grand folks of this grand state to come out here on this grand day and sacrifice your coffee breaks and turn at the pari-mutuel windows to listen to my views on this great election. I want you ladies and gentlemen and that loud-mouthed drunk over there in the corner to know that I feel this is the most vital election this country has faced since the last one.

"My wife and I will never forget the reception you have given us. I wish we could. The pollen count of that bouquet she got at the airport is just dandy for my asthma.

"But we're behind schedule and we must go now. Some rich bore, a heavy party contributor who wants to be ambassador to the Dominican Republic, has just presented us with tickets to the opening game of the World Series."

THOSE SUBVERSIVE HARVARD REPUBLICANS

January 25, 1962

SENATOR GOLDWATER and a number of other Republicans have been pointing with pride recently to the American college and university campus as a wellspring of conservatism. But they can hardly view with anything less than shrill alarm the brand of conservatism bubbling up in the intellectual wells of Harvard. Republican students at President Kennedy's alma mater publish what they call a journal of political thought, entitled *Advance*. The latest issue, labeled in red letters "Revise and Dissent" is just out. If this is a fair sample of what young conservatives are thinking in Cambridge, GOP National Chairman William Miller should be experimenting with methods of thought control, and the party leadership should be calling on Robert Kennedy to demand that the journal and its budding journalists be placed on the Attorney General's list of subversive groups.

72

In its special issue devoted to a study in depth of the Republicans on Capitol Hill, *Advance* has almost nothing good to report. It complains, with some embarrassingly convincing argument, that the dominant characteristic of the men dominating the party in Congress is obstructionism. It maintains that the essential divisions among Republicans in both the House and the Senate are not "liberal" versus "conservative" but "between those who want to do something constructive and those who want to do nothing at all."

Unmistakably, the editors of *Advance* would like nothing better than to see the Republican Congressional leadership retreat to the vanishing point. On the House side, the magazine, on the basis of a large number of interviews with GOP members of Congress, maintains that "Republicans of all views feel they are being less led [by Minority Leader Charles Halleck] than presided over; that the only attempt at hammering anything out comes, not in policy, but in the strategy of obstruction. When there is a Republican 'success,' it is in defeating a Democratic bill, usually with Dixiecrat help; seldom does the House GOP accomplish the sort of substantive victories it did even a few years ago."

As for the Senate, the young-Republican publication maintains that "more Republican talent is being wasted or misdirected [there] than anywhere else in government." It demands the ouster of Barry Goldwater from the important chairmanship of the Republican Senate campaign committee. "The party," says *Advance*, "cannot afford to indulge any longer, in such a crucial office, Senator Goldwater's eccentric ideas about the desirability of certain Democrats and the undesirability of certain voters."

In an editorial, *Advance* declares that "mere obstructionism is a disclaimer of responsibility, not an assumption of it. . . . The Republican leadership looks too much like the baseball team whose strategy was to 'wear out the opposition [by] running them around all those bases.'"

In a surprisingly balanced look at the political scene, *Advance* points up the dismal record of Republicans in Congressional elections over the past quarter of a century. Since 1930 there have been only two Republican Congresses out of sixteen. The magazine urges Republicans to take a look at the British Tories—"the Conservatives who win." The Tory consensus, says an article, "is favorable to the use of government for the benefit of society," whereas Republican conservatism is not conservatism at all, but old-guard recalcitrance.

You have to win to play, is the advice of the Harvard Republican upstarts to their elders, and they even have some ideas on how this should be done: more attention and research by GOP campaign committees of House and Senate in the areas of civil rights, labor, and urban problems; a vigorous drive to increase the staffing of Congressional committees with Republicans. (The charge is that the Democrats have loaded these committee staffs with partisans of their own.) Another recommendation is creation of an "advisory council" of leading Republicans, including former members of the Eisenhower administration, to work with the National Committee in formulating and publicizing GOP policy.* Finally, *Advance* wants the almost exclusively rural Republican leadership in Congress balanced by putting GOP members from metropolitan areas into leadership positions in both Houses.

Lest the Democrats gain a sense of false security from this youthful but uncallow critique, let them heed this appraisal by *Advance:* "The real choice is between anticipating the future, or acquiring a stake in the fading institutions of the past. The Democrats are currently stuck [in Congress] with the stultified men and unjust mores of the declining era of southern parochialism. They are making unconvincing attempts to escape the consequences." Indeed, if the young Democrats of Yale or California or the University of Podunk wanted to borrow a leaf from the book of these impertinent Harvard Republicans, they could give their own elders similar fits, and we might all be better for it.

* On cue or not, leading Republicans meeting at General Eisenhower's Gettysburg farm on June 30, 1962, formed an All Republican Conference, an advisory group of legislators and others, and a National Republican Citizens Committee, comprising volunteers to encourage new GOP groups and voter registration. Senator Goldwater loudly disapproved of these moves, indicating that they would work against the classic conservatism of the party.

FLAPS DOWN ON
THE RIGHT WING

March 14, 1962

SOME PEOPLE think that that sad and lonely appendage of politics, the extreme right wing, is getting too much public attention, and that it could be relegated to the attic where it belongs, among other discarded relics, if the press did not persist, in articles and broadcasts, in endowing it with an importance out of all proportion to its strength. This, I believe, is a dangerous generalization.

Admittedly, the radical right has no central leadership now— no man on horseback—and its fragmentary squadrons of dissident groups are commanded by crackpots. In this state of noisy disarray, it is not likely to take over the country. But, collectively, these outfits are capable of massive mischief. There is no doubt in my mind that by spreading fear, ignorance, and malicious misinformation in the guise of "anti-Communist seminars" and the like, these extremists of the right are doing infinitely more damage to this country than the U.S. Communist party, so long anemic, could possibly do.

Pretending that a situation does not exist is hardly the way to deal with it. Exposés of such nests of unfeathered fanatics as the John Birch Society are necessary. But where newspapers and networks have fallen down, I'm afraid, is in failing to report carefully and in depth the harm that these miserable movements do to the citizens and institutions of an open society, and the almost totalitarian techniques they often use in doing it.

For example, right-wingers have been widely quoting Khrushchev as follows: "We cannot expect the Americans to jump from capitalism to communism, but we can assist their elected leaders in giving Americans small doses of socialism, until they suddenly awake to find they have communism." But when Senator Lee Metcalf, a liberal Montana Democrat, checked with the Library of Congress, the Senate Internal Security Committee, FBI chief

75

J. Edgar Hoover, and the Central Intelligence Agency, they all said they had no record of any such quotation by the Soviet leader.

People who knowingly disseminate such spurious stuff, said Metcalf, "are cut from the same cloth as Communists and Fascists." It is a sad, but interesting, commentary that it was a legislator, not a reporter, who tracked the phony phrase down.

It has become a fashionable guilt-by-association ploy with the radical right to brand anything they do not like as socialistic. Thus medical care, social security, the minimum wage, and other social legislation all become steps toward communism.

Hearteningly enough, some responsible religious leaders have been speaking up lately about the dangerous damage right-wing extremists are inflicting on the fabric of our society. "This is not a theoretical matter," wrote the General Council of the United Presbyterian Church in a letter deploring the "rash of false charges" against churches and churchmen as havens or tools of communism. "There are congregations which are being rent asunder," the letter said, ". . . as church member is set against church member." It warned Presbyterians not to be duped by "a campaign of anticommunism based on a distrust of our free American institutions. . . . In the name of preserving American freedom, they subvert it more effectively by their reckless attacks on the churches, the press, and constitutional government than the Communist conspiracy has been able to do."

Father Thurston Davis, the editor of *America*, a national Catholic weekly, has openly rebuked Catholics for joining the John Birch Society. He stressed that Catholics are "firmly wedded to the best elements in the American tradition. . . . But," he added sharply, "some of our non-Catholic brethren have reason to doubt us when a man like Robert Welch, the non-Catholic founder of that strange phenomenon . . . can make the repeated claims that forty or even fifty per cent of his membership is made up of Catholics.

"Just what we Catholics are doing in the John Birch Society," Father Davis added, "—and what Catholic priests are doing on the roster of its endorsers or its inner council—surpasses my understanding."

An important official of the National Catholic Welfare Council, Father John F. Cronin, in the booklet "Communism: Threat to

Freedom," pointedly warns of the dangers of misuse of the Communist issue, especially by people posing as experts because of some claimed past connection with the FBI. An uncommon number of official right-wing activists tend to glorify some previous contact with the FBI—however fleeting—as a special kind of badge of authority. Whether as ex-agents or informants, their credentials should be scrutinized with care, Father Cronin declares, because it does not necessarily follow that they have any special knowledge of communism at all. This is a highly useful admonition, which J. Edgar Hoover himself will undoubtedly be among the first to welcome in order to preserve the integrity of the FBI— a vital repository of intelligence on communism and Communists.

More broadly, the public itself can welcome these warnings of religious leaders as the most valuable kind of assistance in viewing the radical right in its proper perspective.

Press, Radio and Television

THE VOICE THROWER

January 3, 1955

THIS ASSIGNMENT, inaugurated on this evening of January 3, 1955, is to report the news and try to get at its meaning. This is what orators would call a challenge. The news is everywhere; it never stops happening. And it means many things to many people.

Modern methods of communication, including that indispensable Washington utensil, the mimeograph, have tapped such vast veins of information that the stuff has to be measured by the acre and the ton. If all the pieces of information technically available to the public were laid end to end, it wouldn't matter much— we would never have time to absorb the material.

So the function of a broadcast like this has to be, not just to report, but to try to select, what seems important to report—and attempt to put it in focus, in perspective. In this connection, let it be reported now, for the record, that in the agreements between the American Broadcasting Company, the American Federation of Labor, which sponsors the program, and this reporter there is nothing implied or in print, fine or otherwise, about what is to be reported or what is not to be reported, what is to be commented on or what is not to be commented on, or how.

So, what do we say? Naturally, that will depend on events. The news will come first, and such comments as there are will be reserved for this end-corner. We belong to that old-fashioned school which holds that, insofar as possible, news and opinion should be separated and clearly labeled.

A microphone is a strange and wonderful instrument, not incapable, now and then, of a certain kind of sorcery on the person talking into it. As a distinguished confederate of mine on another network * once observed, a fellow who has never thrown his voice beyond the end of his neighborhood bar suddenly finds himself heard coast to coast, inducing a possible headiness of importance that no bar could supply.

This reporter will try not to forget that danger. He starts this new assignment feeling duly humble, but full of enthusiasm, an enthusiasm made no less sharp by the realization that the sponsor is not allergic to the word "liberal." We do not happen to think that label is an obscenity, any more than we believe that conservatism was conceived in a cave.

To me, the term liberal means, mostly, an open mind, questioning, doubtful, but eager to explore without tearing up all the road maps.

There are many routes to an objective, many facts to a story, and this correspondent will do his level best to find them and put them in balance, remembering that the key to the whole combination is one thing—fairness.

Even senators have learned that they cannot last long without that.**

WHICH TONI IS THE PHONY?

May 6, 1955

CANDIDATES, OREGON'S SENATOR Richard Neuberger once argued, owe it to their audiences to say whether their complexion is pure or powdered on TV, and whether their delivery is the real homemade article or hoaxed up in the studio, as is now the accepted practice. Neuberger introduced a bill † in the Senate which would require office-seekers to state, when they appear on

* Edward R. Murrow, now Director of the U.S. Information Agency.
** Irony of ironies, this inaugural broadcast was almost cut in half on the air because of a mix-up over cues and timing.
† It never got anywhere.

80

TV, whether they are using facial make-up or speech-prompting devices, or both.

"If a candidate gets up and looks an audience squarely in the eyes," he said, "and then reads that in 1922 some 28,833 eels passed through a certain place, everyone thinks he has a great memory and is a fine extemporaneous speaker." As a matter of fact, the candidate is probably using an "idiot board," meaning cue cards or a television prompting device off camera.

A fatty tissue of phoniness, of which television campaigning is only a part, is growing on our body politic. From the time we get up in the morning until we go to bed at night, we live in a world created by the copy writer and the publicity merchant of Madison Avenue, symbolic world capital of advertising, whose legal tender is the outlandish idea and the stomach ulcer. If you do not believe it, leaf through your paper, thumb through your favorite magazines' ad pages, listen to the commercials. How much is real and how much is rich, full-bodied verbal salami? Small wonder if Congressman Claghorn and Senator Snafu feel they have to play the game and cover their confusion with blue shirts, pancake make-up, and cue cards. Their thespian tendencies may have been a bit overdeveloped, too, by the business administration's experiment in government by slogan, and politics glamorized and dramatized by sales techniques.

Left alone, television has a penetrating eye, as the Army-McCarthy hearings so tellingly demonstrated. This is the kind of look at government and politics in action that the public needs. The trick shot should be preserved for the variety shows. It has been charged that the Republicans are making political capital out of televising the Presidential news conferences. It happens that they have an impressive figure in President Eisenhower, who has been playing these conferences straight, without props, with remarkable effect. In these performances, he could hardly run afoul of Senator Neuberger's proposed law. Some other White House-Robert Montgomery productions might conceivably fall into a different category.

Politics is bound to be merchandized to a degree on television, under any law. But the viewer is entitled to know which is the wrapper and which is the product.

LISTEN TO THE LISTENERS

February 23, 1956

I SOMETIMES THINK that commentators are a presumptuous lot. Here we sit, if not in ivory towers, in broadcast booths then, making noises we fancy are important. Some reckless listener tosses us a two-cent-postcard * bouquet of approval, and we wallow in the satisfaction that we have enlightened, if not influenced, public opinion. If the response is negative or, worse yet, if there is no response at all, we hide our piqued or neglected pride behind the rationalization that public opinion has not yet caught up with our thoughts because, after all, the mass mind moves slowly.

Our presumptuousness betrays itself, not only in the arbitrary way we may sometimes attach importance to events and circumstances, but also in the careless way we may come to think of people in terms of lumps instead of as individuals. We identify public opinion with the thoughts of the man in the street, and, since the man in the street does not exist except as a handy symbol for pollsters and pundits, the term "public opinion" can mean anything or nothing. To regard the individual in terms of the mass, or lump, is what might be called "lumpy thinking," because it is to forget his identity as an individual. Despite the tendency to think in terms of the so-called masses, the broadcaster, of all people, should be able to resist it, because the mail he gets is very individualistic, very human stuff, ranging from reactions on the day's news to the delightfully bizarre.

Not long ago, a man from Pascagoula, Mississippi, shared with this reporter his own private project for improving civilization. "I am convinced," he wrote, "that there should be a standardized universal alphabet, and I have made considerable progress by adding six letters to the English alphabet."

A lady from Pueblo, Colorado, had a much more immediate problem on her mind. "If you want to be a dish-washer, clean-up girl, vegetable man, fry cook, car hop, and waitress all combined,"

* It would cost him four cents now.

she complained, "you might get fifty-five cents an hour." No such luck, she said, that the new federal minimum wage of a dollar an hour * apply to her job, and she was asking the authorities, especially the Colorado authorities, why.

A student on a high-school debating team in Niles, Ohio, wanted source material on the proposal to make it easier to finance a college education by allowing the parent to claim at least part of the cost as a deduction on his income tax.

You may say what you like about the disenchantment of the younger generation with important issues, but another high-school student, a girl from Bellevue, Washington, was inquiring about a major one. She conceded that as a northerner she could not possibly know the southerners' problems on segregation. But she noted that some officials in Mississippi were alarmed at the number of Negroes registering to vote, and they were going to stop them. "What I do not understand," she wrote, "is how they could possibly stop them when the Fifteenth Amendment grants the right to vote to Negroes."

A lady in Orange, Texas, wanted me to help her prepare a personality sketch of Walt Disney, whom she had chosen to discuss on a personalities program at her local women's club.

From Los Angeles came the admonition to both political parties, but especially the one in power, to cease the "oppressive overuse of the word 'popularity' in the coming campaign. . . . This," the listener's letter said, "puts the occupant of the highest office on earth on a par with a girl in a beauty contest or an honorary mayor of Hollywood."

Obviously with the same subject of politics in mind, but betraying the quiet desperation of a citizen surrounded by it in the nation's capital, a gentleman from Washington, D.C., wrote, "How many of the voices around us are loaded with a hypocritical piety and humbuggery!"

That should be enough to puncture the presumptuousness in anybody.

* A maximum $1.25 minimum since 1961.

FORGIVE US OUR
PRESS PASSES

September 18, 1959

IT IS HIGH TIME to admit that, in terms of coverage of big events such as the Khrushchev trip, the cherished democratic freedom which we Americans pay such ardent lip service to—freedom of the press—has become a hollow mockery. Minions of the mass media find themselves prisoners of their own massiveness, and the imprisonment is made even more confining by our failure to face up to electronic and other facts which have changed the very nature of journalism.

There are some three hundred correspondents, photographers, newsreel and TV cameramen, and other miscellaneous technicians from all over the world assigned to follow the Soviet premier around the U.S., not to mention equal numbers of local representatives, at each stop, to report, hopefully and individualistically, his every utterance and gesture. "Follow," is the word. We almost never catch up with the central figure in this hectic, jet-propelled carnival. He is simply too far away to be visible to the naked eye or audible to the naked ear. Long gone is the time when journalistic enterprise consisted of a genuine eyewitness account of a story such as this, or of an authentic exclusive interview. Enterprise in the electronic age demands the foresight to carry along a transistor radio or to command access to the nearest television screen. One of the chief correspondents of Tass, the Soviet news agency, covered his leader's arrival in Washington by taking notes in front of a TV set. Yesterday, none but a tiny handful of the mass of reporters riding the railroad with Khrushchev from the capital to Manhattan were anywhere near the center of his activities. One distinguished Washington correspondent of a distinguished afternoon newspaper wrote his account of the New York welcome for the celebrated, controversial visitor from the report on a pocket radio he was holding to his ear, while riding on a press bus blocks away from the actual parade route. Last night, the overwhelming majority of the

84

journalistic entourage sat in a cavernous press room at the Waldorf-Astoria, composing their colorful chronicles on current history from mimeographed handouts, from the cryptic and carefully superficial accounts of official briefing officers, from the bulletin-board-posted notes or word-of-mouth descriptions dispensed on the fly by reporters who happened to be in the day's working press pool, and finally from television and radio sets.

This is ridiculous. The resultant dispatch is no real firsthand "I was there on the spot" account, but a fuzzy hand-me-down synthesis, or maybe a reasonably accurate description of what you at home are seeing on your video screen or listening to on your radio in the first place. One of the reasons for this vicarious vision of events, of course, is that Khrushchev is surrounded by an army of bodyguards. Even if it were possible to dispense with this cocoon of precaution completely, it would be impossible for the other army of reporters and cameramen to draw any intimate journalistic bead on him, because their number is so unwieldy that they are already stumbling over each other.

With the proliferation of population and the perfection—if perfection is the word—of gadgets to serve up mass information to these masses, we have reached, let us face it, the point at which the law of diminishing returns has been lowered against what we still choose to call "personal journalism." It is too bad that this inhibits the individual flavor and flexibility of a free press, but it is a fact, and the sooner we in the profession recognize it and take realistic steps of our own to adapt to it, the better. Because the alternative is a more concentrated dose of bureaucratic spoon-feeding of information than we have already.

This is going to call for some kind of voluntary limiting of demands for coverage of events such as this Khrushchev journey. There are still more than three hundred requests outstanding for reporter and camera places on President Eisenhower's return trip to the Soviet Union.* If this surplusage stands, Moscow or Washington or both may be impelled to cut it arbitrarily. Otherwise, the basic coverage will again be left to rotating pools of irritable

* Far more damaging, I think, than the collapse of the Paris summit conference in the heat of Khrushchev's rage over the U-2 flights, was the aborting of this trip, which might have been the most important good-will visit of modern times.

and exhausted newsmen, and will again consist of fragmentary accounts which the majority of the other haggard travelers will then rewrite after their own fashion into dispatches on which they could have been more reflective and penetrating if they had stayed behind and written them, from the same secondhand sources, at home.

THAT'S A SILLY QUESTION

March 13, 1961

NOT SINCE THE days when Richard Harding Davis made a best-selling success out of personal journalism, have reporters bulged so prominently in the public eye. But, judging by the inflamed feelings of many citizens, we are more of an irritating cinder in that eye than the objects of trusting attention. The reason should be obvious, but, curiously enough, it is not. The increased use of television, and, to a lesser extent, radio, to cover "live" events of news, including the President's meetings with the press, has made the work of the Fourth Estate a kind of spectator sport. More than that, it has made the spectator his own reporter, his own editor, his own analyst of the news. He witnesses the event firsthand and applies his own judgment to it.

There may be something mildly disturbing in the spectacle of millions of Americans becoming their own Walter Lippmann, Joe Alsop, or David Lawrence, but there is something hopeful about it, too, for in it are the seeds of a more alert, better-informed public opinion, and we can always use a bigger crop of that. However, this process is changing somewhat the role of the journalist, though many of us seem to be behind instead of ahead of the change.

According to the White House mail, President Kennedy's televised news conferences are a hit, but the reporters are not. Scores, if not hundreds, of letters complain that our jack-in-the-box procedure of jumping up and down to get recognized is undignified, even disrespectful, and that some of our questions are abusive. Everybody seemed to have his own recipe on how the procedure should work; these ranged from admonitions to the news corps to stop shouting to such gimmicks as placing outside the State Department auditorium door a drum from which reporters would draw numbers as they entered, to indicate their turn on the firing line for questions. If anybody has ever tried to regiment an irascible covey of correspondents, he would know that this is one numbers game that will not work. President Kennedy himself may have quieted some of the public concern, in his answer to a newsman's question last Wednesday about our possibly abusive conduct in what might be called the president's classroom. "Well," he said with a wry smile, "you subject me to some abuse, but not to any lack of respect." He conceded there were difficulties with the present format, but, recalling the adage that you "don't take down the fence until you know why it was put up," he thought we should stick with what we have at least until that "why" is answered.

The main reason for the current apparently hectic pattern of the Presidential news conference is that nobody has been able to agree on a better one. This does not mean that improvements cannot be made. This periodic meeting with reporters is one of the public's most important links with the chief executive. It needs to be kept as flexible and informal as possible. One of the difficulties is that too many people in the information business, more so in publishing than in broadcasting, have not quite accepted radio and television as instruments of journalism that are here to stay. Back in the old New Deal days, when these White House exchanges reached their height of informal give-and-take under FDR, a reporter could ask a silly, cumbersome, or irrelevant question without being instantly exposed to critical public gaze or misinterpretation. Nowadays, particularly under the Kennedy tendency to have so many news conferences covered "live," not only is the President in danger of making an irretrievable *gaffe*, but so are his questioners—and the way Mr. Kennedy has been operating, he is far ahead of his interrogators in excellence of performance.

It behooves the representatives of all media—of the printed, spoken, and televised word—to realize that now we are all an inseparable part of the act. Not an act on the Amateur Hour, but in current history. The public is, or should be, expecting us to press the President sharply and hard on important matters, but with clarity and respect. Too often, I am afraid, we are the authors of fuzzy or inconsequential queries, which could be minimized if we did our homework better or had the topic more securely in hand. The frantic bolt for the door at the end, which seems so disconcerting to the public, might be eased somewhat if more individual papers and broadcasting stations used a little more news-room enterprise of their own and wrote their own interpretive reports of the news conference as it unfolds on the air before their eyes and ears. This might take some pressure off the wire services and give them more time for reflective reporting. It has been observed—not without some accusing bitterness in some quarters—that the President is "using" the news conference to his own advantage. He is, and he is entitled to. When we of the press make our part in it more pointed and responsible, it will be to the advantage of everybody, especially the public.

WE PAUSE FOR A MESSAGE TO THE SPONSOR

January 4, 1962

SOME SPOIL-SPORTS down at the Federal Trade Commission are threatening to take the fun out of television commercials. They insist that ads on video must be truthful or at least not deceptive. Now that the cynicism of the materialistic younger generation has left the illusion of Santa Claus pretty well shot, what is there left for us doddering romantics if the FTC robs us of that lovely land of make-believe we glimpse in the TV plugs for the perfect products in the best of all possible worlds? The answer—to borrow and distort a celebrated quotation by the chairman of another regulatory agency, the Federal Communication Commission's Newton Minow—is a wasteland of realism, and I am not sure we can stand it.

Yesterday in a unanimous and portentous decision which overturned the recommendations of its own examiner, the FTC ruled that TV camera "trickery" must not be used in demonstrating the qualities of a product offered for sale. Involved was a commercial extolling a shaving cream with such qualities that it purportedly could shave sandpaper in one stroke. The main hitch was that the filmed demonstration did not use sandpaper at all but a piece of plexiglass with sand added.

We Americans have come to love this nonsense. With the television fare between the commercials so often so violently dreary, we have come to await with zestful impatience the exciting bit in which the electric razor shaves the fuzz off a peach, a blade mows down sandpaper in a single stroke, a movie camera demonstrates the nondistortional qualities of car safety glass, a cigarette fully filters out tars, or an aluminum foil keeps a ham smokehouse-fresh. These are little dramas that tug at the heart, and who says we want to be told that the peach may not be a peach, that the sandpaper is a phony, that the glass does not distort because the camera shot through an open window, that the filter did not take out any more tars than any other filter, or that the ham looked fresh because the competing one was deliberately dried out? These may be some of the country's most precious illusions.

Then there is the matter of what might be called the cross-fertilization of drama, the commercial's enlivening contribution to the humdrum of the home. A newspaperman I know has a sixteen-year-old daughter who recently was equipped with an evening dress for her first dance. As she descended the stairs, a radiant star in blue satin who reduced her father, quivering with pride, to muteness, her fourteen-year-old brother, an expert on TV commercial tag lines, called out like an evangelist pursuing sin: "Are you betrayed by a fickle deodorant?" No TV offering that I have caught could match the mixture of mirth and tragedy into which that family scene dissolved.

With considerable force, FTC commissioner Philip Elman, in his sandpaper opinion, cites another ruling which said with piercing candor: "If respondents 'do not choose to advertise truthfully, they may, and should, discontinue advertising.'" This brings me back to an earlier point: How much realism can we stand? Here we already have those graphic shots of aspirins and seltzers flaking and bubbling away in the plumbing of our stomachs, and, on radio at least, the word pictures of roll-on deodorant getting stuck to the underarm hairs that men do not shave, the gentle

89

expeditions of laxative pills through the lower tract, et cetera
ad nauseam.

Still, perhaps, the public *can* stand it if radio and TV can stand
Commissioner Elman's abrasive truth which is that it is untenable
to assume that the dominant function of broadcasting is to sell
goods.

WHO WILL BE LEFT
TO PRINT WHAT'S FIT?

January 8, 1962

OVER THE WEEKEND, two Los Angeles newspapers died—
or, rather, were extinguished by their publishers: the afternoon
Mirror, by the Chandlers; the morning *Examiner,* by Hearst.

There is something especially tragic about the passing of a
newspaper, or at least there has been in the past; it was unlike
an ordinary business failure, for a kind of personality seemed to
be involved. Then, too, in addition to the sudden bitterness of
joblessness for reporters, printers, and others, there was the
shrinkage of another source of information, the loss of another
point of view. However, without in the slightest trying to minimize the damage to people intimately involved in the folding of
the Los Angeles *Mirror* and *Examiner,* I suspect the period of
mourning for them will be minimal. So lacking in individual
character were they, so akin to so many other publishing stereo-
types from coast to coast, that indeed they may not even be
missed if, as is probable, their popular features are transferred
to their respective heirs, the Chandlers' morning *Times* and
Hearst's *Herald-Express,* an afternoon paper. As business prop-
erties, the *Mirror* and *Examiner* were simply no longer profitable,
so their days were numbered. The apparent fact is, they were
worth more dead than alive to their owners.

In an interview published by the Fund for the Republic, the
Louisville *Times and Courier-Journal's* distinguished Mark
Ethridge deplores the trend for newspapers "to become only commercial enterprises," when they have such a vital responsibility
right now "to explain what the issues in the world are." Some

publishers, he believes, "think that it doesn't make much difference what a paper says as long as the balance sheet is all right." He concedes that costs are rising all the time, but he is distressed by the spectacle of many papers, in increased competition with broadcasting for the advertising dollar, tending to cut their costs rather than improve their product. Ethridge argues that "the best—and cheapest—box-office attraction for a newspaper is good news and editorial content," and for proof he could point to the financial success of his Louisville papers and the other nine or ten consistently rated as the best newspapers in the country. "My experience has been," he said, "that you will get the economic support when you are determined to put out a good newspaper."

His remarks recalled for me the blistering wisdom charmingly administered to the American Society of Newspaper Editors by that blisteringly charming author and critic, Marya Mannes, a couple of years ago. She accused newspapers of laziness, conservatism, and fear of change, of printing wire-service copy and "canned" or syndicated opinion (good as it sometimes can be), instead of using their own enterprise. Thus has come the tragedy of a decline of public confidence in the press. If, she warned the editors, the public buys a paper to line a garbage can or light a fire, but not to learn, then "you may wake up one day to find you have lost the greatest power entrusted to men: the power to inform a free people."

There is no encouraging evidence that anybody much is following the Ethridge or Mannes advice, except the handful of top papers that do not need it. Newspapers continue to be bought, sold, merged, or dismantled like office buildings. The American Newspaper Guild estimates a dozen mergers since 1959 have cost it 942 jobs. In the first decade after World War II, more than a hundred papers suspended publication and another fifty or so merged.*

* On June 4, 1962, Sam Newhouse became the biggest newspaper-chain operator in the country (nineteen papers) by closing the biggest deal in U.S. journalistic history: purchase of the *New Orleans Times-Picayune* and *States-Item* for $42,000,000. Largely to keep it from folding, the *Milwaukee Journal* on July 19, 1962, purchased the long strike-bound *Milwaukee Sentinel* from Hearst. According to *Time,* daily newspapers have fallen steadily from a 1916 high of 2,461 to 1,760 in 1962; daily-newspaper competition survives in only sixty of 5,911 U.S. cities, "and in two-thirds of these the competition is token, i.e., between morning and afternoon papers."

How many could have stayed alive, how many jobs could have been saved, how many points of view sharpened if the publishers had considered information as important as profit? Arithmetic may not provide the answer, but, paradoxically, Ethridge's formula may: Improve the product, and you need not worry so much about cutting costs. The trouble is, perhaps, that too many publishers interpret improvement as meaning a prettier type face, a new comic strip, a chauvinistic and suspicious view of world affairs, and a suspicious conservative's view of Washington.

The *New York Times*, bless her sometimes stodgy old heart, is hardly the most revolutionary newspaper extant, but she is a precious repository of news in depth and, of late, sharper comment. There are millions of Americans who need and want this kind of responsible journalism, and some of them who need it most, in the Los Angeles area, will find it now in the *Times'* special West Coast edition.

THROUGH MURKY CHANNELS
AND WAVERING
WAVE LENGTHS

April 5, 1962

NEWTON MINOW, chairman of the Federal Communications Commission, once told the National Association of Broadcasters that commercial television was a wasteland. If they did not believe it, he invited them to sit down in front of their sets and watch the programing for one day from sign-on in the morning to sign-off at night. There is no record that anybody in the industry subjected himself to such torture, but there are some heartening indications that Minow's words were not dropped into a vacuum. Indeed, while some broadcasters still brood darkly in their tents about how to waylay Minow's crusading caravan, the public seems to have discovered in him a champion. At any rate, mail has been arriving at the FCC by the bale for many months, and Minow's office reports that most of it is favorable.

Emboldened to pursue even more vigorously what he has called the Commission's only business—the public interest—Minow appeared before the NAB again. This time he turned his major attention to the quality of radio broadcasting. If TV had been a wasteland, radio, he said in effect, was a kind of garbage dump wired for sound. He saluted that rare exception, the station with "well-prepared newscasts, imaginative entertainment, a drama, a children's program, enlightening commentary, breathtaking variety. But," he warned, "in too many cases the results today are incredibly bad. In too many communities, to twist the radio dial . . . is to be shoved through a bazaar, a clamorous Casbah of pitchmen and commercials which plead, bleat, pressure, whistle, groan, and shout. Too many stations have turned themselves into publicly franchised jukeboxes."

It is almost as if radio had become a conveyor belt of endless commercials and moaning music, a seven-day bicycle race for disc jockeys with gluey voices and a comic-book approach to culture. Minow was not the first to discover this phenomenon of noisy decay. There are many responsible people within the broadcasting industry who have been striving long for improvement. One of these, Morris Novik, a broadcast consultant to labor and liberal groups, pointed out major flaws in broadcasting in a speech at an Ohio State University study gathering. He described the typical radio station programing of dubious music and little belches of news bulletins as a "no-talk policy." He produced the embarrassing fact that less than one-quarter of the nation's thirty-five hundred radio stations carried the Kennedy-Nixon 1960 campaign debates, and he noted public complaints to the White House that not enough had been carrying presidential news conferences since. He deplored the disappearance of such programs as "Town Hall of the Air," and the necessity of citizens of Atlanta and other cities to arrange a specially tailored network so they could continue to hear the Metropolitan Opera broadcasts. "Somebody," Novik said, "pulled the plug on public-service programing."

In his NAB speech, Minow saluted the many stations to whom "the public interest is a way of life," but he obviously did not

93

think that the many were enough, and he noted that too many non-NAB stations operated in defiance of the industry's minimal ethical standards. He warned that, unless radio broadcasting can achieve self-discipline to sustain satisfactory self-regulation, the FCC "may have to adopt a rule on commercials which does apply to everyone." *

This immediately provoked howls of "government intervention" and strident charges that Minow was "declaring war" on radio. Often in this kind of battle, the first to cry "fire" are those caught playing with matches. Minow does not want intervention. He is behind enough in his work as it is. If intervention comes, it will be only because the irresponsibility of radio broadcasters asked for it. To grapple with this and other problems, including the considerable financial difficulties of radio, Minow asked for a shirt-sleeve working conference of radiomen with the FCC.

In the interim, he suggested, we should learn from history; we are in haste to improve our communications systems and bounce signals off satellites, but what if we have nothing worthwhile to say? He recalled Thoreau's comment about a projected tunnel under the Atlantic, that "perchance the first news that will leak through into the broad, flapping American ear will be that the Princess Adelaide has the whooping cough."

But he allowed that broadcasting had plenty to say, if it would. "Something happened to America," he said, the day radio and TV carried the consuming chronicle of John Glenn's orbital flight. He asked the radio (as well as the TV) industry to improve its public service programing in proportion to that feat. "Am I guilty of asking too much of broadcasting?" Minow concluded. "Or, are you guilty of asking too little?" The answers are not all in yet.

* In unprecedented actions, the FCC revoked the licenses of two radio stations, in July, 1962: KRLA, Pasadena, California, for "conducting deceptive contests and altering program logs"; WDKD, Kingstree, South Carolina, for repeated obscenity on the air by a disc jockey and misrepresentation of programing. Both stations have appealed for a review. If the FCC does not reverse the decisions, the stations may appeal to the courts.

PIQUE-A-BOO AT THE WHITE HOUSE

May 31, 1962

THE PRESIDENT of the United States and the press are like the constantly quarreling couple who, when asked why they did not get a divorce, replied, "But we can't. We need each other."

Between the White House and the information media—as a reporter's milieu is now cumbersomely called, so as to include us folks in electronic journalism—bickering is inevitable. This is the democratic noise of give-and-take between a reasonably free press and a public official. Something would be very wrong if angry accusations and the squawks of righteous protest were not periodically heard.

Sooner or later, unfortunately, the chief executive finds or thinks he finds his *bête noire* in the press corps, and then a feud begins. Franklin D. Roosevelt was infuriated with the attacks on his administration by the New York *Daily News* in World War II, and one day produced a Nazi Iron Cross with which he proposed to decorate the paper's chief Washington correspondent, the late John O'Donnell.

Harry Truman wrote a letter, threatening bodily harm to the *Washington Post*'s music critic, Paul Hume, for an unfavorable review of his daughter Margaret's singing. He would not allow the *Chicago Tribune* in his office, either, though he swallowed that prejudice with a broad grin the day after his upset election victory in 1948, to allow himself to be photographed triumphantly clutching a copy of the *Trib* with a banner headline proclaiming Dewey the winner.

There were times when President Eisenhower could not bear to be in the same room with a copy of the *Washington Post*, and biographer Earl Mazo writes that Richard Nixon never even subscribed to the *Post*, in order to shield his daughters from the shock of a Herblock cartoon of the Vice-President. And now President Kennedy has canceled the White House subscriptions—all twenty-two of them—to the *New York Herald Tribune*.

Although it is well known in journalistic circles that for months the *Herald Trib* has been about as welcome on the White House doorstep as the *Daily Worker*, the official explanation is that it was replaced by an equal number of subscriptions to the *St. Louis Post-Dispatch* to get a better geographical distribution. The fact is that the *Herald Tribune* has been carping sharply, if not captiously, at the Kennedy administration for some time, and the President's Irish temper appears to have gone up like an unruly window blind.

There is a common denominator of reaction in these Presidential fulminations that reminds us, usefully, that the occupant of the most powerful, exalted, and savagely demanding position in the land is human, too. There is a kind of status symbol in reverse involved here. To know that a President can blow his stack gives the rest of us harassed souls a feeling of identity with him; to see his weaknesses and, on occasion, his faults revealed gives us a sense of sharing his troubles.

Just the same, I wish President Kennedy had not dropped the *Herald Trib*. The nation's newspapers and their predominantly Republican publishers will snatch the story up as a gauntlet and demand to duel with him on the issue of a free press and the virtues of abrasive criticism. On the whole, they will do this clumsily and with more sarcasm than good humor. The result is not likely to wreck the Western alliance or give the Kremlin that opening in the Cold War it is constantly looking for. So that part of the fuss may be shrugged off.

But the President has, if only temporarily, muffed his lines. Who, since that cold and memorable day in January, 1961, has been the fresh, keen wit of Washington, cleanly biting as the air of Inaugural Day? Who has produced more crackling good humor in five minutes at the annual Gridiron banquet than the Washington press corps elite in three hours of attempted political satire there? Who has kidded himself, others of his ubiquitous family, and his "Ev and Charley" Republican opposition more devastatingly than the highest-priced pundit in town? John Fitzgerald Kennedy, that's who. And he could have made the *Herald Tribune* writhe in mortified agony by one well-placed barb in the middle of its shrill caviling. Instead, he seemed to throw stove lids in unbecoming pique.

As for the *St. Louis Post-Dispatch*, the White House should have been getting it all the time. It is one of the best newspapers in the country.

96

People

THE MET MAKES THE GRADE

January 7, 1955

ONE NIGHT about thirteen years ago, this reporter sat in Mexico City's Belles Artes Theater and listened to a woman sing. Perhaps it would be truer to say that her voice was felt more than heard. It was a live, vibrant thing that flooded from her throat and soaked the whole audience in its richness.

I was fascinated to watch her face. When she sang, her physical person seemed to be engulfed by another self. She closed her eyes; the being became the voice and the voice the being. After the concert, I was lucky enough to meet her at the home of a friend, and I couldn't resist asking her why she closed her eyes. She looked at me in surprise. "I didn't realize I did," she said.

Tonight, this same woman, Miss Marian Anderson, at an age within touching distance of fifty, is making her debut at the Metropolitan Opera House in New York, the first Negro ever to sing at the Met. She has the role of Ulrica, the fortune teller, in Verdi's *Masked Ball*. Whatever the critical comments tomorrow on her professional performance, Miss Anderson will have fulfilled a lifelong wish, a secret wish that she had never told her friends about.*

* In a front-page story on January 8, 1955, Howard Taubman, then *New York Times* music critic, wrote: "It was a continuation of a brilliant international career as a concert performer, and for other Negro singers it was the opening of a big, new door to opportunity. . . . Many in the audience knew that Miss Anderson, like Joshua, but more quietly, had fought the battle of Jericho and at last the walls had come tumbling down."

And on January 15, Winthrop Sargeant wrote in the *New Yorker:* "I must confess to a feeling of relief that the publicity and righteous sentiment attend-

The magic happened last October, at a supper party after the opening of the Old Vic Company in *Midsummer Night's Dream*. Rudolph Bing, general manager of the Metropolitan, asked the famous contralto if she would take the part. He thought she would be wonderful in it. She said she would be delighted. Or perhaps she said "we" would be delighted, for she and her voice are partners. She rarely speaks of herself in the first person and never refers to "my voice." If someone asks her how a concert went, she replies, "We did the best we could." This plural self no doubt explains why Miss Anderson had not realized that she sang with her eyes closed; the other person had the stage.

As far as the public was concerned, Marian Anderson did not need this one aria at the Met. She had already entered the second quarter-century of her career as one of the most celebrated singers in the world. But the world is a strange place, and the people in it sometimes do strange things, including denying themselves the privilege of enjoying a great artist because of prejudice against the pigment of her skin.

Until Mr. Bing propounded the policy that if a singer suited the role his genes and chromosomes did not matter, no Negro had ever sung at the Metropolitan. Miss Anderson is too full of humility and grace to make a point about it, but she and her voice must be rejoicing together that their secret dream has come true tonight.

As sometimes happens, this woman became famous abroad before gaining acclaim in her own country, and her appearances at home might have been further delayed but for a happenstance. One evening in the mid-thirties, the impresario S. Hurok was idling down the Champs Elysées in Paris when he noticed that an American singer was billed in a concert. He went. Afterwards, he could hardly get backstage fast enough to sign her up. Hurok has managed Miss Anderson's appearances ever since. Touring the country was not always easy. The person whose voice Toscanini had described as one that "comes once in a century" some-

---

ing the debut of Miss Anderson at the Metropolitan Opera House have finally died down, so that the institution can now proceed to hire the best Negro singers without seeming to be involved in a crusade of sociological rather than artistic significance."

times had to pose as the maid of her tour companion in order to retain her Pullman berth.

Sitting in the audience tonight is her family, including her mother, who used to scrub floors at Wanamaker's in Philadelphia in order to send her three daughters to school. Their faces, no doubt, are shining with pride. The country, in ever-widening fractions, can be proud, too—its vision corrected for color blindness to recognize a voice that is golden and a heart whose music makes humanity a little more harmonious.

DEATH OF A SALESMAN— OF FEAR

May 3, 1957

IT IS CONSIDERED bad manners to speak ill of the dead, but one must wonder tonight whether it is necessary to be dishonest in order to honor the decency of that custom. Men who feared and despised Joseph R. McCarthy in life are mourning the Senator's death with expressions of sorrow that would normally reflect the loss of a dear friend. Surely, it is no disrespect to the sincere bereavement of his widow and intimate associates to suggest that such flowery verbal unctions from his foes are nothing more than wreaths of hypocrisy, better left undispatched.

These nervous utterances may be due in part, of course, to a kind of reflex action betraying the uneasiness of persons in the sudden presence of death, as if mortals confronted with mortality hastened to speak kindly, not out of a feeling of delicacy or compassion, but because of a kind of superstition that grim fate might touch them, too, if they did not. There is, I'm afraid, another reason in this case: fear; fear that, although McCarthy's stature as a senator crumpled long before his death yesterday, there is still a sinister stir of life in the trappings of McCarthyism that he left behind. Therefore, politicians think they must offer condolences they do not believe, in order to court, or at least not alienate, forces they do not respect.

This, I submit, is serious. It betrays the lingering presence of an atmosphere which the senator did not create, but exploited with fiendish artfulness and then left for other demagogues to exploit again. Tortured and tragic figure that he was, McCarthy offered no program, headed no organized movement; yet in his bullying, cynical ruthlessness there was something magnetic which seemed to draw all the disparate little clots of fanatics together behind him. As the *Milwaukee Journal,* which knew him well and fought him hard, says today: "His was a negative function, offering an outlet for uneasiness or hate springing from fears of the outside world, without proposing any positive remedy." Future generations, the *Journal* observes, are likely to find the era of McCarthyism "as fantastic and harmful to the American spirit as that of the Salem witch hunt, the post-Civil War reconstruction or the Ku Klux Klan. McCarthy was not directly responsible for the hysteria (the vague but choking fear of communism) that swept the nation, but he was the man to capture the imagination of those who were susceptible to such an emotional appeal."

The fears, perversities, insecurities, and downright cussedness of human nature being what they are, there will always be, latent or on the loose, the ingredients of what we now call McCarthyism in our society. What have we learned of this malady, of how to recognize its symptoms and deal with its ravages? Communism was, is, and will continue to be a menace. It must be fought deftly, intelligently, and without stint. If the shattering career of Joseph McCarthy has taught us how not to fight it, then nobody can say that this boisterous, unhappy man did not make a contribution of value. But we will not have learned the lesson well—and we may have to pay an even more exorbitant price the next time around—if well-meaning but careless men take a red-herring attitude toward communism's dangers, or if others insist that the half-truth, the innuendo, the trial by headline, the painting of guilt by the brush of association, the smear are (all or any of them) justified as means to an end. They are not. They are the tools of destruction of the very system we are trying to protect.

And, while the flags of the capital are at half-staff for a fallen

100

senator, who is mourning those numberless living souls whose private worlds were split and deadened by the bludgeon of McCarthyism, while we, the American people, did nothing?

SALUTE TO THE SALTY
TWANG OF TRUTH

May 22, 1958

AT NOON TODAY, a modest number of people, decorously dressed and absorbed in solemn thoughts, forsook the full May sunshine and bright midday bustle of the streets for the quietly awesome grandeur of Washington's National Cathedral. They entered in a mixed mood of sadness and respect to pay their silent tributes, each in a private way, to Elmer Davis.

Somewhere in the internal distance, the organ produced the strains of a requiem, binding the men and women there into a kind of bundle of common, dignified sorrow.

Under the massive chandeliers, three or four baskets of flowers sprouted unostentatiously from the base of the pulpit. No sobbing cut out the sound of the organ; no ponderous black veils choked the scene. Down the north transept aisle preceded by the verger, who was bent slightly with the burden of his long staff, accompanied by Canon Luther Miller, moved the tall, straight figure of the dean of the cathedral, the Very Reverend Francis B. Sayre. The congregation and four women in the vivid purple robes and caps of the choir rose.

For a moment, as if in accidental recognition of Elmer Davis' own lack of ease with electronic gadgets, Dean Sayre had trouble adjusting his microphone. Then he began the service, moving quickly through a simple ritual as if in tribute to the tart, nourishing terseness of Davis' own broadcasts.

There was the 23rd Psalm and then the 121st. Certainly, Elmer Davis feared no evil, either in the presence or the absence of his enemies; and he was not ashamed to lift up his eyes unto the hills from whence came his help.

101

Finally, Dean Sayre mounted to the pulpit and quoted from chapter 8 of the Gospel of St. John. The beacon of Elmer Davis' life must verily have been that verse which says, "And ye shall know the truth, and the truth shall make you free." Yet there were those who would have stifled his voice, having heard his truth. And who more than this man could testify, "But I seek not my own glory"?

In just a few minutes more than an Elmer Davis commentary took, the service was over; most of the crowd melted quickly into the dazzling sunshine outside. A few found their way to the north entrance to grasp the hand of a little, white-haired woman in black—the bravely dry-eyed widow. Inside, an acolyte snuffed out the candles beside the altar. The flame of the topmost taper in one candelabrum refused at first to die; even after the acolyte had stifled it again, it continued to burn with a defiance befitting the occasion.

It would be easy and soothing to say that the bright, sharp truths of Elmer Davis will burn forever, but there is a dark danger that this may not be so. A man of his stonelike integrity, his towering, fearless, and wonderful anger, his rasping conscience—such a man does not sit comfortably with or evoke a warm, unanimous welcome from any society in any era. Too many of us do not appreciate the value of his abrasive words. When, I wonder, has there been more need for a scrub brush applied to the pudgy skin of a softening populace? When have we been in such short supply of the probing intellect that deflates swollen, distorted values and pins flapdoodle, claptrap, pomposity, hypocrisy, and fear to the wall? When have we been more thickly siruped with the unctuous, pear-shaped tones poured on by special interests? When have we more desperately groped for the clean, salty twang of truth in the general interest?

A man like Elmer Davis cannot be replaced. His words will live only if people remember them to live by them, determined, as he was, to build a structure of social justice to protect man's sanity from an avalanche of goo.

A TOWERING MAN

October 20, 1959

THE CAREER and achievements of George Catlett Marshall are of the stuff writers use to create a fictional hero. His was a character too peerless to be real. Yet so real was he, so lasting his imprint on the times of tumult in which he lived, that historians already are measuring him as a figure of the century. This general of the army, who died Friday at seventy-eight and who was buried today in Arlington, quietly gave that odd, restless breed, the American, a greater stature.

The high marks of his life are familiar enough: football star and cadet of shining promise at Virginia Military Institute; Pershing aide; brilliant officer; Chief of Staff; architect of victory in World War II and, with Dean Acheson and others, of European recovery through the bold Marshall Plan; Secretary of State; Secretary of Defense; patriot. There were reverses, too, including his notable failure, in months of trying, to bring the warring Chinese Communists and Chiang Kai-shek successfully together.

Other men held more exalted offices. So what was Marshall's mark of greatness?

A scholar who is working on a new biography of the General, Forrest C. Pogue, the director of the George C. Marshall Research Center at V.M.I., puts it in one word: integrity. The General turned down a million dollars for his memoirs. He consented to an "unauthorized" biography only after stipulating that his share of the earnings go neither to him nor his family, but to the V.M.I. Center. His private papers will go there, too, to be available in due course to students and historians, now that he is dead. The lucrative offers of industry luring so many of the retiring military brass were not for him. More than ten years ago, he firmly rejected the blandishments of political hopefuls—Democrats, these were— by declaring he could never be drafted for political office. Here was one man whom the term "soldier-statesman" fits splendidly; it does not droop like the tired cliché it becomes when draped on so many others.

Marshall was absorbed by history from boyhood, perhaps partly because Uniontown, Pennsylvania, his birthplace, was saturated with it from pre-Revolutionary days. With a subtle yet sinewy blending of North and South in his own family heritage, the General's heroes, besides Stonewall Jackson, were Benjamin Franklin and Robert E. Lee; his life reflected the common sense of one, the passionate devotion to duty of the other.

Part of Marshall's genius in World War II was his ability to view the totality of the conflict, understanding but withstanding the fierce pressure of field commanders for special attention to their theaters. It has already been written that he had no room for petty things; yet so brisk and tidy was his mind that, despite the crushing command decisions weighing on him, he was thoughtful and human. He had time to read and act upon soldiers' beefs from the field.

This correspondent harbors two warm personal memories of the General. In the mid-thirties, when two Russian aviators were first to cross the North Pole, I was a reporter in San Francisco, where they were supposed to land. Instead, they came down unannounced at an army base in Vancouver, Washington. I managed to get the commandant on the phone, anticipating a brassy brush-off. Despite the unexpected bedlam made of his Sunday morning, General Marshall—for it was he—took time to relate pertinent and colorful details, including the fact that his wife was at that moment cooking ham and eggs for the visitors.

On D-Day plus seventeen, Marshall, as Chief of Staff, visited Rome, which had been recently liberated. In the Italian theater, we were a motley crew of warriors and war correspondents of a dozen nationalities, ranging from Poles to New Zealanders. Over the doleful protests of censors and security officers, the General consented to have a news conference. Instead of dishing out the dull, deceptive hash of the communiqués, he told us one of the reasons we were winning the war: the marvelous functioning of the floating Mulberry ports off Normandy. This was top-secret. The military functionaries were apoplectic. But Marshall sensed our unity of discretion for a common cause and trusted us. Nobody, so far as I know, even tried to break faith. The Mulberry ports were not taken off the secret list for months.

George Marshall kept faith with a country that often seemed

to have a hard time keeping faith with itself. Monuments may be raised to his memory, but already his character towers like a tree over corn stalks—and, in this year of dubious grace, I use the word corn advisedly.

SALUTE TO A SOCIALIST

November 20, 1959

A MAN who narrowly escaped being jailed during World War I as a pacifist, Socialist, and dangerous radical has been widely feted this week by some of the country's most prominent and well-heeled citizens, including members of that well-known minority group, the Republican Party. The reason is hardly because he was born in Warren G. Harding's home town of Marion, Ohio. The man is Norman Thomas; the occasion, his seventy-fifth birthday, which happens to be today.

In terms of practical politics, a hardened professional would call Thomas' career an idealistic joke. Between 1928 and 1948 he ran six times for the Presidency of the United States on the Socialist ticket and got nowhere. He tried twice, unsuccessfully, for the governorship of New York and twice, with the same results, for the mayoralty of New York City. "In those days," he recalled to me in a telephone visit this afternoon, "I ran for anything that was loose."

In terms of his philosophy, Thomas still believes in socialism, though, judging by his dogged and forthright record, socialism of the climbing rather than the creeping variety. He still is a militant opponent of militarism, and he still is one of capiltalism's sharpest critics. How does such a radical, who should be even more suspect by failing to be elected to anything and thus failing in that category by which Americans most sharply judge their fellows— the tangible trappings of success—how does he rate a ten-dollar-a-plate dinner at the Waldorf, salutes from people of undenied status around the world, and an editorial in this morning's *New York Times?*

I think the principal answer to that question is that, through

105

an age that has seen the American Dream become a frothy nightmare of flapdoodle and downright fraud, Norman Thomas has remained a stubborn monument of incorruptibility. In this era of materialism, such a monument is, encouragingly enough, an attraction, even an inspiration, especially when his posture is not coated with the unction of self-righteousness.

I remember in the late twenties the somewhat sinful thrill (my father was a small-town banker at the time) of listening to this tall, silver-haired, blue-eyed ex-Presbyterian preacher, in a blue serge suit, stiff white collar, and blazing red tie, denounce Wall Street and stand off a couple of sour Communist hecklers at the same time. Even on the carnival midway of the Ontario, Oregon, rodeo, which was where he happened to be speaking, his gladiator's thrust nudged a youngster's vague idealism.

What has he got to say to the fresh generation today? If they are bewildered, he reminds them that he, too, was bewildered. If they are cocksure and content, he warns them of the awful dangers of complacency. And, he says, "I would get quite moral, too. The welfare state is an improvement over what we had, but we have no right to be satisfied with it. The diminution of poverty, as we have seen, does not bring honesty."

Like other thoughtful citizens, Thomas is deeply troubled by the crushing reality of bigness—big business, big labor, big government. If the world somehow escapes the incineration of nuclear war, how can an individual escape suffocation in the thickness of regimentation that is pervading twentieth century life? Thomas sees the great powers of the Soviet Union and the United States moving closer together toward a kind of state capitalism. He does not welcome this because, while it may involve some relaxation in the rigidity of Communist society, it is likely to inhibit the freedoms we are used to—even take for granted.

Norman Thomas' passion remains disarmament and peace. With implacable purpose, despite the frustrations of a lifetime, he is still trying to make men see that the beginning of wisdom must be the end of war. At the moment, he is doing what he can to encourage the efforts of North Africans to organize a march into the Sahara Desert to protest the impending French explosion of an atomic bomb. Many citizens would scoff at this as an empty gesture, a waste of time, or, worse yet, a dangerous distraction from the world's harsh realities. Maybe so. And yet who can say that a man like Norman Thomas may not turn out to be the bravest realist of them all?

THE LOSS OF A MAN

October 6, 1960

Sometimes, when a man dies, his loss tears a hole in the fabric of society, yet from the life he led he leaves behind fine, clean lines of character to bind that fabric into a stronger cloth. Such was the damage done today by a fatal attack on the heart of Joseph Nye Welch, a puckish New England lawyer whose quiet demonstration of decency and fair play helped rouse a nation to its senses from an orgy of hatred and fear called McCarthyism. Our loss is great, but the inspiration from his belief in justice is greater.

In his biography of the late Senator Joe McCarthy, Richard Rovere writes that Welch, who would have been seventy on October 22, was a kind of "aesthetic dividend" from the Army-McCarthy hearings: "a proper Bostonian from Iowa, the son of an English housemaid and a Jack Tar of the Royal Navy," who personified "an Americanism compounded of love of country, a decent respect for the opinions of mankind, and an adherence to the tradition that esteems the public uses of fairness, reason, compassion, wit, and love."

To me, and perhaps to countless other citizens watching the Senate hearings on television in those tortuous days of 1954, the real turning point in McCarthy's career came on the thirtieth day of the proceedings in a clash between him and Welch, who had been summoned as special counsel by the Army.

Tension had been building up between the shrewd, delicate-mannered lawyer and the shrewd, indelicate-mannered Senator for days. On this particular afternoon, Welch was pursuing an especially penetrating cross-examination of McCarthy's chief of staff, Roy Cohn, when McCarthy angrily broke in with a gratuitous

107

attempt to smear a young man in Welch's law firm who had nothing to do with the case.

Stunned and outraged, Welch turned and said in a trembling voice: "Until this moment, Senator, I think I never really gauged your cruelty or your recklessness. . . . Little did I dream you could be so reckless and so cruel as to do an injury to that lad. . . . If it were in my power to forgive you for your reckless cruelty, I would do so. I like to think I am a gentle man, but your forgiveness will have to come from someone other than me."

In the aftermath of that agonizing encounter, it is tempting to observe that good can triumph over evil in real life, as well as in the soap operas and, now and then, the serialized westerns. In any case, the tall, stoop-shouldered Joseph Welch gradually became a national figure, a slightly rumpled repository of wisdom and dry wit, a "lawyer's lawyer" who, again via television, became the people's historian as a commentator on an excellent series dramatizing the meaning of the United States Constitution. More recently, he took an actor's role as a jurist in the movie version of a best-seller called *Anatomy of a Murder*. Welch later quipped he took the job because it seemed to be the only way he would ever get to be a judge.

In one televised episode on the Constitution, Justice Oliver Wendell Holmes was quoted in a historic dissent from a Supreme Court decision denying citizenship to a Hungarian woman, Mrs. Rosika Schwimmer, because of her pacifist views on the oath of allegiance to the United States.

"Some of her answers might incite popular prejudice," Holmes said, "but if there is any principle of the Constitution that more imperatively calls for attachment than any other part, it is the principle of free thought—not free thought for those who agree with us, but freedom for the thought that we hate."

"Holmes puts the test beautifully," Welch commented. "It is only when I am ready to grant to others the right to think thoughts hateful and repulsive to me that I really know what freedom is."

Perhaps Welch's sense of the responsibilities of citizenship under constitutional government bore more impact because he himself was such a human citizen, unpompous, warm, and kind. His hobbies included fishing and loafing, and, he would chuckle,

108

the latter always came first. He played cribbage, drank whiskey sours, and liked to shoot golf balls in the air with a rifle.

Pretense, hypocrisy, and obfuscation were his targets, too. Sooner or later, I suppose, somebody will propose a memorial or a monument to Joseph N. Welch. This is all very well, but I have a hunch that this man would rest in peace and loaf in especially prideful repose if, in the time remaining between now and November 8, the two opposing candidates for the Presidency could find it possible to guide their campaigns toward a shaft of wisdom that Welch himself once raised in describing an honorable courtroom.

"Only truth is important," he said. "Only truth is sought for."

THE CURIOUS IMPACT OF IKE

January 18, 1961

WITH THE TRADITIONAL, "Thank you, Mr. President," and one minute short of the usual, tacitly agreed half-hour, Dwight D. Eisenhower's 193rd and last White House news conference was adjourned at 10:29 this morning. Its content was less historic than the fact that it marked the end of an era, though there were some dabs of color and figurative tear drops of nostalgia which the feature writers picked up.

With the last question answered, as Mr. Eisenhower headed for the door, the 309 ladies and gentlemen of the press rose to their feet and gave him a warm ovation of applause. The President paused in the doorway, smiled, and raised his outstretched hands in a gesture of greeting that has become famous from San Francisco to the Taj Mahal. But he did not tarry long enough to shake hands with everybody, as his predecessor, Harry Truman, had done. Instead, he hurried off with the air of a man who is relieved to have one more terminal chore over and done with. Indeed, some visitors who saw him privately yesterday said he reminded them of a college senior who had just finished his final exams.

James Hagerty once observed that his chief relished these news conferences more than the rest of us realized. If so, he rationed the pleasure carefully. Today's was the first Eisenhower meeting with reporters since last September 7. He averaged twenty-four news conferences a year during his eight years, less than one-third the number that Franklin D. Roosevelt held.

Yet even these relatively rare meetings with the public's emissaries, the press, provided invaluable insights to the character of the man. Mr. Eisenhower has a quick temper and almost invariably bridles at sharp questions, particularly when they impinge critically on his own activities or those of his staff. This morning, he limited his discussion of the subject to the comment that critics have a right to criticize and that wife-beating questions were really the only kind he objected to. Graciously, he did not include stupid questions—of which even Washington correspondents are capable.

Perhaps more than any other device, the Eisenhower news conference dramatized the intangibles of the President's sincerity and proved the mysterious power of his personality. He is probably the only man alive who can make a clear impact with a cloudy generality. The Eisenhower syntax is notorious and unique; in a news-conference transcript, it is calculated to drive a meticulous student of the English language mad. None the less, endowed with the Eisenhower presence and animation, his statements suddenly come alive and have meaning.

"So vivid can this impression be," this reporter wrote after a Presidential news conference five years ago, "that even when you fail to discover a clear meaning in searching the cold text . . . you find yourself wondering if maybe the stenotypist didn't forget and leave it out."

Something in fact was left out: the human vibrations of Mr. Eisenhower himself. This curious quality of projection—some psychology experts might call it empathy—also established the connection the President had with the crowds on his remarkable good-will tours from Argentina to Afghanistan. News Secretary Hagerty sensed this quality and capitalized on it artfully. Exactly six years ago today, he threw these White House news conferences open to coverage by radio and television. Worried reservations were voiced at first over the possibility of cutting the broadcast versions on a partisan basis, of eliminating unfortunate or ill-timed remarks from the tapes. There were also complaints that

110

reporters would become actors. There is a bit of the ham in every-body. It came out, no doubt, in some of us as we turned from white to colored shirts in delighted and dutiful obedience to TV's rule to avoid lighting glare. Whether or not it was due to the glare of publicity, there was no partisan snipping of the transcripts for broadcast; nearly all of them were released verbatim.

But, while the Eisenhower news conferences are now a thing of the past, the President made it plain this morning that he was going to do more thinking and writing and political counseling than he had earlier planned to do. This is not likely to make Republicans unhappy. The party, he said today in something of an understatement, is necessary to the country. And it will not make publishers unhappy, either. Someone, considering the oddity of Eisenhower's spoken prose, once asked one of the General's intimates whether a ghostwriter had done his book, *Crusade in Europe*. "No," came the reply, "Ike writes like a dream."

DEATH IN THE MORNING

July 3, 1961

OF COURSE, the sun also sets. It set for Ernest Hemingway yesterday morning, at the wrong end of the day, but only in a manner of speaking. Whether he killed himself by accident or design is of less importance than the fact that it will be a long time before the sun sets on what he wrote.

Today the world is full of sadness and mourning and self-conscious obituaries. Some writers seemed to set about the obituaries as if to prove it was they who created *For Whom the Bell Tolls*. Hemingway would not have minded. Publicly, he might have uttered an obscenity or two, but privately he would have taken them as compliments, which they were, surely. Some of the tributes were as large and unwieldy as those floral wreaths at the Kentucky Derby and at funerals. But there were two tributes I liked very much.

Of Hemingway's writing, Archibald MacLeish said, "Like all

111

true idioms, it was an idiom of the human spirit, not of the language alone."

After praising him as one of the great writers of the century, whose contribution to literature was a certain clarification of the English language, James Thurber, who has done some superlative things with the mother tongue himself, said, "I met [Hemingway] only once and we went over to Tim Costello's [bar] and had a wonderful time and became brothers." *

I met him just once myself, and in my private thoughts we became brothers, too. Or perhaps I should say more truthfully, if there are no psychoanalysts listening, that he was at least Big Brother. The fact that Hemingway's enduring nickname was "Papa" is probably no accident. He wasn't the head of the family in the *Fumed Oak* sense, but there was a kind of authority in his adventurousness that drew people to him. I do not have the remotest idea what the few words were we exchanged the only time I saw him, which was one soggy afternoon in Paris in the winter of 1944, as he was finishing lunch in that dubious dormitory of war correspondents, the Hotel Scribe. But I do remember very well that my feelings were a mixture of reverence and envy for a man who wrote so cleanly of the big excitements and the plunging poignancies of life, which were the more measurable because he had cut them to personal size, having lived most of them himself, lustily, recklessly, but not unmeaningfully or wantonly.

All right, there were times when he got enmeshed in his own theatrics and looked silly or wrote badly or both, but—basically—

* Thurber, who happened to hear that broadcast, recalled more of that meeting in a letter to me a few days later. "I found Hemingway quiet and gentle that night, even compassionate," he wrote, "because I had been through five eye operations in eight months and he knew it, and, as we all know, he liked a guy who had been through it, in the jungle, on a burning ship, in a street fight, or in a hospital. He kept murmuring 'Jim Joyce and Jim Thurber,' the only time I have ever been linked with Joyce, or ever will be....

"Incidentally," Thurber added in a postscript, "I did not tell the *Times* man that we 'became brothers' but only that we became friends. I was drowsing on my bed when he called me to tell me the sad news and I didn't have time to phrase things very well. One of the few blurbs E. H. ever wrote for another man's book appeared on the jacket of *My Life and Hard Times* and in it he carried on his feud with Gertrude Stein: 'Even when Thurber was writing under the name of Alice B. Toklas ... we knew he had it in him.'"

112

what a giant of the language he was! How tawdry, messy, and even whimpering so many of the manuscripts of the current generation of American writers seem by comparison. That may be a stupidly uttered observation which will live to haunt me, because Hemingway looks more towering in retrospect than he did on the way up, and maybe some new young buck still climbing will look taller. I doubt it. Hemingway was an activist in living, and so he made his writing live, as MacLeish says, with the idiom of the human spirit.

When he worked, morning was the time he wrote. What went through his mind early yesterday morning before the shot was his business. It is not impossible, though, that some of his thoughts drifted back to *The Snows of Kilimanjaro*, the short story he wrote about one of the places he loved best, the great mountain in Tanganyika where he climbed and hunted.

In that story, you remember, a young writer lay dying in the wilderness of gangrene in his leg, infected by a foolishly neglected thorn scratch in the bush. As he lay there, he thought of life and death, and he cruelly taunted the handsome, suffering woman who was with him. Later he lashed himself for that. Then he thought he could beat anything, "because nothing could hurt him if he did not care.

"All right. Now he would not care for death. One thing he had always dreaded was the pain. He could stand pain as well as any man, until it went on too long, and wore him out. . . ."

In his final coma, he dreamed that his friend Compton had come with the plane to fly him out. And Hemingway wrote, ". . . looking down he saw a pink sifting cloud, moving over the ground, and in the air, like the first snow in a blizzard, that comes from nowhere, and he knew that the locusts were coming up from the South. Then they began to climb and they were going to the East it seemed, and then it darkened and they were in a storm, the rain so thick it seemed like flying through a waterfall, and then they were out and Compie turned his head and grinned and pointed and there, ahead, all he could see, as wide as all the world, great, high and unbelievably white in the sun, was the square top of Kilimanjaro. And then he knew that there was where he was going."

LONG LIVE WALTER MITTY

FOR MOST of the day I have been conducting a sort of wake—you might call it a wide-a-wake—over the body of literary works of James Thurber, whom I have rather idolized for more than a quarter of a century. I laughed a good deal. This was both inevitable and, I maintain, appropriate. Thurber, who died yesterday, would not have tolerated a soggy, morbid wake. Furthermore, it is fortunately impossible to mourn a man who is not really gone but who constantly reappears: over the bedstead as a barking seal; in the drawing room as a lancer of pretense and a spiller of drinks; among the daisies as a wistfully troubled dog; on the ingenious and heroic routes of escape from a nagging wife and commonplace reality as the intrepid Walter Mitty; and between the covers, thank Heaven, of more than two dozen imperishable books as the angry, impatient, brave, and hilariously brilliant defender of the hapless human being and his fey but literate world of fantasy, without which we all would perish.

Thurber had the matchless talent of injecting you into the most absurdly impossible situations and making you feel at home because you instantly recognized the plight as similar to one of your own experiences, real or imagined. It didn't matter whether you extricated yourself or not, because you were silently splitting your sides with laughter. Take, for instance, a book which he wrote in 1937 called *Let Your Mind Alone*. In it, he spoofed a manual entitled *Wake Up and Live*, by a Mrs. Dorothea Brande, who had outlined a dozen disciplines for developing sharper minds. Thurber was particularly incensed with discipline number three: "Write a letter without using the first person singular."

"What for?" Thurber demanded to know. "To whom? About what? All I could possibly think of to write would be a letter to a little boy telling him how to build a rabbit hutch, and I don't know how to build a rabbit hutch very well. . . . I remember the time that my father offered to help me and my two brothers build a rabbit hutch out of planks and close-meshed chicken wire.

114

Somehow or other he got inside of the cage after the wire had been put up around the sides and over the top. . . . I don't know exactly what happened, but he shut the door and it latched securely and he was locked in with the rabbits. The place was a shambles before he got out, because nobody was home at the time and he couldn't get his hand through the wire to unlatch the door. He had his derby on in the hutch all during his captivity and that added to his discomfiture."

If Thurber had done nothing else, he would be revered down through time as the man who destroyed, or at least made bedlam of, that "hideosity" of the American social landscape, the cocktail party. Take, for example, a conversation in his last book, *Lanterns and Lances*, between him and a Mrs. Groper, who wanted to know what he thought was the matter with humor in 1951.

"It was suffering from acute hysteria, pernicious fission, recurring nightmare, loose talk, false witness, undulant panic, ingrown suspicion, and occlusion of perception—quite a syndrome," Thurber said. "When reason totters and imagination reels, humor loses its balance, too."

Presently, a man with a highball glass in his hand wavered over and said to Thurber, "You guys give me a pain in the neck. On the other hand, the pain in Twain stays mainly in the brain."

"For such crude intruders," Thurber wrote, setting a beartrap of a pun, "I always carry a piece of complicated academic drollery, and I gave it to him: If you prefer 'I think, therefore I am' to 'Non sum qualis eram,' you are putting Descartes before Horace."

For me, the party ended right there in a delicious shambles. Thurber, who lived in a milky blindness for more than a third of his life, cut through the vapid foolishness of our times with sharp humor and acid satire. He has been compared to Mark Twain; but to me he stands alone, with sorrowing anger flowing from his pen like life's blood, but with a twinkle in his mind's eye, born of the knowledge that nonsense is the most devastating antidote to the nonsensical.

Last July, I got a letter from Thurber, who mourned with me the tragic, violent death of Ernest Hemingway. "To paraphrase General Pickett at Gettysburg," Thurber wrote, "I could say, 'My noble generation has been swept away.' I, too, have been through

115

the deep depression afflicting so many people during the past two years or so. I keep fighting it, though, and I have no shotgun, thank God. . . . Ernest, by the way, had read a piece of mine, circa 1932, called 'Suli Suli,' in which I wrote, 'I do not intend to be dragged from Jacksonville to Key West and back by an enormous fish.' But he [Hemingway] regarded me as a man, in spite of the fact that I never shot anything bigger than a sparrow, or caught anything larger than a lake trout."

Ah, but James Thurber could bring down pomposity, pretense, and utter humbug with a pea shooter; for that, he will be remembered as one of the biggest big-game hunters of them all.

ON A BEAUTY AND BEASTLINESS

April 2, 1962

A PRESIDENT'S WIFE does not have much private life. When she is as devastatingly attractive as Jacqueline Kennedy and has an impeccable if splashily unorthodox taste in clothes, her moments to herself are even rarer. Everybody stakes a claim to her as a public figure, and everybody is quite willing to express a personal opinion about her activities, how she should pursue them, and what color and cut of dress she should wear in the process.

The schools of thought about Mrs. Kennedy's visit to India and Pakistan seem to divide among the approving, the envious, and the critical. Some members of Congress, conscientious Democrats with an eye on the November elections, are fidgeting over the fact that many constituents have written their disapproval of the trip, arguing that Mrs. Kennedy should have stayed home with the children instead of going off alone with her princess sister to strange places, wearing glittering gowns in the palaces of maharajahs, and being candidly photographed on elephants and camels and things. This, some complaints ran, was reminiscent of the India of the British raj—an image which Communist propaganda would be bound to exploit. Besides, though it was true Mrs. Ken-

116

nedy paid her own way on commercial airlines, the man-hours expended by the Secret Service and embassy staffs came to large totals, and what was there to show for it all but a travelogue? Or so the speculation ran.

The facts as they emerge etch in a sharply different picture and a rather delightful one. Prime Minister Nehru, one responsible source estimates, has not been so captivated by a foreign visitor since Lord and Lady Mountbatten were in India to seal the nation's independence fifteen years ago. The Prime Minister and the President's wife talked endlessly, and Nehru seemed to begrudge the two hours daily that he budgeted himself for appearance in the parliament. President Ayub Khan of Pakistan was equally charmed. At one point, in India, autographed photographs of the First Lady were given to the household servants; later, one was spotted affixed to an Indian shrine. People on the streets struggled to express their gratitude that she had come so far to see them.

According to economist Kenneth Galbraith, the American ambassador to India, who had perhaps the most influential hand in planning this journey, it must not be viewed as a single adventure, but as part of a series of trips he has been quietly promoting for a wide variety of Americans to the Asian subcontinent. The "image" Galbraith found when he arrived in New Delhi last year was of a U.S.A. narrowly dedicated to capitalism, obsessed with its clash with communism, but brashly boasting of victory and goading onlookers to board the bandwagon. He found this picture warped and insufficient and set about to prove to the Asians that our pluralistic society did many things besides eat Marxists for breakfast.

Among those he has exposed to acquaintance with Indian officials, editors, philosophers, artists, and others, were: a Nobel Prize-winning scientist; George McGovern, head of the President's Food for Peace program; historian and White House adviser, Arthur Schlesinger, Jr.; Dr. Jerome Wiesner, the President's science adviser; Bil and Cora Baird, the fabulous puppeteers of the theater and television; and now, Jacqueline Kennedy. No Gallup poll was taken, but the word is that the Baird Marionettes bewitched the Indian audiences, that Wiesner's discussions of the application of new scientific techniques to the problem of disarmament opened new vistas of contemplation to Nehru, and that "Jackie" topped everybody.

But does all this prove anything? Not positively or tangibly. Mrs. Kennedy did not come back with a treaty. She did not discuss the cold war with her hosts, in either India or Pakistan, or ask them to take a political position. She discussed history and art and culture and children. "Children," she said, "speak the same language the world over," which, she added warmly, is perhaps why we value them.

Her presence moved Nehru to remark, "She has brought grace and charm to the international scene." Which scene, one might add after looking at the headlines, could stand a pinch more of both.

Mrs. Kennedy is herself pleasingly tangible as well as intellectually stimulating. We are lucky to have such a charming and versatile symbol working for us, whether or not she invades coal mines with her radiance as Eleanor Roosevelt used to do.

DARKNESS IN JULY

July 6, 1962

AFTER WILLIAM FAULKNER declined with regret the White House invitation to the dinner President and Mrs. Kennedy gave for the hemisphere's Nobel Prize winners last spring, somebody asked him why he had been unable to attend. "Well," the great southern novelist reputedly replied, "it's a long way to go just for a meal."

Although his touch for describing human turmoil moved men in far places and although he knew something of the world himself, Faulkner did not need to travel beyond the confines of his imaginary Yoknapatawpha County in his native Mississippi to establish his fame. Indeed, that is where it came from, and it is from there that it will endure "to illuminate the restless searching of all men," as President Kennedy gracefully put it in eulogizing Faulkner, who died this morning of a heart attack at the age of

118

sixty-four. Faulkner's search done, the President added, he now rests, "his place secure among the great creators of this age."

No doubt, controversy long will rage over exactly what it was that Faulkner created. He often wrote obscurely. *The Sound and the Fury*, his first book to win wide critical acclaim, opens with the babbling of an idiot. But the starkness of his characters, the depth and color of his moods, the true deftness of his vernacular, and the richness of his writing all add up to unforgettable artistry. When, as a callow undergraduate, I read *Light in August* in 1932, I seemed to be undergoing an experience, rather than reading. Even though its details escape me now, the intimate feel of it is still there.

My ABC colleague George Watson, a southerner himself and a student of the master's work, wrote me a memo which sums him up far better than I can. "Faulkner," Watson said, "transformed the public's literary image of the South from the veranda-sitting, julep-sipping gentry, listening to the gentle rhythm of darkies happily strumming banjoes down on the levee, to the brooding, dark, and ultimately tragic fact of southern life. This was not done in an accusatory way. Indeed, the South was for Faulkner a microcosm of America. But, in religious terms, the South was indelibly tainted with an original sin—the Negro's bondage, and that was and is the central, inescapable fact that persisted to plague the South.

"This sense of tragedy, of impending doom," Watson went on, "is what the brilliant young Negro writer James Baldwin says is desperately lacking in America, to counterbalance our glib optimism and sense of life's possibilities. This did not mean for Faulkner that life was humorless or without hope. He had a marvelous comic sense. (Indeed, his last novel, *The Reivers*, is something of a romp.) But his feel for tragedy did temper the easy optimism with which we tend to view our society."

As I riffled through the pages of *Light in August*, this afternoon, trying to pick up the thread of the trials of Byron Bunch and the others, this passage leaped out at me:

"The mild red road goes on beneath the slanting and peaceful afternoon, mounting a hill. 'Well, I can bear a hill,' he thinks. 'I can bear a hill, a man can. . . . It seems like a man can just about bear anything. He can even bear what he never done. He can

119

even bear the thinking how some things is just more than he can bear. He can even bear it that if he could just give down and cry, he wouldn't do it. He can even bear it to not look back, even when he knows that looking back or not looking back won't do him any good.'"

As if he were still tugging on that thought, Faulkner told the cadets at West Point, not long ago, that as a writer he tried to show a man "in all his phases, his conditions, his base attitudes and spirit—that he goes on, he continues, he has outlived the dinosaur, he has outlived the atom bomb, and I'm convinced in time he can even outlive the wheel. There is something that makes him endure. . . ."

Faulkner was obviously moved to deep respect by the Negro's capacity to endure, and recently he established a foundation to provide literature scholarships, principally for Negro students in the Deep South. But in a "Letter to the North" in *Life* magazine in 1956, though he spoke of the "incontrovertible immorality of discrimination by race," and his being drawn also to the Negro's side by "the simple human instinct to champion the underdog," he declared he was just as strongly against compulsory integration as against compulsory segregation, and he begged northerners to pause in the "forced" enforcement of civil rights.

The bitterly ironical fact was, of course, that the force of violence came from the racists, prominently including some of Faulkner's fellow Mississippians. But, for Mississippi's sake, and the country's, it is appropriate to point out that her richest legacy will come, not from the Senator Eastlands or even her bevy of Miss America beauty queens, but from the Nobel- and Pulitzer-Prize-winning works of the shy little squire of the farm north of Oxford on Pusscuss Creek, who was the third American literary great to die in one brief year: Hemingway, Thurber, and now William Faulkner.

DISQUIETING DEVELOPMENTS ALONG THE POTOMAC

July 13, 1962

Art Buchwald, says a column by Art Buchwald, is moving from Paris to Washington. If the mountain were suddenly to come to Mohammed, I could not be more stunned with surprise or filled with suspicion.

Something is going on here which does not meet the eye. This is no routine transfer of journalistic body from capital to capital, with family and furniture to follow. This is Buchwald, the syndicated satirist, the companion of kings, the sassy adviser of statesmen, the judge of wine, women, and White House news secretaries, transferring his domicile from the sophisticated City of Light to the raw-hewn center of the New Frontier. The question on everybody's lips on both the right and left banks of the Potomac is: Does this mean that Washington has arrived or that Paris has missed the boat?

My own theory is that this is a cover, as the boys in the CIA would say, for bigger things. One possibility is that Buchwald's employers on the mother paper of his syndicate, the *New York Herald Tribune*, are using him as bait to lure President Kennedy into resuming his subscription—twenty-two subscriptions, in fact —to the wayward *Trib*.

With the possible exceptions of sports writer Red Smith, pundits Walter Lippmann, Joseph Alsop, and David Lawrence, Buchwald is the *Herald Tribune*'s greatest living status symbol. (Horace Greeley is now dead.) The management may well figure that, if he can personally hand Mr. Kennedy a few needed tips—picked up at Deauville, if not from Dun and Bradstreet—on how to handle businessmen and the stock market, then the President will not have to bother calling in Bernard Baruch or Nichols and May, and in gratitude might restore the *Trib* to its accustomed place beside the morning milk, the *New York Times,* and other nourishment.

121

There is an even more sinister possibility in Buchwald's decision to take up residence in Washington. He may be a paid agent of de Gaulle. After all, he has lived abroad for fourteen years and speaks French with a Brooklyn accent; his ruddy and rotund configuration bespeaks his intimate knowledge of such Gallic state secrets as vintages and *cordon bleu* sauces; and—well, let's face it—he is practically a *foreigner*. I have an inkling of his dark mission. It is to kidnap Mrs. Kennedy. When General de Gaulle last visited this city, in the amiable twilight of the Republican regime of President Eisenhower, he reportedly said, in effect, with a mixture of gallantry and good taste that marks the true, discriminating Frenchman, that, of all he had seen, Jacqueline Kennedy alone was worth the trip. The motive is there, plain as the navigational warning lights on the Washington Monument, and Buchwald, whose journalistic charms beautiful women in countless world capitals have found irresistible, is just the man to do the dirty work.

In any case, Art Buchwald's arrival will be the greatest challenge to the Washington press corps since *Evening Star* society columnist Betty Beale started counting the fallen bodies in Attorney General Robert Kennedy's swimming pool. Buchwald is the kind of reporter who can turn a news leak into an artesian well, drying up everybody else's sources in the process. Once the Buchwald version is out, it defies all rational comment.

Worse yet, this man consistently writes with humor. This, manifestly, is something which Washington, in her present hour of trial, simply cannot stand. There is no field here for wit or satire. This is serious-minded *Advise and Consent* country, bub, where ruthless officials go their devious ways and the doddering chairmen of the House and Senate Appropriations Committees duel to a deadlock over Congressional privilege and protocol, denying the government the billions it needs to spend and create a budget deficit. This is where businessmen demand action and then howl when they get it, where organized labor and the U.S. Chamber of Commerce make common tax policy, where the sweetest lobby is in sugar, where about all the Disarmament Agency has to read for the nonce are dispatches about our hydrogen-bomb testing, where "Ev and Charlie" make you wish vaudeville had died earlier and where eggheads write eloquent public speeches and wince at private jokes about the Kennedy dynasty. The only things that draw a laugh around the nation's capital these days are the farm policy and the Washington Senators baseball team.

Plainly, there is nothing here for you, Buchwald. Take my advice, and not Horace Greeley's. Don't come west. Stay there, Yank, where you've got it made. But, if you must come, then welcome, or, as they say in New Frontier social circles, "bienvenu," and get in the swim—fully clothed, of course.

Labor and Management

COLLIER'S *CHRISTMAS PRESENT*

December 17, 1956

Friday night, between five and six hundred business and editorial employees of two of the country's oldest and best-known magazines, *Collier's* and the *Woman's Home Companion*, went home worried about their jobs. There were eight more shopping days until Christmas. Rumors had been winging around the Fifth Avenue building of the Crowell-Collier Publishing Company all day that the two magazines were going to suspend publication. Another Crowell-Collier perennial, the *American Magazine*, had folded last summer. But, just before quitting time, top management passed the word down to disregard the rumors and come back Monday as usual.

Yet only a few hours later in mid-evening, management revealed to a hastily formed employees' committee, which had been standing by, that telegrams were going out over the week end to virtually the entire staffs of both publications. The personnel would be notified that their jobs were finished and that their pay checks for that week would be their last. They could come in Monday and have a brief time to clean out their desks. Only incoming telephone calls would be permitted. That was it; no severance pay, no pension system, no benefits. The notifications went to the newest staff members and to the oldest, including a woman, now in the hospital, who had been a Crowell-Collier telephone operator for some fifty years, and a circulation man who

125

had taken one full vacation in his thirty-four years with the company.

The status of approximately four thousand employees is involved. The employees' committee is to meet with management Wednesday morning to discuss what severance settlements, if any, may be arranged. But the two magazines are dead.

Brush aside as sentiment, if you like, the fact that *Collier's* and the *Companion* had nourished such writers as Hemingway, Damon Runyon, Jack London, and Richard Harding Davis. But there is no sentiment in the story behind the story. The bare bones of it are these: *Collier's* and the *Companion* were at record highs in circulation, but they were losing money. The staffs argued that they had a bright future because recently reorganized formats were attracting more readers. It was learned, however, that a fierce struggle had ensued within management, and a Chicago broker named J. Patrick Lannan came up with the winning hand. He had bought into the company heavily with debentures reportedly convertible to stock, and had been elected to the board of directors last Monday. Crowell-Collier does an enormously profitable book-publishing and printing business, but the magazines had pulled it into the red. Lannan heads a special executive committee, which revealed the end of the magazines Friday night. Crowell-Collier stock went up almost a point in Wall Street today.

Collier's and the *Companion* weren't exactly fearless in their editorial content or stand, but they had positive points, and now they are gone—two more magazines swallowed up in "bigness." *Collier's* subscription list goes to *Look* magazine. The publishing business is feeling the weight of the giants that are left.

There is no rule which says a business must be operated as a charitable institution, but, if we pretend to exercise a "moral force" on the world at large, there is something the matter with a system which permits a human tragedy such as befell the employees of Crowell-Collier over the week end.

DAVE, THE GOLIATH

March 26, 1957

As DAVE BECK was shouldering his way out of the Senate Caucus Room at noon today, a young woman approached him and, in a voice shrill with anger, cried, "I have never heard such a liar in all my life."

Fixing her in the cold stare of his beady blue eyes, the president of the country's biggest labor union replied with sarcastic courtliness, "Thank you, thank you for your courtesy," and barged off to lunch.

In this conversational cameo was caught the kernel of the whole drama in the Beck affair: the rising fury and frustration of an awakening public, as expressed by the anonymous girl, and the shield of callous cockiness thrown up, almost in a reflex action, by Beck to protect himself from the inescapable realization that the arrogance of his power has finally cornered him.

From the transcript of this morning's proceedings before the McClellan committee investigating racketeering and other scandals in labor-management practices, it would be nearly impossible for the most astute of prosecutors to pin a rap for falsehood on the Teamsters' Dave Beck. Burlesque? Yes. Hypocrisy and cynicism? Certainly. Shocking disregard for the obligation of responsibility attached to his high position in organized labor? Without a doubt. But Beck took meticulous care to stand on technicalities in a stratagem which, he monotonously reminded the committee, had been thought out for him by his chief counsel, Senator Duff. His endless references to the lately defeated Republican senator from Pennsylvania as being responsible for his burly embrace of the Fifth Amendment bid fair to become a trademark of this hearing.

In the fog of emotion rising from the unpleasant marshes of testimony in this investigation, it is hard to remember that Beck, as a citizen, under the law and the Constitution, has a right to plead the Fifth Amendment on grounds that his answers to questions on what he did with union funds might tend to incriminate

127

him. He also has a right to challenge the jurisdiction of the committee, even though he compounds his risk of being held in contempt of Congress. The inquiring senators must have known this when they insisted on trying to nudge Beck from his narrow legalistic position into a confession. Their impatience and their appeals to patriotism and conscience were human and understandable, but clumsy.

It remained for Michigan's Senator Pat McNamara, a man from organized labor's own ranks, to hoist onto Beck's back the full weight of his responsibility. The act was all the more courageous and impressive because of the pain and embarrassment it involved for the Senator, a union pipe fitter from Detroit and a member of the McClellan committee.

The essence of McNamara's questioning of Beck was this: Granted your constitutional rights as a citizen, don't you feel you have a duty to the ranks of labor you represent? You are not here only as head of the Teamsters, the country's biggest union; you represent—to the public—all fifteen million members of the AFL-CIO. Do you not realize that by your conduct you are jeopardizing the rank and file, that by your position you are inviting federal legislation that might be repressive to labor?

But Beck was not moved. He shrugged off his responsibility, intoning that he bowed to no man in his patriotism in war and peace, or in his devotion to the union man and to the Benevolent and Protective Order of Elks, which he also served.

Whatever the outcome of Beck's legal battle, the public can only conclude that his usefulness as a labor leader, if not as a toiler for the Elks, has expired.* Happily, in the quiet outrage of such men as Senator McNamara, the conscience of the responsible leadership of labor rises to prove, if belatedly, that Beck's sordid saga is the exception and not the rule.

* On June 20, 1962, Dave Beck entered McNeil Island penitentiary in Puget Sound. He must serve at least twenty months of two concurrent five-year sentences, on convictions of filing fraudulent income-tax returns in 1950 and 1952 for the Joint Council of Teamsters Building Fund of Seattle.

THE CASE OF THE
BOUNCING CHARTER

August 5, 1957

THIS IS A SORDID little saga of what should not have been, but is. It is, of course, anything but a typical story of American enterprise, of legitimate labor-management relationships. But even one of its type is too much. It is the sort of dirt-under-the-rug operation which is currently being revealed by the Senate's McClellan committee. Committee Counsel Robert Kennedy, at the hearing this afternoon, called it the "Case of the Bouncing Charter." The moral of it would seem to be that anything can happen if people let it; or, putting it another way, racketeers don't care whom they play for suckers—the working stiff, the boss, or the district attorney.

The charter that bounced belonged to Local 228 of the old AFL United Auto Workers, a union now known as the Allied Industrial Workers of America which, according to McClellan committee evidence, figured prominently in the underworld domain of racketeer Johnny Dio. Dio allegedly has had more than dreams of sharing a powerful New York labor-union empire with the astute ninth vice-president of the International Brotherhood of Teamsters, James Hoffa. The full pedigree of Local 228's charter has not emerged, but in 1955 it dropped, or bounced, into the hands of a little man named Sam Getlan.

Getlan, a native New Yorker, age fifty-four, sad of face, but sly of eye and sardonic of tongue in the old Damon Runyon manner, told the committee a little about it this afternoon—less about himself. He did say that in the late twenties he worked for Frank Costello. Activity: servicing slot machines. Locale: Harlem. In Florida in the mid-thirties, he operated 250 slot machines at a gain to himself of $7,000 a week.

"Save anything?" Kennedy wondered.

"Didn't have time," was Getlan's philosophic reply.

When Florida banned slot machines, Getlan eventually found

129

himself back in New York, in, to be exact, the respectable reaches of Westchester County, where suburbanites and exurbanites used cigarette and other vending machines in the machine-age manner of millions of other Americans. However, Westchester's coin-machine business was not organized, and that's where Getlan came in.

At one point, he found himself looking for a union charter, and that's where Local 228 bounced in. He didn't apply for it; he just heard it was kicking around. Got a phone call one day, went down to the office of Milton Holt of Teamsters Local 805—a reputed headquarters of Johnny Dio—and there it was, framed and everything. "Take it," Holt said. "Improve your membership. Go to work."

"I hung it on the wall," Getlan testified, "and that was it. I didn't pay anything for it."

Getlan's local, headquarters at 10 Park Avenue in Mount Vernon, New York, got about one hundred members, who each paid dues of $5.00 per month. They handled four thousand coin machines; for each machine, the local got a fee of fifty cents a month. All this worked out to some thirty thousand dollars a year, from which came union officials' salaries and, sometimes, wages for pickets. Pickets, Counsel Kennedy brought out, might be thrown around somebody's bar if the proprietor didn't get his coin machines from the right association. About thirty per cent of the local's membership, it developed, were employers—operating their own machines. What did the union do for them? Nebraska's Senator Curtis wanted to know; help them negotiate a pay rise with themselves? No, Getlan said, what the union did was see nobody jumped his location.

As he talked, the unscrupulous skein of operation almost sketched itself. It had not been a management-union operation. Rival racketeer groups, with their fingers in the coin-machine business, had been warring for territories, fortified by phony or subverted union contracts and the pitiful paraphernalia of fixers and sharp lawyers and the rest—the accumulated dirt under the rug. With the aggressive, if belated, help of responsible labor leaders, businessmen, and public officials, the Committee is moving at last to clean it out.

130

But Getlan didn't keep that Local 228 charter long—only ninety days, in fact. He is affiliated now with the International Jewelry Workers, Local 26 of the coin-machine employees union, of which he is secretary-treasurer. Why did he drop 228? "The service from the international wasn't worth it," he said. But, just a few minutes earlier, he had testified that the local "didn't pay no per capita tax" to the parent union. Reminded of that, Getlan said, "We didn't want something for nothing." So he sent the charter back, frame and all.

It turned out that Sam Getlan's brother Izzy runs a club in Westchester County, but he doesn't belong to Sam's union.

"Why don't you make him join?" Senator McClellan asked. "Why don't you picket him?"

"I don't talk to him," Getlan replied. "I'm afraid he'll come to you people."

Chairman McClellan thanked him and called the next witness.

TEAMSTERS OFF THE TEAM

Atlantic City, N.J.
December 6, 1957

AT 1:46 THIS AFTERNOON, the International Brotherhood of Teamsters, Chauffeurs, Warehousemen, and Helpers of America found themselves without a home. On the floodlit stage of the Atlantic City auditorium, framed with the inevitable potted palms and a gaudy, discolored strip of red, white, and blue bunting overhead, George Meany banged down his gavel. "I declare the report of the Appeals Committee adopted," he shouted. So, after a tense, smoke-filled session lasting more than four hours without a break, a session charged with emotion, weighted with oratory that was now wounded, now defiant, now righteously admonitory, but always cumbersome, the Teamsters were formally expelled from the AFL-CIO.

What did it mean? It meant, for one thing, that power and money, for a trade union, are not enough. With nearly one and a half million members,* the Teamsters are the biggest single union in the country and boast a bankroll of forty million dollars. But they have lost the badge of respectability and decency which affiliation with the AFL-CIO represents. This is an important point. There are those who view the picture cynically, who say there are scores of unions and unionists still in the fold who, to put it mildly, are less pure than the driven snow, and they are right. What these people forget is that the labor movement has had to fight, historically, for its life, and respectability hasn't come easy. When those elements of business that are out to destroy or emasculate unions couldn't fight them frontally, they often sought "accommodation" with certain union leaders. This kind of temptation was high among the many lures to which individual Teamster officials succumbed. It wasn't that some company vice-president found it outraged his moral code to do business with a Beck or a Brewster or a Hoffa. On the contrary, testimony shows a business-man often preferred dealing with such buccaneers; there was a certain piratical stability to it which allowed both parties to concentrate on the profits, with a mutual disdain for the interests of the customer and the union rank and file.

Although the expulsion of the Teamsters does not assure an Ivory Soap purity to the AFL-CIO, it is a highly significant earnest of intent. Corny as it may sound, today's action must be put down as a sacrifice in the name of decency. It may backfire. The merged labor movement has had its population decimated in the last twenty-four hours. It will lose nearly $1,000,000 a year in Teamsters' dues and faces a bruising, expensive battle should the Teamsters try to go it alone under Hoffa, with all the raiding and jurisdictional rowing that would involve. Also, the Teamster ouster was not unanimous. The voices in opposition were plaintive and pathetic, but they represented a die-hard psychology of unionism which argues that ethics are incidental to power, a sort of "to hell with everybody else" school.

* Half jokingly, I asked Philip Pearl, then the AFL-CIO's director of public relations, what this loss would do to the sponsor's opening commercial on my broadcast, which began, "Fifteen million Americans bring you Edward P. Morgan and the news." On the spot, he changed it to thirteen and a half million. I don't know whether anybody noticed the difference in the billing of my report from Atlantic City that night, but the item made the gossip columns.

The painful decision to evict the Teamsters proves the sense of responsibility of the current AFL-CIO leadership, with all its internal faults. The order to the Teamsters did not read, "Never darken our doorstep again," but, "Welcome back as soon as you dump the rowdies and racketeers." * If businessmen and politicians take that at its face value and respond in kind, we can really get somewhere in eliminating corrupt practices involving labor and management.

GHOST TOWN

Charleston, W. Va.
May 6, 1960

THIS IS A SKETCH of the life and death of an Appalachian town.

Forty-five miles south of Charleston, five miles up Seng Creek from Coal River, there sits by the side of the road, as if heaved there like an abandoned packing box, a little gray smudge of a building, with an American flag drooping over the door in the hot stillness of the morning. This is the U.S. Post Office of Highcoal, West Virginia. Above and below it, in the narrow hollow, sprawl the miners' empty houses, crusted with coal dust, their white paint peeling. Somehow, they resemble a pile of bones bleaching in the sun. Like a dirty doormat in front of the post office, a mongrel dog, whose mother must have known a beagle, lies sleeping. Across the road, trying bravely to hide the black trickle of a drainage stream running through a gash in the rock from the mine tipple, a catalpa tree lifts its soft lavender blossoms in profusion. Buffered from the blows of reality by nothing more than the fresh spring green of the oak, maple, poplar, and tulip trees on the ridges, Highcoal at high noon is as quiet as a graveyard.

Four years ago, there was a loud, grimy bustle to the place.

* Despite internal restiveness and pressure from a boasting Hoffa for readmission, the AFL-CIO reaffirmed its position at its biennial convention in Miami Beach, in December, 1961.

One hundred and twenty-five families filled the company-built monotony of houses, white and Negro living side by side. The pig-squeal of the conveyor-car wheels agonized the air as the coal moved from the mine along the trestle to the tipple at the railroad siding. The sign on the foreman's shack said "Work Tomorrow," and that meant another twenty dollars a day, or more, for the union miners, who spent only some of it on the jukeboxes and pool tables in the ugly cement-block building which passed as Highcoal's community center.

Then the coal vein wore thin. Costs rose, and down the valley, mines with new job-saving machinery crowded Highcoal out of the dwindling market. The mine shut down. Now there are only fifteen families left, and they must move soon. The company is selling the houses at $150 a frame carcass, to be hauled away to other sites or torn down for scrap lumber. Only one of the fifteen families has a breadwinner—he works at the Eunice mine, several miles across the hills. The rest are on relief or are drawing other temporary benefits. Today, some of the men-folk have gone down to Whitesville to queue up for their unemployment-compensation checks.* As these men wait their turn among three hundred others in front of the office in the Moose lodge at Whitesville, there isn't much talk of politics, though an ex-prizefighter named Protan is electioneering for sheriff, and, next door, the linotype of the now-defunct weekly paper is clanking out material for campaign hand-bills.

A quick, superficial check reveals Humphrey and Kennedy supporters in puzzlingly even numbers. "We don't care who wins," one earnest young fellow tells an inquiring stranger. "We just want to get some jobs in here." Was bigotry coloring the campaign? Some, maybe, he allowed; then he pointed in the direction of a trim new church. "That's the Catholic church," he said. "Protestant volunteers helped build it. One man lent his bulldozer for a week. He's a Presbyterian."

Community co-operation can raise churches, but not necessarily

* Despite New Frontier relief measures, West Virginia is still a critically depressed area. Unemployment in May, 1962, was 59,900, 9.9 per cent of the total labor force—only a shade below the 10.3 per cent of May, 1960. Welfare cases rose from 50,906 in May, 1960, to 58,968 in May, 1962; but the latter figure included aid to 12,500 dependent children, some of whom obviously had not had the needed assistance before.

jobs. Does the coal company share a responsibility in the re-educa-
tion, resettlement, and readjustment of men squeezed off the pay-
rolls by machines or shrinking markets for coal? "The big outfits
and other industries can afford it," brusquely says the operator of
a going mine outside Whitesville. "We can't. With rising costs,
we're fighting to keep a market."

Meanwhile, back in Highcoal, Postmaster J. D. Morton, who
runs a little store on credit in the back of the post office, is about
to close up for the two-hour midday break, when a fragment of
his own shrunken market materializes in the dirty-faced form of
a five-year-old boy, Dean Meade. With that proud Scots name,
chances are Dean's forebears settled in these hills about the time
coal was first discovered in West Virginia, more than two centuries
ago. The postmaster fills Dean's grocery list and adds a package
of Juicy Fruit. Clutching his single paper bag and the gum, Dean
scuffs up the dusty path home to lunch, in one of the ghostly white
houses of the hollow.

Heading back down Seng Creek toward the highway and the
air-conditioned economy of Charleston beyond, the stranger
glimpses a booted miner attacking a sidehill garden plot with a
grub hoe. Suddenly, the tragedy of Highcoal swings into focus.
No single conspirator, but a combination of circumstances, plotted
its death. Perhaps it is too late to salvage more than temporary
relief for the empty-faced men in the unemployment line at
Whitesville; at least, the miner with the hoe can grow a stubborn
stalk of pride in his miserable garden. But five-year-old Dean
Meade deserves more of a future than this, and he cannot possibly
grapple with it alone.

WHERE DOES CULTURE
COME OFF HERE?

June 6, 1960

THE SHOW MUST, in fact, go on if an important, intangible
something in American life is not to perish. Tangible, material
things, like pensions and the production of chrome-coated car

bumpers, are involved in most labor-management disputes, as well as the hard realities of economics. There is something else at stake in the deadlocked dialogue between New York theater owners and members of Equity, the actors' union. It is the perishable commodity of creativity. Call it, at its best, art. The more comfort-conscious and materialistic we become, the more we seem to neglect the shriveling stockpile of artistic values. Broadway is one of the country's last repositories of this shrinking treasure, and Heaven help us if the disputants and the public don't keep that fact firmly in mind.

Costs of producing a musical or a play on the legitimate stage have soared in recent years; pressures from labor unions explain a large part of the rise. Does it follow then that unions are clobbering culture with greedy demands for fatter contracts? Without doubt, the bargainers for organized theatrical folk, from artists to stagehands, usually have been less concerned about art than arithmetic, and the extremes to which some unions have gone in the name of job protection have been selfish, silly, and quite unjustified. Having made their featherbeds, they have too often insisted on lying in them, not infrequently to their own long-range detriment.

Still, you cannot eat art. Life in the theater is a very hazardous profession; people in it are entitled to be as concerned about security, fringe benefits, and the tangibility of the weekly pay envelope as the next group, if not more so. Furthermore, Actors Equity, the union involved in this Broadway dispute with theater owners and producers, is one of the most responsible in the entire labor movement. It commands the high loyalty of its members and demands the faithful observance of a strict code of rules; an artistic temperament is no excuse for not abiding by a contract. It has had a strong hand in forcing the elevation of theater working conditions above the primitive. Through its own emergency funds, it was helping broken-down actors, than whom there are few more tragic figures, long before fringe benefits were a negotiable item. Equity's preoccupation with this growing problem, plus the contrast of enviable advantages in the contracts of the American Federation of Television and Radio Artists, made a pension fund a major point of contention in Equity's quarrel with Broadway management.

136

Both sides will have to give a little to liquidate the current impasse. Both sides must remember that they are dealing here with something more delicate than the production of refrigerators or power-driven cocktail shakers.* But in the protection of this thing called creativity something more complicated is involved than pricing an orchestra seat or balcony perch out of the market, and here the public has a responsibility, too. The legitimate stage cannot endure if the public will not be a little daring itself, and support the adventures of experiment.

"Broadway," wrote *New York Times* drama critic Brooks Atkinson yesterday, "is a form of excitable anarchy. In a business that deals in ideas, points of view, art, and spectacle, anarchy is an asset. It preserves individuality during a cultural period in which individuality is eroding. It is also a defense against the standardized product—the curse of industrial entertainment. If Broadway were a well-run industrial enterprise," Atkinson said, "without temperament, it would be so dull that audiences would stay at home, where a standard product is available in the family idiot box."

Ironically and paradoxically, while the failures of this rather disastrous Broadway season have been attributed largely to low quality, the public has not responded much to the high quality of off-Broadway productions, either. Broadway darkened by a labor-management row is a disturbing spectacle, but not half so disturbing as a legitimate stage darkened by a public's lack of appetite for anything except predictable, pre-packaged culture.

BUSINESS AS USUAL?

January 5, 1961

MAYBE IT IS a legacy from the time when few dared to question—aloud—the behavior of the so-called ruling classes, but the unpretty fact is that we Americans still use a double standard

* The dispute, which kept Broadway "dark" for ten days, was settled by an agreement which included substantial fringe benefits and increases in minimum wages, rehearsal pay, and road-show salaries.

in measuring the morality of management and of labor. One of the most eloquent examples of this duality emerged in the government's victory in the largest antitrust case ever tried.

In early December, 1960, nineteen big manufacturers of heavy electrical equipment pleaded no defense in federal court to criminal charges of price fixing. Among the principal defendants were firms whose brand names—General Electric, Westinghouse, Allis Chalmers—are household words; but the word of their criminality simply did not get around as widely as it would have if a similar rap had descended on a trade union. The story was not suppressed; because of our American sense of values as measured by the information media, it just did not get the play given, say, exposés of labor racketeering in the heyday of the McClellan committee.

The extent of the conspiracy boggles the imagination and, by comparison, makes the arrogant sins of a Beck or a Hoffa or the sad scandals involving the leadership of the Carpenters union look almost like the pranks of juvenile delinquents. What happened, briefly, was this: In the 1950's, by a simple but secret system of faking competitive bids, these companies carved up markets and rigged prices on sales, amounting to a total of seven billion dollars, to industry, private utilities, and other corporations—and a billion dollars in federal, state, and local government contracts.

With factual reporting and a series of biting editorials, the *Washington Post*, to its everlasting credit, endeavored to put this whole mess into a little sharper perspective. The *Post* today provides a fascinating peek into the workings of some corporate minds by excerpting from a General Electric task force report some recommendations on public relations:

"Business," the excerpt begins, "might subsidize a 'brain trust' of competent writers (novelists, playwrights, etc.) to begin an active campaign of turning public attention away from the left through the source of popular-attitude formation (television, movies, stage, radio, novels, magazine articles, etc.).

"It is important to pick out opinion molders in every community and 'work on them.' However, as a rule, a specific story should not be given to them directly by just anyone at random. For example, if the opinion molder to be influenced is a news-

138

paper publisher, it might be best to have him approached by one of his biggest advertisers."

In an interestingly refined concept of executive responsibility, the board chairman and ex-president of General Electric, Ralph J. Cordiner, says he knew nothing of the conspiracy in which GE was so deeply involved. But it is as if this whole pattern, from the sly public-relations approach outlined above to the actual conniving to cheat other businesses, the government, and the public out of millions, had become an accepted way of life.

What a hollow, hypocritical sound there is now to the arguments of "'patriotism" and "national security" which the industry has tried to use, sometimes successfully, to defeat foreign competition. In 1959, TVA bought a British turbine generator for a low bid of $12,100,000. Though GE and Westinghouse bids were each more than $5,000,000 higher, appeals were made—unsuccessfully —to the White House to revoke the British bid. One GE vice-president complained that foreign bidders had the advantage of lower wages. But economists for the International Union of Electrical Workers figure the forty-five per cent difference in bid prices more than exceeds the difference in labor costs between the American and British electrical manufacturing industries; that, in other words, GE and Westinghouse could have met the British bid and still have made a profit, despite higher American wages.

The behavior of business, as revealed in this vast and shocking price-fixing conspiracy, should not only impel sober self-appraisal by the captains of industry, but also stir deep public concern.* The same concern and soul-searching, I hasten to add, should apply to unions wherever wrongdoing is involved. Of course, the racketeering or misuse of power by certain labor leaders is not mere juvenile delinquency. Any vestige of either is despicable and unacceptable. But let's begin now to apply the same standard of morality to both union and management. We should have realized long ago that, insofar as human weakness and strength are concerned, we do indeed have a classless society.

* See "Confidence Men," page 152.

I DIDN'T RAISE MY BOY
TO BE A MINER

Lexington, Ky.
March 2, 1961

LAST FRIDAY, the bituminous-coal mine of the Joe Knob company closed down at Kenvir in Harlan County, Kentucky. One hundred men lost their jobs. Among them was Nathan Bailey, aged thirty-five, a lean, sandy-haired, blue-eyed, modest, good-natured native of the East Kentucky hill country. By shoveling an average of eighteen tons of coal a day, on his knees, for $3.20 an hour, Nate Bailey made $4,200 in 1960. With this, he supported his wife, Ines; his thirteen-year-old daughter, Helen; his ten-year-old son, Douglas; and a fire-engine red 1954 Pontiac sedan, on which he has $32.00 left to pay.

This morning, a few miles up the Clover Fork of the Cumberland River, above the town of Harlan, Nate worked in the sunshine outside his drab, but tidy five-room house, washing and polishing his car and thinking vaguely about the future. Inside, Mrs. Bailey was busy painting the kitchen. Nate will soon be eligible to draw $37.00 a week in unemployment insurance for twenty-six weeks. "I'm going to wait just a little while," he said, "and see what the company is fixing to do. I load coal. That's all I was cut out for, I guess."

Nate finished the third grade in school. If the Kenvir mine stays closed—twenty-seven have shut in Harlan County since 1957—Bailey will look for a pick-and-shovel job on an independent truck-mining operation for $10.00 a day when he works. A fatherly friend, Rufus Bailey (not a relative), who is safety director for the Harlan County Coal Operators Association, suggested that Nate had "too much pride to draw them surplus-food packages from the government."

"No," Nate said slowly. "I ain't a bit too fine for that. I'd go get it if I had to."

Would he be willing to learn a new trade if the company or

140

the United Mine Workers Union or the government or somebody came up with a retraining program?

"If a man couldn't find a job in the mines," Nate answered, "he'd have to look somewhere else, wouldn't he? Still, I don't just know what I could do."

The Nathan Baileys are luckier than a lot of their Harlan County neighbors. There are forty-five hundred Harlan miners working today.* There were twelve thousand ten years ago. Many moved away when the mines closed, but there are still six thousand jobless men in the county—fifteen hundred more than are employed. Most of them have been idle far too long to be eligible for any more unemployment benefits. About thirteen thousand people in the county are drawing weekly surplus-food packages, according to Coal Operators President Cloyd McDowell.

John "Snuff" Coffee, a Negro coal loader in his sixties, is not one of these—yet. Laid off for ten days, he headed for the river with a bamboo pole and a can of worms this morning, hoping to catch some catfish and rock bass, or "red eye," as they call them in the Appalachians. Snuff's three children are dead, and he has only his wife and himself to support. Last year he earned $1,302. Could he live on that? "We just do," Snuff replied, as he ambled toward the river down a muddy, unpaved street past a cringing row of miners' shacks. In the front yard of one, his neighbor Gus Owens had just hung a freshly butchered hog. Gus had no deep-freeze, of course, but he would salt down the pork for storage. "These people know how to cure meat," Rufus Bailey said. "It's the best-tasting stuff you ever laid over your chin."

A generation ago, Harlan was a battleground. Less than a year ago, a highway sign with the legend "Welcome to Bloody Harlan" still stood; out-of-date now, this wound to civic pride has been removed. In the depression years of the thirties, Kentucky National Guardsmen had to patrol Harlan County for months at a time. John L. Lewis was trying to organize the workers, and the mine owners resisted. There was open warfare. Kerosene was poured

---

* According to U.S. Labor Department figures, Harlan County unemployment by the summer of 1962 had been reduced somewhat, to 16.3 per cent of the labor force; but there were fewer miners working. The total work force in three counties of the Harlan area had been reduced by more than six thousand people in two years. Presumably, many had left to seek jobs elsewhere.

into the kettles at farmers' soup kitchens for the striking workers. The Guardsmen had to soak their garbage in coal oil to keep hungry children from eating it. Violence came from both sides. Now Harlan County is a battleground again, but the enemy is the infection of economic blight. The community is trying to fight it.

Harlan has raised $125,000 so far for its vest-pocket airstrip, carved into a rocky knob high above the town. The Mine Workers are maintaining their union hospitals. Coal operator McDowell has been fighting for lower freight rates to compete with water carriers and for more research in the use of coal as a binding tar to replace oil in highway construction. An aggressive state administration is trying to help. Expanded federal relief is on the way. But the problem somehow seems bigger than the total of all these efforts, standing out as a stubborn, goading reminder that, as much as our help and leadership are needed in the rest of the world, we have not paid enough attention to our own underdeveloped areas and the human problems created by automation, management-labor stress, and other aspects of our sensitive, staggeringly complex economy.

Nate Bailey's children were away at school this morning. Already they have received twice as much education as their parents, but their future is clouded and uncertain. One thing is certain. Nate Bailey doesn't want his son to be a coal miner.

A SIMPLE MAN

July 7, 1961

THE TIME has come to pay tribute to a great American, James Riddle Hoffa. Homage is due this fearless citizen because once more he has been raised—apparently legally this time—to the very pinnacle of power as president of that humble, public-spirited instrument of our democratic way of life, the Teamsters Union. President Hoffa also deserves the cheers of his peers because he is the very embodiment of red-blooded, two-fisted Americanism—indeed, his coat of arms might well be a brace of blood-smeared fists rampant on a field of trampled responsibility.

142

As every schoolboy knows, or will soon be taught, Hoffa's rise to the top was accompanied at every step by his reverent devotion to the same traditions and principles so dear to the hearts and vital to the success of other great patriots, such as Boss Tweed, Jay Gould, and Al Capone. He has shown the weak the way to be brutally strong. He has taught the selfish to be more lustful, and the lawless to be more defiant of the law by exercising the virtues of deceit, intimidation, and ruthless power. James R. Hoffa is, clearly, what the country and the times call for—a simple man of direct action, though it is true he needed thirty-seven lawyers in residence at his union convention in the Napoleon Room of the Deauville Hotel in Miami Beach, to see to it that his inspiring mockery of democracy did not make his re-election by acclamation illegal.

Perhaps his crowning triumph was not that renewed five-year lease on the Teamster presidency at a modest fifty per cent rise in salary to $75,000 a year, but the wonderful changes wrought in the union constitution. They authorize him and his henchmen to alter any action taken by this week's convention. They convert the Teamsters Union, in effect, into a new federation of labor claiming organizing rights in every segment of industry; and, in a drive to bring all trucking under a single national contract, they further deny Teamster-local autonomy. The new constitution also drops a clause forbidding union membership to racketeers. It greatly simplifies the handling of union funds by, among other things, permitting locals to pay cash when desired and to keep the cash in safe-deposit boxes instead of bank accounts. In sum, Hoffa winds up with the biggest war chest (dues were increased by twelve million dollars to twenty million dollars a year for the one million seven hundred thousand teamsters), with the highest personal salary, the largest organizing staff, and the most centralized authority possessed by any labor leader—probably in the history of trade unionism.

If I were Khrushchev, I would tear up the constitution of the U.S.S.R. and wire over to Miami Beach for a copy of Hoffa's monolithic contract with his members. Indeed, the John Birch Society itself better look to its laurels if it intends to retain preeminence as an authoritarian institution. The convention did toy with a few open procedures. The legal beagles made sure that

Hoffa, calling the signals from the rostrum with an electronic console device, permitted dissenters—the few that there were—their turn at the microphones. However, no damage was done by this democratic action. A call to elect officers by referendum was referred to a committee which Hoffa headed. Yesterday, when a California delegate charged that a Hoffa machine dominated proceedings, the master teamster steered through a motion to expunge the Californian's remarks from the record. "Hoffa don't have no machine," Hoffa said reprovingly. ". . . Now we'll have no more of that." Today, one of the president's backers was so incensed by whatever protest remained that, as he rose to object, he spit out his false teeth, but he neatly caught them on the fly.

There is little question over what Hoffa will try to do with the power now locked in his jaws. He will use it to acquire more. To him, power is both tool and target, the means and the end; and to this Machiavelli in the driver's seat, one fully justifies the other. He has no compunction about strong-arm tactics or spitting in the eye of the law if he can get away with it. He has utterly no use for the broad social responsibilities at home and abroad assumed by the leaders of the merged labor movement who kicked him out in 1957. He is interested only in fat pay checks for his teamsters and the expansion of the power complex by which he can extract those rising wages and fringe benefits.

His threats against the AFL-CIO contain much bluster. But they contain some bite, too. Within the labor movement there is some damaging disunity, which Hoffa is attempting artfully to play upon. He boasts that a half a dozen unions or more want the Teamsters back in the fold, that two or three may join his "federation" anyway. The troubling fact is that some AFL-CIO leaders—minority though they be—think in Hoffa's narrow, selfish terms and are magnetized by his power. Hoffa can't destroy or dominate the labor movement unless he corrupts it with his concept that the public be damned. If that happened, nothing could save it.

A FUTILE FAMILY FEUD

Miami Beach, Fla.
December 8, 1961

By SMOOTH double talk, diplomats may contrive to conceal, temporarily, the ruptures between sovereign states. But family feuds are impossible to disguise. Somebody is always bound to blow his top in front of the picture window. Thus it is with the internal rows besetting the AFL-CIO.

Some of these difficulties are embedded in the history of competition between the trade and industrial unions. Some of that competition was sharpened as joblessness grew during the recent recession. Without wiser counsel and more tangible help than he has been getting to ease his own adjustment to change, the workingman can hardly be blamed if he sees increased imports, flight of capital, and automation as further threats to his shrinking job opportunities.

Too many unions reflect these worries in attitudes of quarrelsome defensiveness, darkly tinctured by the bitter, real, but not always realistic personality clashes among labor's leaders. A tough, dogged George Meany and a tough, restless Walter Reuther do not get along like Damon and Pythias. They and others have engaged in cruel exchanges over the approaches to such union problems as raiding and jurisdictional disputes, membership drives and racial discrimination. There are piercing ironies here. Only a few unions and relatively few jobs are involved in jurisdictional rows, and the impassioned quarrel on the race issue is not over principle, but over methods and timing for progress.

The uncomfortably cohabiting AFL and CIO have avoided the showdown of actual divorce. But can the country expect nothing better than a paper truce, a figurative India-Pakistan partition within a labor movement which is bleeding from incessant internal strife? Few people, if any, know better the strengths and weaknesses of unions or can view them with more respect and critically fair-minded detachment than the man who, as a special union counsel, was one of those instrumental in the 1955 merger of the

145

AFL-CIO, Secretary of Labor Arthur Goldberg.* On the sixth anniversary of the uneasy remarriage between the older AFL craft unions and the younger industrial unions of the CIO, his speech to the labor convention was loaded with significant suggestions and admonitions to labor about its role in American leadership.

Goldberg appealed to labor to assume new responsibilities and new attitudes; it had to fight for its recognized place in society. But with that place now won, labor's role, the Secretary said in effect, is less of combat and more of co-operation with the community, business, and government.

Restrictive practices that cut industrial efficiency and impair competition will not stop unemployment, he said; they will create more. Resistance to automation will not help to accomplish full employment; it will hurt. Protectionist trade policies won't aid in creating jobs; they will take more away. A squeeze on business profits, from which new enterprises must be financed to provide new jobs, will not help; it will hinder. Wage increases, as a rule, should be earned by increased productivity.

There must be no question, he said, about trade-union unity in supporting full citizenship for all Americans. (But there is.) Law or no law, labor has an eternal obligation to maintain vigilance against corruption. (But labor does not exercise it fully.) Labor, he indicated, was wasting its substance in expensive jurisdictional disputes in which the number of jobs involved, in total terms, was downright insignificant. Compromise, Goldberg said, is a rule of life in the union movement, and its leaders ought to have no trouble in compromising their differences on this divisive issue. (But they do have.) **

* Goldberg, one of the most brilliant minds in the Kennedy cabinet, was elevated to the Supreme Court after the resignation of Justice Felix Frankfurter in August, 1962.

** After an all-night session of principals, the 1961 Miami Beach convention hammered out a plan to handle jurisdictional disputes. A key cog in the machinery is the "impartial umpire," David Cole, ex-head of the Wage Stabilization Board and one of the most accomplished arbitrators in the country. If cases cannot be solved at two lower levels, he makes a decision. This is appealable to a three-man committee of the AFL-CIO Executive Council, but if the decision is upheld and the offending union does not comply, the union becomes classified as a "raider," sanctions are exacted

146

Organized labor, he reminded his audience, stands upon an ethical base and has a moral purpose—the increase in human welfare for all. This reminder was needed. Coming from a hostile camp, it might be ignored. Coming from the friendliest and most empathetic of critics, it will, one hopes, register a maximum impact on all concerned.

WHO WANTS TO
JOIN A UNION?

Miami Beach, Fla.
December 11, 1961

AN IMPRESSIVE NUMBER of foreigners, including African trade delegations and European correspondents, have been observing the convention proceedings of the AFL-CIO on the sun-kissed sands of Miami Beach. Several things puzzle them.

Some wonder about the appropriateness of a labor convention in the midst of the garish opulence and extravagant comforts of a leading resort. This particular puzzlement, however, is not profoundly thoughtful. It does not follow that, to do their convention work with dedication, union delegates must descend into a coal mine or caucus on the fringes of a foundry. After all, business groups have been known to seek out the healing atmosphere of a spa for their get-togethers, and British trade unions repeatedly succumb to the seaside charms of Blackpool, the Atlantic City of England. Geneva, hardly to be classified as the River Rouge of Switzerland, continues to beckon international union, industrial, and governmental gatherings.

Perhaps what bothers the observers about Miami Beach is, not the site itself, but the incredible material, synthetic, gimcrack richness of the civilization it represents. In that context, the ques-

---

against it, and it has no further recourse to the dispute-settling procedure. Of some eighty cases filed in the first six months of operation, only two have required the application of sanctions.

tion fairly leaps up at them: Is organized labor displaying the dynamism and responsible toughness necessary to support and justify its role of power and leadership in the American society? The answer must be, regrettably: No, it is not.

The public image of this convention has become, largely, a panorama of pettiness, of bitter internal bickering, intensified by sharp personality clashes, over whether one union group can gain an economic advantage over another. There is, of course, much more to the picture than this. President Kennedy himself recognized the invaluable support the AFL-CIO has given to the development of free and democratic trade unions in the emerging nations on other continents. Only last Friday, the merged union movement's help in establishing an anti-Castro, free-labor front in the Dominican Republic was revealed here. Labor has given $680,000 to the Eleanor Roosevelt Cancer Foundation, though this is more than $300,000 short of its announced goal.

Undoubtedly, superficial reporting is partly to blame for not putting the full labor picture in perspective. The Sunday edition of the *Miami Herald* totaled 278 pages; not one page was devoted to a thoughtful, dimensional report of this critical meeting going on in the *Herald*'s own back yard. Perfunctory news of convention proceedings was buried on inside pages.

But journalistic bad judgment is not labor's basic problem. Labor's basic problem is within its own ranks. Another point puzzling to foreign observers is that union membership, inside and outside the AFL-CIO, represents less than a quarter of the total U.S. civilian labor force. In many European countries, more than ninety per cent of the workers are organized. Indeed, the American union movement has lost membership, although the work force has been growing by leaps and bounds. Why?

Restrictive practices by business and state legislatures, especially in the South, are an important part of the answer. But thoughtful labor leaders are worried privately about something else. Where is unionism's popular appeal? Where is the influx of college graduates and other technically trained youth to comprise labor's leadership force for tomorrow? It is not there. Although they are not hostile, undergraduates regard trade unionism today with open doubt and skepticism. Organized labor is still a minority group, yet its approach to other minority groups is too narrow.

148

A moral force is lacking to attract workers into organized ranks.

Sometimes innocently, sometimes arrogantly, unions have neglected the impact of their actions on the public. Skimpily informed on labor-management issues, the public is often more sympathetic to management's view in a dispute. It would not be if unions gave more thought to presenting their cases—including careful consideration of how justifiable a particular case is. Business exploitation of the featherbedding label has often completely obscured a union's deep and legitimate fear of job losses because of automation and other technological improvements. But some unions are dragging their feet against reasonable adjustment. Here, it is easy to hear one union criticize another's practices as insupportable featherbedding.

Today's papers feature the story that union electricians in New York are going to demand a twenty-hour week and a four-hour day. There may be sound economic reasons for this move, but they are not apparent to the public or to the Kennedy administration, which opposes shorter hours in a period of continuing international crisis.

To the criticism that labor is taking too narrow a view, some of its spokesmen may well reply, "Who isn't?" That is not the answer. Labor must expect more from itself, whether other segments of society do or not. Its main reason for being is, not to hold the interests of a particular group above the whole, but to improve the welfare of everybody.

IMPROVE THOSE
SHINING HOURS

January 22, 1962

Last week, nine thousand union electrical workers in New York City won the shortest work week in collective bargaining history—a five-hour day in a five-day week. In South Bend,

149

Indiana, the president of Studebaker-Packard, Sherwood H. Egbert, an ex-marine, was arrested on a charge of disorderly conduct. A picket said that Egbert dared him to a fist fight in front of the automobile company plant, which has been struck by the United Auto Workers over such issues as wash-up time, premium pay for night and week-end work, and vacation benefits.

Though these developments in New York and South Bend were not related, they may well have been linked in the public mind as cause and effect: exorbitant, unjustified demands for which organized labor deserves a punch in the nose. This, of course, is not the way these two separate situations should be judged, but entirely too many labor leaders are unaware that the public judges trade unionism, not on the basis of its over-all contributions to society in improved welfare and living standards, but on controversies which get into the papers, and on conflicts in which the public is caught in the middle.

Some business executives, naturally, exploit this state of affairs to put unions on the defensive. But there are exceptions, and I ran into an interesting one over the week end. At a formal dinner, I found myself seated between a business executive of one of the nation's leading newspapers and the counsel for a group of eastern railroads. The attorney was heatedly condemning the contract just won by Local 3 of the International Brotherhood of Electrical Workers with New York builders as the latest wrinkle in featherbedding.

"In my plant," the newspaper executive replied, "I deal with sixteen unions. Each has a different problem, and I have found by experience that I can't discuss an employer-employee relationship until I know what the problem is and understand the union's point of view. I don't know anything about the construction business, so I don't feel competent to criticize that electricians' union contract. It sounds awful, but it may have some fine things in it."

Then he turned to the South Bend ruckus. "I don't know the merits of this case, either," he said, "but that Studebaker fellow was silly. You don't settle industrial disputes with your fists any more. Men in management are supposed to have enough intelligence and training to understand their workers and get at the heart of their grievances. I don't blame a union for demanding shorter hours and more pay. And I don't blame a man operating a machine for being afraid the machine will soon operate itself, and consume his job in the process.

"But," he went on, and here was the newspaper executive's punch line, "I simply do not understand why, when they win better contracts, unions won't produce in proportion. And it's not just the man-hour charts; it's the worker's attitude of 'Aw, the hell with it. I'm protected by the contract.'"

It strikes this observer that bargainers on both sides of the industrial table have paid too much attention to arithmetic and too little attention to attitudes. Too much emphasis may have been put on economic formulas and not enough on performance. Is the manufacturer proud of his product, and are his workmen proud of their work, or are both sides simply going through the motions of turning out an article of dubious value from which they can suck sweeter profits and juicier wages?

I know a government official, borrowed from business, who built a house outside Washington not long ago. Some of the crews were union, some nonunion. But his individual experience was that the nonunion men were better in industriousness and workmanship. "I wouldn't have minded the union wages I paid," the builder said, "if I had got more for it. But I was paying more, not only for less, but for inferior work."

Union electricians in New York belong to an efficient work force which can build a skyscraper almost as fast as nature rears a mushroom. However, their twenty-five-hour week is not being hailed by the Kennedy administration or by the AFL-CIO leadership as a breakthrough for progress. Both are unhappy about it. The AFL-CIO holds that reduction from a forty- to a thirty-five-hour week could help combat unemployment, but fears that a twenty-five-hour week where there is a shortage of men, not jobs, may damage and delay its basic argument. Labor Secretary Arthur Goldberg agrees, and reminds labor that, considering world competition, the electricians' plan is not a sound pattern; higher costs are a more obvious result than higher productivity.*

* But by the summer of 1962, organized labor's leadership, disquieted by prospects of a recession, took a more urgent view toward the possible need of a shorter work week, and Secretary Goldberg himself warned that if the unemployment picture did not improve, trade unions would surely demand shorter hours.

The union counters by saying it has agreed to double its number of apprentices—to include, it is hoped, eligible Negroes—and reportedly it will make certain concessions on wage-hour rates for private-home building. But now, clearly, the burden is on the union to fulfill, not just the letter, but the spirit of the contract it has won.

CONFIDENCE MEN

April 27, 1962

AT AN IMPRESSIVE social gathering of businessmen in New York, Roger Blough, board chairman of U.S. Steel, said, "One of the most necessary things this country must have is confidence in the business of this country."

Would, Mr. Blough, that we could.

The record of recent months is not only distressing. It is alarming, and the alarms are still coming in. Let us cast a quick glance at only major developments:

In February, 1961, climaxing the largest antitrust action ever tried, heavy fines were meted out to twenty-nine major manufacturing firms of electrical equipment and to forty-four of their officials (some of whom even went to prison) who had pleaded no-defense to criminal charges of price-fixing. Involved were more than eight billion dollars' worth of government and commercial contracts.

Last May, a father-son brokerage team, Gerard A. and Gerard F. Re, were expelled from the American Stock Exchange on charges of illegal stock manipulation. A sweeping investigation by the Securities and Exchange Commission ensued and is still in progress, but an interim report released in January was sharply critical of several Exchange practices.

On February 27, 1962, James Truman Bidwell, chairman of the New York Stock Exchange board of governors, was indicted by a federal grand jury on charges of evading more than $55,000 in U.S. incomes taxes. He has resigned his post.

Yesterday, in New York, the nation's two top steel producers,

152

U.S. Steel and Bethlehem, were indicted by another federal grand jury, together with two other steel companies, five executives, and a trade association, on charges of violating the antitrust laws.

In only fifteen months of the Robert F. Kennedy regime at the Department of Justice, there have been thirty-four federal indictments for price-fixing and bid-rigging.* In March, two big milk distributors in the state of Washington were indicted on these counts, and Wednesday, in Boston, three Massachusetts milk companies were similarly charged; in addition, they were accused of defrauding the government. Also in March, four ice-carnival shows were indicted on the charge that they had divided up the country to corner the trade. A New York venetian-blind firm has been indicted for price-fixing and, allegedly, for paying off a union official.

As far as the pending court cases are concerned, all the defendants must be presumed innocent until proved guilty. Proved wrongdoing, ranging from sharp practices to gross criminality, is, or should be, too shocking to tolerate, and there are certain to be a lot of scandals that have not yet come to the surface.

In an article in the *New York Times* three weeks ago, the ex-president and board chairman of Inland Steel, Clarence B. Randall, who has served three administrations in Washington with distinction, wrote that "it is clear that industry in this country is facing a moral crisis." He went on to mention a little-publicized situation: American companies doing business especially in the emerging nations of Asia and Africa, presumably with or without foreign-aid contracts, were bribing officials of those fledgling governments in order to buy their way into mineral concessions or other operations. What a standard of American integrity; what a measure of American democracy in action abroad!

The situation at home may well be worse. Last November, in a speech before the Economic Club of New York, Attorney General Kennedy said: "The sad truth is that, although price-fixing conspiracies are the exception rather than the rule, in almost every major community in the country a number of businessmen have conspired or are conspiring in secret, not only to fix prices, but to make collusive deals with union officials, defraud their cus-

* By late October, 1962, the Kennedy administration had brought a total of forty-seven indictments for price-fixing and bid-rigging.

tomers, and even, in some instances, cheat their own government."

It is vital at this point to recall the counsel of a fair-minded man, Secretary of Commerce Luther Hodges. In a speech on business ethics in February in Miami, he said we should remember that "business morality all through history has mirrored the morality of society as a whole. . . . Business ethics, as a whole, have never been singularly different from those of society at large. And they have changed and improved only as society . . . has evolved, by law or private conviction, a more enlightened standard of what is right."

Let the corrupt or unscrupulous labor leader, too, put that in his pipe and smoke it. The still larger point is that none of us can escape the weight of that admonition. Voluntarily, labor has done much to clean its own house, but comparisons do not necessarily get us anywhere. It has been demonstrated clearly that in our reactions—strong or weak—to temptation, we are pretty much a classless society. However, with the onus blisteringly on business for the moment, it would be inspiring to see businessmen set a quickened pace toward better ethics for everybody. Give us something to believe in, Mr. Blough, and we'll believe it; and please, make it a little more than a quarterly report to stockholders on earnings.

Censorship

THROUGH THE
BRASS, DARKLY

January 29, 1962

AT THE SO-CALLED military-muzzling hearings in Washington, the retired Air Force Chief of Staff, General Thomas D. White, neatly shot down the ballooning impression lofted by South Carolina's Senator Strom Thurmond that patriots in uniform were being denied the fundamental right of free speech by administration censorship policies.

Before and during the inquiry into Pentagon and State Department procedure to clear public statements by high military and civilian officials of the government, bitter complaints had been raised that the brass (both in and out of uniform) were not only having some of their most original, virile, and trenchant anti-Communist remarks suppressed, but also were being squashed by lowly, nameless censors hidden away somewhere in the vast bureaucracy of Washington.

Then General White let the cat, or rather the gas, out of the bag. Somewhat diffidently, as if he sensed that some of his colleagues with a proud pretense of authorship considered this classified information, the general confessed, with brave and refreshing candor, "I rarely personally wrote a speech myself. There were relatively low-level persons who wrote the speeches in the first place." He noted that "as a matter of practicality most speeches are written by junior officers and reviewed by junior officers of a similar rank."

So, instead of a battle of the giants, we have a kind of minuet

155

of midgets. It is even possible that on rare occasions some of the brass were not intimately acquainted with the details of the speeches they were delivering. This, admittedly, is a trifling point, because no junior officer would last long as a ghost writer who fed his superior a line that the latter or the superior's service would not swallow. Indeed, one of the duties of these anonymous authors is to familiarize themselves with the general thinking of the men whose speeches they are assigned to prepare.

Still, General White's revelation tends to deflate the whole controversy to more dispassionate proportions. The spectacle of lower-level censors blue-penciling the prose of ghost writers of equal rank strikes a balance that makes the problem somehow more democratic all the way round.

Off that background, Senator Thurmond's charges of a dark conspiracy bounce with a more hollow ring. The senator, however, perseveres. In a letter to South Carolina's weekly newspapers, he declared that the censorship of military speeches shows that the State Department "has sold our leaders on the idea that we do not want to win the cold war.

"What remains to be answered," he continued, "is whether the censors are acting capriciously on their own or acting in accordance with established national policies which have not been made readily available to the public; there is strong evidence indicating the latter."

By charging that the government is following a "no-win" policy, the senator implies that somebody, or an unidentified sinister group of somebodies, is trying to lose or throw the cold war. This is nonsense. The parallel implication is also nonsense: that the way to win it is to give individual officials, military or civilian, unlicensed expression of their own ideas (which could easily be misconstrued as official statements), however violently they may oppose U.S. foreign policy.

Every witness so far has supported the basic principle of civilian control over the military, and there has been wide agreement that the military must not participate in partisan politics. "It is difficult," ex-Defense Secretary Robert A. Lovett wisely wrote to the Stennis committee, "to imagine a more dangerous situation for the military or the country" than to have certain officers identified with one party or faction. "If you have doubts on this," said

156

Lovett, "look at unhappy France." He paid rich and deserved tribute to the dedication of U.S. career officers as a whole. He had one particularly pointed word of wisdom. "I cannot escape the feeling," Lovett said, "that, as a government, we tend to talk too much." *

HORSEMAN ON FOOT

April 4, 1962

THE SCENE in the Senate caucus room today was, as Missouri's Senator Symington so aptly described it, a sad one, and it was too bad the hearing even had to be held. Here, on one side of the long, polished table, sat the members of Senator Stennis' special Armed Services subcommittee examining the Pentagon's alleged "muzzling" of the military. And there, in the witness chair, sat a tall, black-haired, heavy-browed ex-soldier who had a brave and distinguished combat record, but whose skirmishes with the enemy in the cold war had led him into a bog of nightmarish unreality and obviously lost him there in pathetic confusion.

At one point, the troops of the radical right had high hopes that former Major General Edwin A. Walker, the "muzzling" inquiry's star witness today, would be their man on horseback. There were elements of a useful martyrdom in his case—he had been relieved as commanding general of the twenty-fourth division in Germany a year ago for trying, among other things, to influence his soldiers and their families, on the eve of the 1960 Presidential election, to vote a rigidly conservative line. His answer, which stirred zealots

---

* Presumably with the praiseworthy objective of assuring that, when the government does talk, it does so with more prudence, consistency, and good sense, Under Secretary of State George Ball told the Senate Special Preparedness Subcommittee, on June 4, 1962, of three changes being wrought in the reviewing of speeches by military and civilian brass: (1) smoothing and tightening procedures; (2) assignment of a Defense Department officer to the State Department for closer co-ordination of this function; (3) establishment of a full-time State Department post to supervise the speech-review function. Obviously, the system has yet to be invented that will satisfy both muzzler and muzzlee.

157

of the right wing, was that he was simply pursuing a hard line of militant anticommunism. But the more the ex-general expounded his views in public, the more cloudy they became. Reportedly, some of his erstwhile supporters even opposed his appearance before the Stennis committee, for fear it would damage their cause. Their fears were well founded.

Walker stumbled through a thirty-two-page prepared statement, in which he charged he had been the "scapegoat of an unwritten policy of collaboration and collusion with the international Communist conspiracy," implicating both President Kennedy and Secretary of Defense McNamara. He hardly answered a single senatorial question, however straightforward and simple, without first getting whispered or written advice from two men flanking him. This provoked impatient protests from at least three senators, but Senator Strom Thurmond, who has been the right-wing protagonist of these hearings, protested that Walker had the right to counsel, which indeed he had. But even when the ex-general, his jaw trembling with emotion, faced a battery of microphones outside the caucus room after the morning session, the hoarse whisper of an adviser could be plainly heard before Walker answered reporters' questions. He had identified his advisers as two fellow conservatives and friends: C. J. Watts, a retired brigadier general in the army reserve, from Oklahoma City, and Medford Evans, a Yale Ph.D. from Dallas.

Here, plainly, was no man on horseback, but a bewildered and bewildering citizen with no mount at all. Here was no captain of the right-wing guard, but a captive of it. How thoroughly a captive of it seemed to be made clear inadvertently, when Walker conceded that he had never even read a book by the eminent social scientists Harry and Bonaro Overstreet, which he had denounced in his prepared statement as implicitly encouraging accommodation with the enemy by taking the Communist line of competitive coexistence. It developed that the book was the best seller *What We Must Know About Communism*, which the late John Foster Dulles had recommended to President Eisenhower as an excellent manual. In questioning Walker, Senator Symington said he had been impressed with the book, too, and asked the witness what there was about it he did not like.

"My knowledge of the book is only by hearsay," Walker re-

158

plied with ingenuous candor. When Symington pressed the point, Walker said he would be glad to read it and give an opinion. In the process of his answer, he also invited (but denied) an inference that General Eisenhower's book, *Crusade in Europe,* was somehow open to question.

Bafflingly, he went on to laud the writings of a member of the John Birch Society, whose book he had never read, either. At this point Symington said, wearily, "General, you have lost me."

It was plain at the noon recess, however, that Walker had admirers whom he had not lost. A small but buzzing swarm of middle-aged ladies engulfed him and one of them, a plainly dressed woman quivering with dedication, volunteered to read the Overstreet book for him and give him a brief.

The sadness of the day was marked by this scene, too. These citizens were confused, but sincerely alarmed, convinced that the government was riddled with Communists and appeasers, but not even informed on the material they had denounced. They were reaching out for a St. George to slay the dragon, oblivious to the fact that their attitudes and actions were serving well the very totalitarianism they professed so passionately they wanted to destroy. But they found no saint or knight in shining armor today, only a comrade more thoroughly confused, if possible, than they themselves.*

FREEDOM IS MORE
THAN ACADEMIC

June 8, 1962

WHAT MIGHT BE most simply described as a collision between political and sociological ideologies has occurred on the

---

* It was as if the eyes of Texas voters detected this confusion. In the state's Democratic gubernatorial primary, May 5, 1962, Walker ran last in a field of six, scraping together roughly ten per cent of the votes. He still maintains an office in Dallas and makes occasional speeches. Like a cinder, he was caught in the public eye again when he emerged with the mob in that fateful night of violence, Sept. 30-Oct. 1, 1962, opposing the entry of a solitary Negro into the University of Mississippi.

campus of a small college in western Pennsylvania, bruising the feelings of faculty, students, alumni, and townspeople alike. The victim suffering the deepest wounds was an intangible called academic freedom. The question is whether, or how fully, this delicate but vital ingredient of American education will recover.

The scene is Grove City College, sixty miles north of Pittsburgh. The first nudges of the clash came into public view just a year ago, in letters to the editor of *The Collegian,* the campus newspaper. The issue: war or peace. The opponents: Professor Larry Gara, a devout Quaker and avowed pacifist, who was chairman of the History Department; and Professor Hans F. Sennholtz, former *Luftwaffe* pilot, now a naturalized American citizen and chairman of the Economics Department. The debate, including angry arguments over whether we would be "better Red than dead," was indecisive, but it mobilized liberal and conservative forces for further combat behind two figurative field generals who could hardly have been more irreconcilable in their views.

Gara, a Ph.D. from the University of Wisconsin, spent three years in jail during World War II as a conscientious objector. In 1949, he was sentenced to eighteen months' imprisonment for counseling a student at Bluffton College in Ohio against registering for the draft. He was paroled after six months. He has taught at Grove City for five years, and the college was fully aware of his record when it hired him. He has published four books, including one about the underground railroad of the Civil War. Many considered him the most distinguished scholar on the faculty—until he was fired, last winter. But that is getting ahead of the story.

Sennholtz, who has been at Grove City six years, is an ardent right-winger with a lively interest in right-wing causes. He is a contributing editor of *American Opinion,* published by the John Birch Society, whose editorial advisory committee happens to include eighty-year-old J. Howard Pew, former president of the Sun Oil Company. Pew is now president of the Grove City College Board of Trustees and a militant proponent of extreme conservatism. Pew's father founded the college in 1876, and Howard Pew's sister, daughter, nephew, and grandson are also all on the Board of Trustees.

Last fall, Sennholtz got the curriculum committee to substitute

160

a "social-science" requirement for the history requirement. This, in effect, would have meant diverting students from Gara's history classes to Sennholtz's economics classes. The faculty overruled the committee, but this feud only added fuel to the ideological fire.

In January, two private detectives, both ex-FBI men, checked into Grove City's Penn-Grove Hotel, and spent nearly a week "investigating" Gara. One of them, John J. Frank, once worked for the late Dominican dictator, Trujillo, and recently was accused of "bugging" a hotel suite in Washington. It was occupied by a utility lawyer, pressing before the Federal Power Commission, a case in which millions of dollars of natural-gas sales were at stake.

Shortly after the investigators' visit, college President J. Stanley Harker notified Gara that his contract would not be renewed. Reports have been printed that Pew wired Harker to "fire Gara." Quickly, five faculty members, and then a sixth, resigned in protest. They were especially riled by the reason given for Gara's dismissal: "incompetence as a teacher." They recalled that he had received substantial yearly rises in salary, as well as letters of commendation from the administration. President Harker had declared that his background as a pacifist was not the issue. Gara denied the accusation of Professor Sennholtz and some others that in teaching history he "skipped wars."

When the American Association of University Professors sent a three-man committee to Grove City, late in May, to investigate the circumstances of the Gara case, Harker issued a memo to the faculty stating flatly that the Board of Trustees had instructed him to give them no co-operation. The pretext was that the A.A.U.P. had violated a pledge not to publicize its mission. Several faculty members interpreted the memo as a threat to them "not to talk," either. Subsequently, however, Harker did select some teachers to meet the committee.

The committee is completing its findings in secret, and the whole affair has cast something of a pall over Grove City's commencement exercises, to be held tomorrow. Professor Gara meanwhile has found another post at a college in Ohio.

But the issue of academic freedom for Grove City remains unresolved. In a letter to Harker, which so far has gone unacknowledged, alumnus Donald M. Maclay, now a U.S. foreign-

161

service officer, just assigned to Dahomey in Africa, summed up the problem this way: "Somewhere between the... intellectual anarchy of unbridled academic freedom and the protective custody of sophisticated brain-washing, there lies a middle ground. A great many small schools in the United States have found it. I fear that Grove City has not. Even worse, I am afraid she is not even seeking it."

Holidays and Heroes

DO WE KNOW THE NEXT
UNKNOWN SOLDIER?

May 30, 1958

THIS IS A DAY when old soldiers relive old glories, when small boys squat at the curb to cheer the band and the colors past, when Gold Star mothers gather at gravesides to touch grief again, when citizens at large think solemn thoughts of the fallen; and when statesmen pledge the dead shall not have died in vain. Memorial Day is a time, too, when reporters, straining for Pulitzer Prizes, unfurl patriotic paragraphs about the nation's observance of a brave and militant heritage.

Through such an atmosphere in Washington today, two mute, anonymous citizens moved from the rotunda of the national Capitol, along Constitution Avenue, and across Memorial Bridge over the Potomac to Arlington National Cemetery. They were the unknown dead of World War II and Korea, dispatched to lie with the nameless doughboy of World War I in the white marble tomb of the unknown soldier, that mystic monument on a lovely, wooded bluff above Lee's mansion, overlooking the quietly splendid skyline of the capital.

The flat, blue-white heat of a Maytime sun stretched like a metallic sheet over a strangely stirring scene: a human mixture of reverence and reverie, of pomp and picnicking. Pleasure boats darted from the edge of the river as the cortege slowly bridged it. Watching history move, a man in a sugar-cane hat lounged in the shade on a GI blanket. A woman, who had lingered at the edge of the open graves of the unknown since breakfast time, collapsed at midday because of the heat.

163

Only the swivel-chair military mind could have planned this reverential pageant with such fatuously painstaking punctilio— even to the point of marking in tape to the inch the positions where dignitaries would stand, and mobilizing their public-relations staffs to engulf the press tent with thirty-one separate piles of news releases on the event. Happily, these canned handouts languished, and the schedule went just enough awry to furnish reassurance that the republic is not quite ready for full regimentation. In the sun-drenched pool of the amphitheater, the President himself bobbled, placed the posthumous Medals of Honor directly on the two caskets, instead of on the little black stands provided; his erroneous gesture, I thought, was the more appropriate. The small, self-important staff colonel, with twitching left elbow, tried in vain to bar late-arriving photographers from the arena. A mortified mother was obliged to exit with her bawling boy-child in the middle of the invocation. At the final rites at the tomb, the spectators included not only the august figures of the government and the embassies, the head and vice-head of state, the living Medal of Honor winners—aged and young, bending and erect—but also an unsegregated cluster of dark- and light-skinned urchins clinging to the branches of a pepper tree, just behind Mr. Nixon.

What drew them all to that consecrated spot?—the curious; the solemn; the steel-jawed legionnaires, their overseas caps fairly quivering with patriotism; the sweet and silly girls snatching flirtatious fragments of conversation with handsome young men in uniform.

One may gently scoff at some of the extremes of ritual, hoping thus to preserve balance and perspective and not be washed away in a sheer torrent of chauvinism. And yet there was something which melted the motley, distinguished congregation together. The living, fluid identity of a people rose here like an invisible force, pushing a sad lump of pride up into the throat as the carillon bells gave a soft, round whisper to "Faith of Our Fathers," and the President, an old soldier himself, standing in the sun, now staring at the past, now squinting into the future, saluted the soldiers in personal silence as the cannon boomed, followed by the muted bugle wailing taps.

It is fitting and proper that, in the name of all, these nameless ones rest in a place of honored glory, providing that we remem-

164

ber, for their sake and for ours, that war has finally lost its glory, and that the tomb of the next unknown soldier may simply be the mass grave of mankind.

SANE FOURTH IN
A MAD WORLD

July 4, 1958

FROM HIS CARTOON CORNER in the paper this morning, that syndicated scalawag, Dennis the Menace, suddenly lit the fuse of memory and rocketed me back to July Fourths long forgotten.

"You never heard of a *sparkler?*" Dennis is remarking incredulously to a baggy-panted playmate while holding two of those wonderfully sputtering firebrands high. "My gosh, kid, where have you *been?*"

In what I will insist is the not too ancient past, the glorious Fourth was embellished with family fireworks displays that had loud, rewarding grandeur. The community rocket shoot was admittedly bigger, and we faithfully drove down by the river to watch it, but it was always a little remote, a little out of reach. There was nothing quite like igniting your own inferno in your own back yard.

Sparklers were only a minor part of the party, the hors d'oeuvres, so to speak, of the great shebang. There was a build-up, too, of tension and expectancy to the evening's star-burst. You knew you were headed somewhere purposeful, that the climax would be a dazzling, authoritative thing, not the damp-match-box kind of safe-and-sane glimmers and thuds that pass for household Independence Day fireworks today. It began in the fresh, flat, dry hotness of early morning with the explosion of a medium-sized firecracker under a tomato can. This singular salute sent the dog scurrying to his private bomb shelter under the bed, where he stayed, tail cringing at half-mast, for the duration of the ceremonies.

Then came the connected, contiguous crackle of a whole pack

of midget Chinese firecrackers. The luxury of that deliberate waste of noise at one wanton touch of punk! As the ammunition wore thin, you husbanded your shots a little more carefully; even if you spent the store too fast—which you inevitably did—there was always the Technicolor anticipation of rocket and Roman-candle riots for the evening.

Interspersed, of course, were the picnics in the poplar grove on the Flat, with fried chicken and lemonade and those confounded games: the potato, sack, and three-legged races. I do not think I ever placed or showed in a single one, but my younger brother— oh, crowning ignominy!—used to sweep first honors with ease. If there was time and enough coin left over before supper, there would be the hasty excursion farther down the country road to Campbell's Hot Springs for a swim in the pungent sulphur water, warm as stale beer, but refreshing in an acrid fashion—embellished, no doubt, by furtive, painful glances at the consciously posturing items of maidenhood adorning the pool.

Then came the pinnacle of pleasure, the homemade, or at least home-assembled, pyrotechnics; being able to shoot your own stars from the side lawn into the soft summer darkness. The sparklers, as I said, opened the show, revolved in furiously spraying arcs at arm's length. Next came the hot hiss of the pinwheels, punctuated by the lazy, lofting color balls from the Roman candles, and finally the rockets. Nobody below voting age was allowed to fire these monsters, and I sometimes think now that Father laid down this rule, not entirely as a precaution, but to assure himself of one secret throwback to boyhood. Even that sophisticated menace, Dennis, would have been thrilled.

Those days, for the most part, are gone now. We never quite learned how to handle fireworks safely, and laws have been strung in a kind of chicken wire of constraint around the carelessness of youth. Still, an eye, a full-fingered hand surely are a fair, if difficult, trade for the maiming threats hidden under a tomato can. War has long since lost its sparkler-sized glamor, so it should be less difficult for civilization to lay aside the deadly fireworks of a nuclear rocket. It should be, but it is not, human nature being the foolish, stubborn article it is.

166

A TOWER FOR TAFT

April 14, 1959

IN THE CHILL WIND that blew at the dedication of the tall Taft tower in Washington this morning, House Speaker Sam Rayburn clapped his hat back on his gleaming bald head. Then, addressing the crowd of five thousand, as well as the memory of Mr. Republican, Rayburn barked: "I desire to say I have as much respect for you with my hat on as I have with my hat off."

As Robert A. Taft sometimes did to his own adversaries, the 100-foot monument cast a cold shadow over the official participants huddled at its base, even as a bright April sun shone on the open Capitol grounds. But the eulogies to the late great Senator from Ohio were warm and florid and flowed from the rostrum in a veritable flood of superlatives and emotion.

"One of the great Americans of all times," said Speaker Rayburn.

"An inspiration to Democrats and Republicans alike," said Vice-President Nixon.

An "illustrious . . . commanding figure," who was "many things to many people," said his admiring friend Dwight D. Eisenhower, who had fought and beaten him in 1952.

A loyal, courageous bulwark, declared ex-President Herbert Hoover, not only against communism but against "centers of irresponsible intellectualism."

"A tower of strength," said Senator Harry Flood Byrd of Virginia.

It remained, however, for Republican Congressman B. Carroll Reece,* to outpeal the very bells of the Taft carillon with paeans of praise. A "great soul" who "symbolized the highest concept of the divine nature of man." "An apostle of virtue." "The noblest American of his time." These were some, but not all, of the laurels heaped upon the fallen Senator by the honorable Representative from Johnson City, Tennessee.

Senator Taft died of cancer, less than six years ago. He had not been gone two years before Congress, not without bitter

* Congressman Reece died on March 19, 1961.

controversy, authorized the erection of this privately subscribed memorial on federal property, the first time in history a monument has been raised to a senator on the Capitol grounds. The controversy has not abated. Congressman Stewart Udall,* Democrat of Arizona, has just introduced a bill forbidding construction on federal property in Washington of any further monuments to anybody who has not been dead for fifty years.

This is no reflection on the person or the personage of Bob Taft. This, rather, is a precaution to preserve national perspective and, one might add, dignity. Who is there, at the moment, equipped to measure the stature of Senator Taft? Hardly the spectators who viewed today's ceremony from the roof of that white marble mausoleum, the international headquarters of the Teamsters Union, which looms across the greensward only a long stone's throw away. Hardly someone in the crowd or on the official platform, foe, neutral, or friend, not even B. Carroll Reece. This is a task for the historians. And it is quite possible that the measurements they take of Taft for posterity will be taller than the rectangular marble tablet with the twenty-seven French bells in the top.

Expressing the family's profound thanks for the tribute, one of Taft's four sons, William Howard Taft III, observed with candor, "What my father would have thought of a physical monument in his name is very difficult to say." There arises the embarrassing question, too, of the consistency, not to say sincerity, of some of those who made the eulogies.

In the printed program for the dedication ceremonies, there were three pages of excerpts from the writings and speeches of the senator: fragments of Taftian philosophy about democracy, freedom, citizenship, solvency, willingness to work, justice. But there was not a word on one of the subjects that was closest to the Ohioan's heart—the necessity for adequate, decent shelter for all the country's citizens.

Almost exactly ten years ago, on April 21, 1949, Robert Alphonso Taft, to the astonishment and consternation of his conservative colleagues, stood up in the Senate to plead for passage of a public-housing bill which could not, in all likelihood, clear the Congress

* Now Secretary of the Interior, Udall is still fighting a battle against premature monuments and "expendable" statues already erected.

today. In fact, a similar bill, more conservative in its public housing provisions, faces the immediate prospect of ruin in the House next week, though it passed the Senate.* One of its opponents in the Senate was Harry Flood Byrd, and one of its most implacable foes in the House is B. Carroll Reece.

A CERTAIN FABULOUS
FELLOW

February 12, 1960

YESTERDAY, I WENT over to the Lincoln Memorial to think me some thoughts. They had a formal little program there at noon today in observance of Lincoln's Birthday, but I preferred the relative privacy of an unscheduled visit, so I went in advance. There was a soft hint of spring in the air. The sky was filled with the fresh petticoats of pearl-gray clouds, showing here and there a flash of blue. The trees were a blur of bare brown branches, and on the winter-faded, yellow-green grass starlings scratched and squawked. The clean white spike of the Washington Monument wavered like a water color in the long, breeze-flecked reflection pool. And there, behind, just inland from the left bank of the Potomac, rose in rhythmic Doric columns that harmonious mass of marble, a sort of American Parthenon, the country's tribute to its homely sixteenth president.

There were not many visitors: a young man with a camera; two government girls; a bespectacled air-force tech sergeant with a baby in his arms; his wife and two other children, a boy and a girl, bringing up the rear. While his blanketed armful squirmed, the airman stood at the base of Daniel Chester French's statue and stared up into Lincoln's sad, strong face. Then he gazed reverently around the temple. "It's fabulous," he murmured in a

* The Taft-sponsored act was a guide line for public housing for more than ten years. Finally, in 1961, the first year of the Kennedy administration, a new public-housing act was passed which did liberalize the 1949 legislation, mainly in the field of housing for the elderly.

Carolina drawl to his wife. She nodded and took the baby from him as if fearing he might drop it while absorbed in his absent-minded moment of inspiration.

"Fabulous," was not an adjective that I had associated with Lincoln before. But, as I contemplated it, I realized it was just the word to describe the impact of his character on the current American scene. Here indeed was a fabled figure, gauntly, grotesquely unbelievable in the easy ooze of the opulent sixties. He was a bumpkin whose awkward dress would be as anachronistic as his honesty. He was only fifty-six when Booth's bullet killed him, but the tragic responsibilities of the Civil War had long since lined his face with the scars of pain, sacrifice, and burdens which successful men unload nowadays on the analyst's couch and in the steam bath at the club.

Very likely, it is easier to rise to greatness in the hoist of historic cataclysm. From the memorial's wall, inscriptions carrying the awful weight of Lincoln's days bear down on you with an almost palpable crush. The Second Inaugural Address, delivered at the height of the war, rings with words of heartbreak, determination, and hope: "With malice toward none, with charity for all, with firmness in the right as God gives us to see the right let us strive on to finish the work we are in. . . ." And from those scribbled comments at Gettysburg: "It is for us the living rather to be dedicated here to that unfinished work which they who fought here have thus far so nobly advanced."

The work they died for is still unfinished, and other tasks command our dedicated attention, too, but it is very hard now for us to sense the terms of our emergency with the sacrificial urgency that war can bring. So it was that day before yesterday at a Congressional hearing, a disc jockey defined the "wonderful, romantic" American way of life with the motto: "I'll do for you. What will you do for me?" And so it was, too, that by far the longest dispatch on the news wires today chronicled the crisis between a television comedian and his network over a censored joke about a water closet.

Mr. Lincoln would have chuckled over that: not the joke—the situation. But he would have been deeply troubled, surely, at the spectacle of a great country shrinking from adventure, sliding into a secondary place with a misguided, if somewhat guilty, satis-

170

faction. A century and a quarter ago, at the ripe old age of twenty-nine—a little younger than the mature years of current payola witnesses—Lincoln told a Young Men's Lyceum in Springfield, Illinois, "Towering genius disdains a beaten path. It seeks regions hitherto unexplored."

At the memorial, I asked the handsome National Park Service guide, a Negro and native of Jefferson's Charlottesville, whether visitors asked him questions. "Yes," he said, "they keep asking how tall the statue is."

COMMEMORATING A
CATACLYSM

December 7, 1960

IT IS TOO BAD we could not find a better symbol for the celebration of the anniversary of Pearl Harbor than publication of the pictures of the types of atomic bombs that we dropped on Hiroshima and Nagasaki. Yet there is a likeness of ourselves herein which we would do well to recognize and not forget.

In the first place, there is something revealing in the official bureaucratic flap over whether these photographs should be released even now—more than fifteen years after "Little Boy" and "Fat Man," as the original combat packages were whimsically called, were arched off on their deadly, fateful missions over Japan, feeding the Communists and their fellow travelers fresh and purportedly tangible evidence of our "bloodthirsty imperialism." This is an understandable and legitimate worry, but it seems to me slightly misguided, as if by suppressing the prints it would expunge from history the cataclysmic fact that the United States of America, the leading power of the so-called civilized world, was the first to use atomic weapons, which, in the two first droppings, netted a total of one hundred and fifty thousand dead Japanese.

The point is not whether "Little Boy" and "Fat Man" should or should not have been dropped. That issue will be debated inconclusively, perhaps to the end of time. The question is aca-

171

demic because the *fait*, as they say in Berlitz, is *accompli*. The point is that the bombs were dropped and that we dropped them. The treachery of the Japanese on December 7, 1941, is easy to recall, and, as Franklin Roosevelt predicted, this date will live in infamy. The dates of what happened at Hiroshima on August 6, 1945, and at Nagasaki on August 9 are not so comfortable for us to recall, but they, too, are a part of the record of World War II.

It develops that the shapes and sizes of the two bombs were declassified a long time ago, but not their actual photographic likenesses. There have been numerous and insistent requests for the latter from the press, from scientists, from historians, and, presumably, from literal-minded, if not prideful, types in the Pentagon itself. When a House subcommittee on freedom of government information got wind of this, Chairman John Moss, Democrat of California, struck up an aggressive correspondence with the Atomic Energy Commission that lasted until the pictures were finally released yesterday.

They might have been more appropriately published on Christmas Day, and I do not mean that cynically. With a well-chosen foreword from the proper authorities on the juxtaposition of symbolism involved, we could have studied the black, evil, corpulent, but surprisingly classical bomblike lines of "Little Boy" and "Fat Man," and then contemplated—with more detachment and perception on December 25 than on Pearl Harbor Day, perhaps—our contributions to peace on earth and good will to men.

These contributions, I hasten to add, have been vast, generous, and meaningful. But their value and their meaning shrink when we refuse to remind ourselves, as we too often do, that, in addition to our benefactions and sacrifices, we also have contributed something to the world's woes. Let us remember that only the tyrants, of left or right, are infallible in their own image.

Remembering this should make it easier for us to look at ourselves and the world a little more realistically, to be less introverted with a brooding guilt on the one hand, less smug in self-righteousness on the other. Such an attitude might provide us with a more penetrating approach to the conflicts and tensions now besetting the globe. We cannot solve the problem of the arms race with a miracle, but we had better ask ourselves whether we are not discounting with more impatience than sound judg-

172

ment the depth of the sentiments of neutralism, not just in the world's uncommitted areas, but in such friendly lands as Great Britain.

A heartening prospect for countering resentment and recapturing the imagination and enthusiasm of foreign peoples emerged during the Presidential campaign. News Secretary Pierre Salinger says that apparently nothing Senator Kennedy proposed during his run for the Presidency produced more exciting response than his idea for a peace corps,* so-called, as a replacement for the draft for qualified youths wanting to serve on aid projects abroad. This idea will have to be carefully activated, but the bomb pictures should help speed it into being. There is a parallel inspiration which should not be overlooked: On November 22, an ex-air force major named Claude R. Eatherly,** aged forty-four, vanished from the Veterans Hospital in Waco, Texas, where he was being treated for mental and emotional disturbances. He had piloted the lead navigation plane over Hiroshima in 1945.

AND NOW, BACK TO JESUS CHRIST

November 23, 1961

IF YOU RISE still hungry from your seven-course Thanksgiving-dinner snack, there remains the bulging cupboard of Christmas goodies advertised in the magazines of the season, to

---

* See "The Peace Corps Scores," page 224.

** Eatherly's legacy from that Hiroshima mission is a tragic one. For the past fifteen years, he has been in and out of hospitals and jail. He suffers, Veterans Administration doctors say, from an anxiety neurosis. He has been divorced by his wife, who remarried and has their three children. He has been alcoholic and suicidal. Now an ardent pacifist, he has "quieted down" and visits a psychiatrist several evenings a week. As this was written, he was living alone in a motel on the outskirts of Galveston, Texas. Eatherly's income comes from a government disability pension—fifty per cent at first, later raised to one hundred per cent when he was ruled psychotic—and from royalties on a book, *Burning Conscience,* a collection of his correspondence with Dr. Gunther Anders, a Viennese pacifist philosopher. The book has been published in fourteen languages.

nibble on. For me this has become a kind of holiday ritual, replacing brandy and the after-dinner mint.

But, late this afternoon, as I lay on my couch lazily sampling the plums of gift suggestions fairly tumbling from the slick pages of the current periodicals, I was brought bolt upright by that glamorous handmaid of God and mammon, Mrs. Clare Boothe Luce. In her monthly commentary in *McCall's*, she was heroically defending the commercialization of Christmas. Indeed, her theme seemed to be that if it were not for the valiant efforts of the American advertising man, the Christian spirit born with the Babe in that Bethlehem manger might have died long ago.

"What, after all, is wrong with Christmas advertising?" she wanted to know. "We are enjoined to give generously, especially to children. I cannot recall a Yuletide advertisement," Mrs. Luce went on, "that did not emphasize giving rather than getting."

Surely, such Luce thoughts are food for thought. They caused me, for one, to see in an entirely new light a silversmith's ad I had just encountered in *Esquire* under the challenging caption: "She loves sterling almost as much as she loves you." Also, I found myself taking a wholly fresh approach to another layout, in which a genial fellow under a simulated halo was plugging the merits of a traveling bar with the now-loaded question: "Who says you can't take it with you?" At first glance, I had thought the halo was supposed to be an amusing gag, but now, with Mrs. Luce as my guide, I was able to see what should have been obvious—that this was the manufacturer's graceful attempt to get in step with the holiness of the Christmas season. In a way, the silversmith's pitch was more subtle. Juxtaposing, as it did, the material with the sublime values of human relationship, it made it crystal-clear that it was more blessed to give than to receive, especially in view of the fact that if, you did not give your girl more silver, she might love thy neighbor better.

I am beginning to grasp more and more fully the truth of Mrs. Luce's observation that business and advertising not only may be helping to keep the Christmas spirit alive in the West, but also are happily and selflessly spreading it around the world, as well. Particularly convincing was her emphasis on the advertisers' emphasis of the importance of giving to children. How many times in the past, in devouring the displayed desirability of diamond necklaces and mutation minks, have we all glided unappreciatively over the reminders to remember the children of Greece and the Congo, of Peru, Persia, and Hong Kong?

Mrs. Luce reserves her most moving defense for the Christmas-card people. "The Virgin," she writes, "has never made an apparition in the United States; but her cardboard image numbers perhaps millions every December—thanks to commercialization. The cards with families grouped around a tree, tables loaded with turkey and plum pudding, emphasize the bonds that unite husband and wife and children. Only a cynic, reviewing a sample thousand Christmas cards, could think that the true spirit of Christmas—good will and love—is dead in the American people."

I agree. It is not dead. Indeed, one of the most heartening testimonials to the amazing virility of the American spirit is that it has managed to remain alive and dispense the warmth of human kindness and love despite the suffocating load of materialism that the crass commercialization of our civilization has heaped upon it. Nothing is sacred any more. Even religion feels it must resort to advertising to thrive. "The family that prays together stays together," says the public-service plug over the air and on the subway cards, as if what you could expect to find in church were a kind of glue, sponsored by the Almighty, to repair the emotional and spiritual cracks in your home. The admen begin their Christmas merchandising in July, and the finest artists of the land interrupt their broadcasts to plug a powder to kill body odor, a pill to ease congestion in the lower tract, a magical medicine, or a humming machine to remove hair from milady's legs and armpits. A less hardy population would have long since perished under the weight of this crushing vulgarity. Thanks perhaps to the heritage of a tough Pilgrim stock and the rough seasoning of the pioneers, we have not only survived, but may well be beginning to rebel against the limits that commercialization has reached.

Indeed, I wonder whether Mrs. Luce's interesting defense of the advertised sponsorship of almost everything does not reflect the guilty realization by the business community—and its contingents of employees, as well—that there is such a thing as the oversell of material values. If it does, we may have even more to be thankful for in this beautiful and blessed, but sometimes biliously bountiful, country than we thought.

175

Civil Rights

THE MISSILES OF HATE

Y OU MAY HAVE SEEN the news picture in *Life* magazine of a fifteen-year-old Hungarian boy standing guard on a street in Budapest, before Russian tanks and troops came back to crush the revolution. A safety pin in his overcoat lapel, a rifle slung over his shoulder, a haunting look of brave determination on his face, the very purposeful stance of this lad testified that he was a son of freedom who knew what he was fighting for.

Not a very pleasant pastime for a teen-ager, and it makes you shiver to think what may have happened since to this boy—Pal Pruck, the caption said his name was. But I cannot help wondering what would happen to his thinking, what his impressions would be if, somehow—assuming he is still alive—he could be lifted from Budapest and set down in Clinton, Tennessee. If he had got there a couple of days ago, he would have seen teen-agers fighting in the streets, too—not armed with rifles, to be sure, but with eggs and rocks. And, irony of ironies, in this great republic which we take pride in referring to as a bastion of liberty, Pal's contemporaries in Clinton High School were not fighting for freedom, but against it. They were throwing the eggs at Negro classmates, protesting the freedom which integration was supposed to give them.

If Pal also had been taken to a town in northern Georgia called Summerville, he might have been even more perplexed. Two Negro high school football teams, Lafayette and Summerville, were supposed to play there tonight on the athletic field of the seg-

177

regated white high school—the only place available. Spectator seating was to be segregated, too, in accordance with state law and long custom. But, despite a protest from the junior chamber of commerce, the field has been padlocked. The county board of education forbade its use after Sheriff Fred Stewart of Chattooga County received a telegram from a man named Wesley Morgan, who called himself an imperial vice-president of the Ku Klux Klan. Allowing two Negro teams to play on a field built for white students would violate the law, the Ku Kluxer said, and that, apparently, was that. The proceeds of the game, incidentally, were to go into a fund for the white high school band.

Now that our young Hungarian freedom fighter had got this far, he might have extended his trip to Atlanta, where, last night at a fund-raising dinner of the States' Rights Council, Georgians were asked to present a "massive united" front against integration. Pal's bafflement, I suspect, would have been complete if he could have heard the speech of Senator-elect Herman Talmadge. "If we're organized," Talmadge said at one point, "we can demonstrate the will to resist that the people of Budapest showed only a short time ago in an effort to govern themselves." *

But if Pal, the Hungarian lad, would have been confused, I wonder if we Americans are not really the ones who are far more confused on the meaning of freedom. True, the principal of Clinton High in Tennessee has threatened to expel any student attempting further intimidation of Negroes. True, the Summerville incident is so desperate in its ridiculousness that its ultimate effect can be only to help crumble the crust of prejudice. As for Herman Talmadge, not many people will continue to confuse the passion of race extremists with the passion that has fired the Hungarians against their oppressors.

This stark question remains: Who is providing whom with a living lesson in the meaning of democratic values? Pal Pruck of Budapest—since he reached the age of reason—was taught nothing in school except the dogma of communism. He has never known

* Massive resistance is slowly but surely crumbling in Georgia, and one of the reasons is that officials, including Senator Talmadge, realize they cannot buck the inevitable forever. Token desegregation has already come to Atlanta schools, and race relations in general are perhaps more civilized and promising there than in any other city in the South. Smaller cities and rural areas present a more stubborn problem.

life in a free country such as ours. He was nurtured from kindergarten by the state and was supposed to become a flower of
tomorrow in the Marxist garden. Yet, when the time came, he
somehow knew the lessons of freedom by heart. I wish there were
enough Pal Prucks to remind the student bodies of Clinton and
Summerville and our own home towns that the missiles and mis-
sives of hate and fear can in their way be as deadly to democracy
as a totalitarian tank.

A MATTER OF
UNDERSTANDING

Durham, N. C.
October 23, 1957

THIS REPORTER received a liberal education in a matter of
minutes on the campus of North Carolina College, in Durham.
Some fourteen hundred Negroes, mostly from this state and other
parts of the South, but representing the farthest corners of the
country, too, comprise the student body in this state-supported
institution. Since their whole future, not to mention their everyday life, is saturated with the race problem and attempts to solve
it, it is not surprising that they are absorbingly interested in it.
It was not on this point that I got my lesson, however.

I learned it from President Alfonso Elder, a graduate of Atlanta
and Columbia Universities. We were talking about Little Rock.
I mentioned, as I had mentioned publicly before, that to me one
of the most moving aspects of that tortured story was the courage
and dignity of the nine Negro students, particularly on the first
day, when one of them ran or rather walked the gamut of Governor Faubus' guardsmen in front of Central High and was denied
entrance. "I am not sure," I said, "that anybody else could have
done that."

Dr. Elder caught me up. The Negro, he said, does not like to
think that the courage, self-restraint, and even the dignity he may
exhibit in the clutch of crisis and the glowering shadow of physi-

179

cal violence are peculiar to him or his race. He wants them recognized only as *human* qualities; indeed, if the situation at Little Rock had been reversed, if a minority of white students—with a legacy of deprivation—had been confronted with an armed black guard standing between them and their classrooms, the chances are that they would have shown brave determination, too.

What an eloquent tribute and testimony this is to the innate dignity of man, regardless of the color of the wrapping on his individual human package. Here is a Negro, not only declining to take credit for patience and moderation and courage, but also protesting that these things, after all, are only human attributes and should not be used to set his race apart. I cannot think of any more convincing argument for the proposition that all the Negro basically wants is full recognition as a human being, no better or worse than any other, with the inalienable right to be treated as a human being, equal under the law. It could be that the people who want to deny Negroes this right are a little less human than they.

I learned something else. A reporter, A. M. Rivera, Jr., roving correspondent for the *Pittsburgh Courier*, one of the biggest Negro newspapers in the country, raised another point. Little Rock, he said, proved the good qualities of whites, too. For a moment, I thought the mellow warmth of Indian summer had got us both, but his reasoning was that neither courage nor armed escorts could have landed those Negro students in class if they had not known or sensed that inside there were enough persons equipped with reason and decency to keep them from grievous harm. A few white students—though by no means all—have shed their preconceived prejudices against integration by the simple measure of confronting the reality of these Negro boys and girls, and having the honesty to realize that their former views were based on hate, fear, ignorance, or all three.

There are racial bigots everywhere, but one of the favorite cries of this ilk in the South is that "Nobody understands the Negro like the southern white man does."

"You know," journalist Rivera was saying, in effect, "the white man has kept apart from the Negro. Yet we have had an intimate look at him. Negroes have cooked for him, waited on him, nursed his children, rejoiced in his successes, grieved at his failures,

180

watched him in his own house under stress and strain and celebration. The white man has not had that same opportunity of insight. Now, with that experience plus some education, we are facing him."

I wonder whether it would not be wise to amend that cliché to read: "Nobody understands the white man as the Negro does."

SMU SURVIVES SUBVERSION

April 24, 1958

WORD FILTERS THROUGH the Cactus Curtain that the Lone Star State has undergone an ordeal by fire and emerged, as from a kind of intellectual Alamo, with flaming if not really radical colors. Yesterday afternoon in broad daylight, an ex-Communist appeared on the campus of Southern Methodist University in Dallas. Lo and behold, the citizens of the state awoke this morning completely intact, and not a Cadillac or an oil pump has skipped a beat.

Alerted by organizations of unsleeping patriotism, the community was able to brace itself for the worst. In the van was the Public Affairs Luncheon Club, a group of ladies whose buxom ambition, reportedly fulfilled, is to stay to the political right of the DAR. The club smelled the blackest mischief in the invitation of a student committee to John Gates, ex-editor of the *Daily Worker* in New York, to appear on the campus and describe something of the anatomy of communism. One of eleven leading Communists convicted under the Smith Act for plotting the violent overthrow of the U.S. government, Gates publicly broke with the party last January, two years after having been paroled from a federal penitentiary. But the ladies took no stock in his ideological reform and argued that, in any event, a person of his atheistic views should not be allowed within a Christian institution like Southern Methodist. They generated a good deal of heat; at the height of it, some unimpoverished Texans threatened to suspend their financial contributions to the university. But SMU President Willis Tate stubbornly stood his ground in support of the student

181

committee, with the quaint argument that one of the functions of an educational institution is to educate, and that this can often be done by examining conflicting opinions and philosophies.

The upshot was that Gates's appearance, instead of collecting the expected handful of listeners, filled the school's McFarlin Auditorium with more than three thousand students and townspeople, reportedly outdrawing such luminaries as John Foster Dulles and Harry S. Truman. In a pretty turn of etiquette, Gates, at the outset of his not necessarily valuable remarks, thanked the ladies of the Public Affairs Luncheon Club for making the meeting such a success.

Under the pressure of community clamor, extreme pains were taken to see that Gates—forlorn figure that he is—did not somehow spin a cobweb of conspiracy before the very eyes of the crowd. He was questioned by a panel which included the university chaplain and two professors—one of religion and one of government—and he was rebutted by Herbert Philbrick, erstwhile counterspy for the FBI.

As one Dallas lady put it, "We had the horrible experience of hearing an outside view and, remarkably enough, we survived." With a little more of such recklessness, Texas and the rest of the country may well survive, too.

CONTACT THROUGH A STORM

December 12, 1960

THE PARALYZING VIOLENCE of a winter storm reminds me of the violent convulsions the country is undergoing as it struggles with the harsh, bitter conflict of racial prejudice. If you stop to think, this parallel is not so strange as it may seem. A blizzard can move with the sinister sound of silence. A brooding hatred is sometimes spread that way, pushed by a whining wind of fear. One of the first things a heavy snowfall does is to break down communications. In the sociological spasm of desegregation and its related crises, contacts are almost totally broken. A quick glance at a panorama of snow reflects a deceptive dazzle that is almost all white and black. But a closer look at the picture reveals complicated shadings and countless little cameos of individual problems—a frozen railway switch, a blocked driveway, one stalled car by the roadside, a solitary soul bending bravely against the wind to clear a path.

To understand the storm the Negroes are struggling against as they inch forward to grasp their full constitutional rights as first-class citizens, this deep disturbance must be broken down into the intimate, bitter, moving pictures of personal experience which comprise the whole. Over the week end, at a seminar on human relations at the University of North Carolina, in Chapel Hill, I had the rare privilege of examining some of these poignant portraits of private human problems firsthand.

To stretch the image further, I felt as if I were looking at fragments of a vast mosaic which earnest people were trying to put together on an uneven surface. Just as one fragment would seem to fit, the surface would quiver and push it out of place. Here are some of the pieces, candidly displayed by Negro and white students of twenty-three southern colleges and universities attending the seminar:

One day, after city buses had been desegregated in Charlotte, North Carolina, a white girl, who thought she believed passionately in equal rights, ran home from school in tears. There had been one empty seat on the bus next to a neatly dressed Negro woman. The girl could not summon the courage to take it.

At a dormitory bull session in Chapel Hill, eight students were discussing segregation. Suddenly one of them, from Georgia, clapped his hands to his face and rocked back and forth on the bed. "I know segregation is wrong. But I cannot bring myself to reject what I've been reared to believe."

At one of the seminar workshops, a young man from Duke University hesitatingly confessed, "Why, I've never even shaken hands with a Negro." Quietly, a North Carolina University Negro freshman extended his hand across the table. For agonizing seconds, the hand hung there. Then, slowly, tensely, the veins standing out on his neck, the Duke man took it.

Restless to break away from a background of aristocratic southern prejudice, a white student joined a mixed construction gang last summer. Though the Negroes were better skilled and one or two of them even had more education, they were classified as common laborers who could not claim the higher pay of the white carpenters, despite the fact that they often did the latter's jobs. There was, however, a curious camaraderie among the Negroes and whites. As the building went up, one of their pastimes was to whistle down at pretty girls on the street below. But they were protectively careful to segregate their whistling. If a white girl passed while a Negro was watching, he would shout, "Get over here, David." And vice versa it would be, "Hurry up, Moses, and get a load of this."

This same North Carolina University student, who had never traveled north of Richmond, Virginia, recently went to New York. In a bar, he fell into lively conversation with a man about, among other things, poetry and literature. The man was colored. Hurrying back to his hotel at 2:30 A.M., the student burst into his room and excitedly woke his traveling companions. "Listen, fellows," he shouted. "I've just met a cultured Negro."

The fragments are innumerable. There was the Negro exchange student in Germany who mused that German students could enjoy in the United States rights and privileges which Negroes and other Americans had fought for against the Nazis in World War II, but which he and his dark-skinned fellows had to come abroad to taste.

Some of the fragments are beginning to fit. The white girl on the bus later joined Negro sit-in demonstrators. The handshake broke the ice for the Duke and UNC men, and the two of them spent much of a seminar reception talking together. But the mosaic of understanding has only been begun. Such seminars as this one on human rights at the University of North Carolina quicken the process, although similar ones cannot be held in the Deep South, where they are needed the most. There is so much to do and so little time to do it in, against the world's rising storms of racial strife.

A SCENARIO OF PARAMOUNT IMPORTANCE

June 15, 1961

YESTERDAY, IN NEW YORK CITY, four girls and eleven young men, who had picketed the executive offices of American Broadcasting-Paramount Theaters, Inc. the week before, were found guilty of disorderly conduct by a judge in Manhattan's adolescent court. The judge lectured them and gave them suspended sentences. The company owns a number of big theater chains throughout the country and is also the parent of the ABC radio and television networks. The peaceful demonstration had been in support of the efforts of students, professors, and other citizens of Austin, Texas, to desegregate movie houses. The young people's path led to the doorstep of ABC-Paramount president Leonard Goldenson, because, they said, they understood the policy he set was the key to the operation of the theaters in Austin. Interstate Theaters Incorporated, a subsidiary, owns three theaters in Austin, all of which had been, and still are, among the principal targets of the desegregationists.

Goldenson refused to see the demonstrators, four of whom had penetrated to his outer office, where they staged an overnight sit-in. And later, pleading prior conferences, no company official was available to Norman Thomas, former Socialist candidate for president and a leading American liberal, who called in person at the New York offices to support the protest against theater segregation in Austin. While in the ABC-Paramount lobby, Thomas told reporters it would be "outrageous hypocrisy" for ABC commentators to criticize segregationists when their own organization has been a "far more powerful obstruction" to racial equality.

Earlier, Goldenson had issued a statement emphasizing that all the company's theaters, including those in the South, were operated on an autonomous basis by local subsidiaries. He added, however, that "the company has expressed to its theater affiliates its point of view that they should proceed with desegregation as fast as

185

they possibly can within the limits of their responsibilities for the welfare of the particular community and the theater located there."

But, when the manager of the Austin Paramount, Charles Root, was confronted with this statement, which seemed to place some responsibility on him, he replied, "Nonsense," adding that the authority is in Dallas, the headquarters of Interstate, ABC-Paramount's Texas subsidiary. At the moment, nobody seems to know where the buck stops, and there is still no desegregated movie theater in Austin.*

There is something painfully ironical about this. On other fronts, Austin, which is the home of the University of Texas, has made remarkable, almost model and peaceful progress in clearing the hurdles of racial prejudice. The university itself has been open to all qualified students since 1956. Restaurants have been largely, though not totally, desegregated. At one point in this drive, more than 2,000 persons in three days signed pledges to patronize only desegregated eating places. But, strangely, theaters resisted, despite long and patient pleadings led by a young Jewish rabbi, Charles Mintz. In Austin, it is not a question of segregation. Negroes are not admitted to the movies even on a segregated basis. The manager of a fine-arts theater across from the campus indicated clearly that he followed the policy of the Interstate chain; at least, he would not buck it. In April, the manager of the State Theater, owned by Interstate, wrote to the father of one of the box-office-line stand-ins, complaining that his son was one of the "most outspoken (at times disrespectfull [sic]) leaders" of the desegregation group. The boy was asked to quit the demonstrations by his father, a state employee whose supervisor had learned of the boy's participation.

The demonstrators have had difficulty in convincing some of the theater-management people that they are not Communists or paid by Communist sympathizers. Part of this is due, no doubt, to the fact that management has not really given them a hearing.

When a group called "Students for Direct Action" tried to discuss with Interstate headquarters in Dallas the question of why one Austin Paramount theater could not desegregate now, headquarters replied, "This is a business matter which we do not choose to discuss further."

* The three theaters in question are now desegregated.

It is indeed a business matter, but it is also a human matter and therefore a public matter. It is a paradox and a pity that ABC-Paramount, whose liberal policies in broadcasting allow commentators, including this one, to speak their minds critically on the air, cannot more consistently activate a policy of desegregation to which it is committed. It is an admirable policy. More than that, it is a vital policy because it means—if it means anything—that human rights are as important as property rights. Some enterprises, interestingly enough, have even found it to be good business.

THE BLUE YONDER
OF THE COSMOS

January 9, 1962

THE QUESTION before the house tonight, ladies and gentlemen, is: When does a private club lose its right to privacy? One broad answer is, surely, that it does not lose it, that it has the right to pick and choose its own members. Then it must also follow that, if its method of selection is not in tune with the society in which it exists, the club may find itself eventually too exclusive for its own purposes—not because it did not invite enough people to join, but because not enough eligible people will be interested in joining.

That may be stretching the point a little, but not much. This, roughly, is the dilemma in which one of Washington's old and distinguished clubs, the Cosmos Club, finds itself after its admissions committee last night blackballed the proposed membership of Carl Rowan, a deputy assistant secretary of State for public affairs. Rowan is not only an official member of the Kennedy administration—which has made a point of fighting segregation, whether in private clubs or public bus stations—he is himself a Negro.

The effects of the blackball were immediate and are certain to be far-reaching. It killed the prospective membership of the President of the United States in the Cosmos Club, by causing his

187

sponsor, John Kenneth Galbraith, U.S. ambassador to India, to resign. Other resignations in protest will follow. Another proposed membership, that of Edward R. Murrow, chief of the United States Information Agency, is also being withdrawn. The situation recalls a similar ruckus some months ago, when the President's brother, Attorney General Robert Kennedy, resigned from the more sedate Metropolitan Club because it had rebuked a member for bringing a Negro into the club as his guest.

The Cosmos Club does not bar Negroes as guests; this policy long predated the Kennedy administration. Its criteria for membership, which do not include race, do include contributions to some branch of knowledge, cultivation in the arts or letters, and accomplishment in fields involving the public interest. Today some members were astonished to find that no Negro has ever been a member of the Cosmos Club. The chairman of the admissions committee, Harold Graves, who is director of information for the World Bank, said the committee considered it improper to divulge anything beyond its decision in Rowan's case.

Rowan's own reaction was both graceful and gracious. He said that the question of race was not raised when his name was first submitted, and he would not raise it now. "It is my understanding," he said, "that this is Washington's club of intellectuals. If it is the intellectual judgment of the membership committee that I do not merit membership, I can do no more than note this judgment and wish the club well."

The question arises, inevitably, of the dimensions of the Cosmos Club's intellectuality as reflected in the arts and sciences and public affairs. If it rejects a man because of his color, rather than his failure to make a colorful contribution to culture, the public has a right to question its pretensions to intellectuality and culture, if not its method of selecting members. This questioning is painfully timely. In this changing world, where old habits and old prejudices are crumbling, one hopes that the intellectuals—particularly those in a prominent club in Washington, which is not only the nation's capital, but in a sense the civilized world's capital —will set the pace in adopting the broader view.

If intellectuals, especially those so mistrusted and feared by the radical right, namely, the liberal intellectuals, do not show a con-

188

sistency of conscience in matters of principle, who will? The Better Business Bureau?

What is the recipe of procedure for a private club nowadays, particularly one in the goldfish bowl of Washington? Ambassador Galbraith put it to me this way when confirming his resignation from the Cosmos Club: Its formula, he said, must be "something that reflects the values—hopefully, the civilized values—of its members." When it fails (though it has the legal right to do so on the issue of membership), it puts the obligation on the individual to make a choice. Galbraith, once, years ago, the youngest member of the club, has made his choice.

In fairness to any harassed membership committee, it must be said that, the world being what it is today, almost nobody would believe a committee if it said that a Negro prospect was rejected, not because of his race, but for other reasons—for which many non-Negroes do not get into clubs. If this were true in Rowan's case, the Cosmos Club could rightfully complain of unjustified criticism, and it could eloquently and quickly prove how unjustified the criticism was by electing, say, a Ralph Bunche to membership.*

DEMOCRACY IS MORE THAN A GAG

April 10, 1962

EVERY NOW AND THEN, the apparatus of democracy revs up to a reassuring hum; the road opens; the sky lightens; and the

---

* Shortly after the club's rejection of Rowan, there was a large protest meeting of members, which adopted a resolution condemning a segregated membership policy. Officially, a club spokesman refused to admit that this meeting was even held, and insisted that the Cosmos practiced no exclusion on the basis of race, creed, or color, but only on the basis of a candidate's failure to qualify on "meritorious, original work in science, literature, or fine arts." It is understood that the names of one or two Negroes have been proposed for membership since the incident, but, reportedly, no member who resigned in protest over the Rowan incident has rejoined.

hearts of men of good will are lifted by the sight of a society purposefully at work. A case in point involved the community of Berkeley, California, and Gus Hall, the hapless secretary of the American Communist party. The incident is worth recalling because it means far more than all the doomsday lessons of the passionately pious, but conveniently commercialized, anti-Communist crusades which are so fashionably haunting the country.

The story begins with a letter I received from a young fellow at the University of California, reporting anguish, disillusionment, and distress over the towering uproar created when officials of Stiles Hall, the off-campus YMCA where he worked, had agreed to let a student group meet there to hear Communist Gus Hall speak. Communists are not allowed to appear on the Berkeley campus itself.

But some Berkeley businessmen banded together, determined to keep Gus Hall out of Stiles Hall, too. They threatened to block the $20,000 Stiles Hall gets from the United Crusade by boycotting the whole $11,000,000 community-chest drive if the meeting were held. There were angry visits, even threatening phone calls to the "Y," and indignant letters to San Francisco Bay papers. One of the spokesmen for the business-chamber of commerce group was quoted as saying, "We're against all this liberal thinking."

Such exasperated huffing and puffing was not enough to blow Stiles Hall off its thirty-year course of protecting the rights of free speech. In a public statement, the YMCA's board chairman, J. Clayton Orr, said, "The position of Stiles Hall with respect to communism is clear and unequivocal. We are opposed to all forms of totalitarianism, communist or otherwise. On the other hand, we are dedicated to the maintenance of Christian and democratic values. That is the reason for our policy . . ." of supporting the constitutional guarantees of free speech and assembly for the student community.

United Crusade officials stood fast, too, and did not exert an ounce of pressure on the "Y" to change its position, and the "Y" share of the chest fund was undiminished. The San Francisco *Chronicle* editorially congratulated Stiles Hall "for its refusal to panic under the shrill threats of a frightened few, who are overworried about domestic Communists and underinformed about the rights of free speech and assembly." The next day, Gus Hall

190

spoke to a standing-room-only crowd in the modest 170-seat auditorium of the "Y" and predicted that all Americans eventually would be Communists, through a bloodless evolution.

At last reports, the university walls were still standing. There has been no detectable rush to join the party, but there does seem to have been considerable response to the speaker's parting shot: "I hope I have stirred some element of thinking here." Indeed, there is evidence that the community did some rethinking on the values of constitutional guarantees: In letters, phone calls, and comments, at least four times as many citizens supported Stiles Hall and the United Crusade as opposed them, though neither institution asked for any response.

And the University of California may have struck a bonus bonanza in the bargain. Just before the commotion about Gus Hall broke, an eighty-three-year-old Oakland real estate man, Fred E. Reed, promised to leave UC a million dollars if it would keep Communist speakers off the campus. After talking to students who had come to hear Hall, Reed changed his mind and drew up a new will giving five million to the university, no strings attached. He said he had underestimated the intelligence of the average student and that he now had "absolute" confidence in the student body, the board of regents, and President Clark Kerr.*

How much the example of Stiles Hall has contributed to the clear thinking of undergraduates and other citizens who have come in contact with it cannot be calculated, but it has been considerable. In the Communist case, the hall's present executive secretary, William J. Davis, was building on a Stiles Hall tradition that reaches back almost two generations, a tradition that impelled one of his predecessors, Harry Kingman, now head of the Citizens Lobby in Washington, to fight successfully for the rights of loyal Japanese-Americans against the hysteria that harmed them after Pearl Harbor. There is nothing the matter with democratic institutions that the active courage of men and women who believe in the American revolutionary principles of a free and open society cannot cure. The inspiring story of the Stiles Hall YMCA is fresh proof of that.

* Reed has been enormously pleased with the favorable notices his change of legacy brought, and seems increasingly convinced that students on the Berkeley campus "have their feet on the ground."

CHRIST AND
GEORGE SINGLEMANN

April 24, 1962

THE CHRISTIAN WORLD has just celebrated the joyous festival of Easter, marking the resurrection of Christ, the prince of peace and brotherly love. And now, in the dubiously sovereign state of Louisiana, citizens who undoubtedly profess the Christian faith have just resurrected the symbol of slavery.

They have done it with a cynical veneer of refinement thinly disguising the savagery of their act. They have gone to a native American citizen, a jobless longshoreman named Louis Boyd, who has a wife and eight children, and said, in effect, "Nigger, git." Oh, to be sure, they concealed the order behind a kind of mock courtliness, and generosity fell from their fingertips like hominy grits from a spoon. "Here is $50.00 in cash and a one-way bus fare north," George Singlemann, head of the racist Citizens Council of New Orleans, told Boyd. "You'll soon find out how you're treated up there."

What certain citizens of New Orleans were really saying, in open defiance of the Bill of Rights, was: You are inferior, Boyd, you and your kind. You are not entitled to the rights and privileges guaranteed by law, because here we are a law unto ourselves. Under our law, the freeing of the slaves was a joke. We do not recognize it, though Lincoln's Emancipation Proclamation will be one hundred years old next New Year's Day. Oh, you may have a certain qualified physical freedom, Boyd; we couldn't get away with auctioning you off the block nowadays—but we still enslave your spirit. And we don't like your rebelliousness; so we've sold your constitutional American right to live where you choose. Now beat it. And don't come back.

Singlemann's slave trade in the degradation of the human spirit seems to be picking up temporarily. He and his racist kind are now gleefully talking about sending north a special trainload of one thousand Negroes, not on the underground railroad, but above ground in broad daylight, to demonstrate their rare version of southern hospitality. This can only end in heartbreak and disaster.*

Although the story of longshoreman Louis Boyd has had a happy first-chapter ending, it is not the way to solve the problem of race relations, as any thoughtful citizen knows. Boyd, who had never been out of Louisiana before in his life, has begun a $100-a-week job as a handyman for a medical-equipment firm in Jersey City, New Jersey.** Willing agencies and new friends are trying to settle the Boyds satisfactorily in a home near the plant.

"I'll never go back [to Louisiana], never," Mrs. Boyd said. "In the past three days, we've been treated better than we were for the past five years at home. I knew they wanted us to leave, and I thank them for it."

What pride Singlemann and his fellow White Citizens Councilmen must take in that testimonial to the kind of civilized community they stand for! But that is not the point. Nor is it the point to launch a nation-wide contest to see which community can be nicest or most beastly to the Negro. The point is to mobilize the nation's conscience, intelligence, and ingenuity in a campaign to end the second-class citizenship of twenty million people, North and South, so that they may contribute the full share of their talents to our society at a fateful juncture in history when we need every vestige of human strength, mental and spiritual, to face the future.

The order went out today to explode nuclear bombs again in a series of tests designed, so the reasoning runs, to protect our way of life and save us from destruction. Is George Singlemann's way of life what we mean to protect, or is it the way provided so foresightedly and with such guarantees of equal justice by the federal Constitution and the Bill of Rights? Whatever precarious stability a nuclear stalemate may bring, how safe from destruction is a society corroded by the acid of racial prejudice?

Nor will any northern "holier than thou" attitude in the sad saga of the Louis Boyds be helpful. Sooner or later, they will find

* The "free rides north" movement fizzled out. Exact figures are unavailable, but it is reliably estimated that less than a hundred Negroes were inveigled into this crude operation, including the publicized handful sent to the town of Hyannis Port, President Kennedy's Cape Cod home.

** Boyd lost that job when the firm went bankrupt in May, 1962. Later, he worked in a laundry briefly, still hoping to find a steady job.

there is segregation and race hatred north of the Mason-Dixon Line, too. Ruthless injustices in the South can be blamed in part for the flooding of Chicago, Detroit, Washington, New York, and other unprepared northern cities with Negro "refugees" and an attendant rise in crime and delinquency. The raw truth is that those problems would have been far less difficult to handle, even in their artificially swollen condition, if northern police, politicians, and plain people had shown more responsibility and less prejudice themselves.

It would be reassuring if, in the face of this vast sociological problem and the threat of that great leveler, the hydrogen bomb, we would find Congress grappling with these matters with realism and candor. But what do we find? We find at this very hour the Senate of the United States bracing against a filibuster, in which all other critical legislation will grind to a standstill, while southerners try to block a bill to strengthen the voting rights of Negro citizens.* How much longer can we afford the luxury of such tragic nonsense?

* This bill, to abolish poll taxes cleared Congress, languidly enough, as the only piece of civil rights legislation passed by the 1962 session. A proposed constitutional amendment, three-fourths of the states must ratify it before it becomes law.

A Reporter Abroad

JOURNALIST LOST
IN THE JUNGLE

Monrovia, Liberia
March 8, 1957

In Liberia, the jungle, which marches up to the very edges of Monrovia, is as thick as a tangled head of hair and lushly green. Stately palm trees edge the white-sand strand that is the Atlantic coast. Coconut palms and oil palms are everywhere. In clearings and on high ground, one of the most magnificent trees I have ever seen, the silk-cotton tree, rises in statuesque grandeur of greenness and straight, great white trunk. There are rubber plantations, as well. The rivers are broad and as dark as melted chocolate, and natives cross them in canoes hollowed from tree trunks.

There is a strange clash here of African and so-called Western civilization. For the most part, the bush tribes cling to native costume, vivid in color; flashing loincloths hang like little aprons on some of the women. Other women are naked from the waist up. In the same village with them will be natives in sport shirts and shorts, looking so American that they might have just landed from Atlantic City. An expensive American motorcar rumbles through a settlement of mud huts, squat circular dwellings covered with thatched roofs.

You are at once so near to what you are used to seeing and so terribly, terribly remote from a world that is familiar to you. Perhaps I can illustrate a little by telling what happened before I could do my broadcast yesterday. Liberia has been a republic for more than a century. It is solidly friendly to the United States, but it is a case of arrested development, even though there have been some heavy, if isolated, American investments here, topped, of course, by the Firestone Rubber Company.

The native broadcasting station is run by a group of American missionaries of the Sudan Interior Mission. Their station, ELWA, is ten miles out in the jungle from Monrovia and down the coast. They have no telephone, so they did not know exactly when I was coming yesterday. When I arrived by car from the airport, they were busy broadcasting their religious programs across Africa.

I seem to remember an A.T. & T. advertisement to the effect that one is never any farther away from home than the nearest telephone. I am going to amend that now to read "the nearest ham radio operator." We had no way of calling the American Broadcasting Company in New York except by amateur short wave. ELWA has an amateur station, call letters ELCS, and for the better part of an hour we kept calling "CQ New York City, CQ New York City," meaning: Any ham in Manhattan, please come in. We got Washington; we heard Capetown in Ontario, Canada; but finally, bless his heart, Fred J. Harter, a ham operator in Syracuse, New York, answered us, and we managed to get a message to him which he telephoned to ABC News Director Fritz Littlejohn in New York City, saying that I was standing by in Monrovia and, please, would RCA tune us in.

When RCA began calling us, ELWA was beaming to Nigeria a program called "Back to the Bible Hour." It magnanimously interrupted this broadcast so it could handle my report to New York, but it could not do this instantly, partly because, quite properly, it did not want to cut off the reading of the Scriptures until the announcer had come to the end of the chapter. Somehow, this seemed the longest quotation from the Bible I have ever listened to.

We communicated swiftly with New York and were back in the modern world. In Africa, you swing almost violently back and forth between modern conveyances and the primitive life of pre-biblical times. The human problems here are admittedly immense, but Liberia is hardly the best example of how these problems are being met. Erase the color of African tribal dress and a few other purely local fixtures from the scene, and the capital of Monrovia would easily pass for a dilapidated, impoverished town in the back country of the American Deep South. American capital and the United States government have done a little here to assist progress, but the result so far makes much of British imperialism, now in its fading stages, look like a shiny example of humanitarianism and foresight by comparison.*

STORM SIGNAL IN SIBERIA

Warsaw
August 3, 1959

IN THE SOVIET UNION there is a vast difference between the people and the government which rules them. The Soviet public is not radically different from the public of any other country, reflecting as it does a mixture of pride, nationalism, an aloof curiosity, and a certain amusement over foreigners and their costumes and antics. The last reaction melts from a kind of haughtiness in Moscow to passionate interest and open-faced friendliness in the hinterland of, say, Siberia.

But the government is a cold, inhuman machine. To try to deal with a bureau or the Communist party hierarchy is like being led blindfolded into the bowels of Mammoth Cave and then told to find your way out. You cannot do it without becoming impaled on the stalagmites and gashed by the stalactites of madly illogical logic, of calculated inaccessibility, of crushing inefficiency, and implacable treachery deliberately designed to only one end—the overreaching purposes of the party.

When Deputy Premier Koslov came to Washington, I met the deputy director of the Soviet Foreign Office Press Section who was traveling with him—a thick-lipped, thickly bespectacled, canny

* Now, belatedly, big things are happening in Liberia. The government is spending between sixty-five and seventy-five million dollars on such projects as roads, a federal-court building, and an executive mansion. A $23,000,000 Export-Import Bank loan for a hydroelectric project is in the works; a $7,200,000 Voice of America relay station has been ordered; office buildings and a missionary hospital are new landmarks. A palatial multimillion-dollar hotel in Monrovia has been so successful that its size is being doubled.

young man whose name (appropriate, it turned out) was Popov
—A. J. Popov. He assured me that in covering Vice-President
Nixon's trip I would be able to broadcast from Moscow and
probably from Leningrad without difficulty; but from the Siberian
Steppes it would in all likelihood be impossible. The actual expe-
rience, it turned out, was almost precisely the reverse.

Heavy traffic, disorganization, and what I like to think were
bureaucratic sunspots, made the origination from Moscow anything but satisfactory. Leningrad was absolutely hopeless, although
we knew the facilities were there, and we dogged Popov constantly to be allowed to use them.

Afterwards, his explanation for the failure was that nobody had
reminded him of the problem until too late—that it was an organizational, not a mechanical, difficulty. Another official said the
trouble was mechanical, not organizational. Forewarned, I de-
spaired of any circuits out of Siberia, except for telegraph; but,
on the flight from Novosibirsk to Sverdlovsk, Comrade Popov
astonished me with the statement that he believed we could
broadcast from that old city on the edge of the Ural Mountains.
Hopes rekindled, my radio colleagues and I spent most of the
next day trying to pin Popov down to the essentials of when and
where and how. He produced utterly and completely nothing—
not even a clean-cut "yes" or "no" on the possibility. The run-
around was eloquent in its perfection.

A Bolshoi prima ballerina could not have executed a more
elusive pirouette. By nightfall, we were seething with angry frustration. Having finally cornered the enemy at a vodka and caviar
press reception in the local hostelry, Sverdlovsk's own Waldorf-
Astoria, which was called the Bolshoi or Grand Ural Hotel, we
wheeled up our wrath like an artillery piece and let Popov have it
point-blank.

We announced we were going to ask Vice-President Nixon to
make an official protest against our cavalier treatment in violation
of an agreement of reciprocity which assured us of all possible
facilities. We were not asking for miracles, we emphasized, but
we had not even been told what facilities existed, if any. We were
blunt and firm and undoubtedly undiplomatic. Nobody, the old
Moscow hands assured us, somewhat aghast, but nobody, had
ever talked to a minion of the Soviet Foreign Office like that. It

had not occurred to us hot-headed novices that, since we were already in Siberia, a salt mine might be within walking distance.

We will never know how much our outburst had to do with it, but the situation changed almost immediately. The next morning, when the party went to a tube rolling mill, Popov stayed behind; at last, he was grappling with something. I may have been mistaken, but I thought I sensed a more genial attitude from the Soviet correspondents. Had they admired our brashness in a very public row with an official who could not have been very popular with anybody? Or were they trying gently to calm us down? I simply do not know.

At any rate, Popov caught up with us at a copper mine at noon and flatly announced that he had established a broadcast circuit from Sverdlovsk for one hour that evening. The three major networks could share it equally among them.

The plot instantly thickened. No sooner had Popov made his announcement, emphasizing condescendingly that this was all a special favor magnanimously dispensed by the honey-hearted Soviet government, than the ranking Kremlin official of the entourage bitterly denounced the National Broadcasting Company. Into a banquet toast to peace and friendship, the head of the Soviet Cultural Exchange Program, Georgi Zhukov, incongruously wedged an attack on NBC for its handling of the now celebrated Nixon-Khrushchev television debate.

When we got back to Sverdlovsk, however, Popov declared that Zhukov had been misinformed, that he had really meant to denounce ABC. Whereupon he produced a Siberian edition of *Pravda* for July 30, quoting a speech two nights earlier in which Premier Khrushchev told a workers' group at Dnepropetrovsk that ABC was the worst culprit in the way it broadcast the magnetic-tape interview. He did not specify what ABC in New York was guilty of, but that was enough for Popov, who knows the party line when he sees it.

He immediately ruled that, as punishment, ABC could not use his special Sverdlovsk facilities, but NBC and CBS could. They gallantly demurred. This time, neither angry nor unctuous entreaties could budge this bumptious, brazen bureaucrat.

In retrospect, we should thank Comrade Popov for his effrontery. He did not bar us from using the telephone. We all called up the BBC in London and recorded our broadcasts on a clear line. They were graciously relayed to our respective networks, and used. If we had taken Popov's special, but untried, Sverdlovsk facilities, we might still be attempting to get a signal out of Siberia.

MARBLE AND THE MASSES

New Delhi
December 14, 1959

IT IS USELESS to try to describe the Taj Mahal, no matter where you sit. I went expecting to see a Hollywoodlike materialization of a tinted post card. The reality was overwhelming, but overwhelming in a gentle sense—as if one had been bowled over by a feather. The gleaming whiteness of the marble, the lacelike lightness of carved marble screens, and the delicate floral inlays of semiprecious stones added to the sweet balance of proportions without creating—for some strange reason—a sticky, cloying total effect.

In a green garden of spiked cypresses, pine trees, blazing blossoms, sweeping lawns, and caroling songbirds, here indeed was a temple of love—a monument built by the Mogul Emperor Shah Jahan to the memory of Mumtaz Mahal, his departed queen. From Agra, where the Taj stands on the banks of the Jumna River, President Eisenhower helicoptered the 120 miles back to New Delhi to make his final public appearance in India. This was in the late afternoon, yesterday, at a civic reception at Ram Lila Ground, a large, long strip of open parkway, between two avenues dividing Old Delhi from New Delhi, and used for public meetings. On a caramel-colored platform, whose base was decorated by a series of carved heads of chocolate-colored elephants, the President looked down on fifty solid acres of humanity. On this sea of upturned heads bobbed thousands of little white Gandhi caps, like small boats. Nobody will ever know how many Indians were squatting there in the dying sun, listening to the President quote the Mahatma himself about the gift of freedom.

200

Some said there were far more than half a million; others, veterans of such affairs, simply said there had never been such a throng as this, with the possible exception of the day India won her independence from Great Britain. It was a strange throng. It sat almost silent throughout the program, and even for Gandhi's heir, Jawaharlal Nehru, there was little more than a polite spatter of applause. But there is an intangible thing in India called *darshan*. It is not quite definable, but it radiates from a personage as a kind of benediction, and it is *darshan* which Indians seek in a great presence. Gandhi had it in abundance. In a somewhat lesser degree, Nehru has it, and even the young Dalai Lama is said distinctly to have it. And now the President is being endowed with it by the Indians themselves. As totally improbable as it sounds to Western ears, the appellation "Mahatma Eisenhower" was, in effect, officially bestowed on him the other day by Nehru, and his accompanying press corps is not likely to let him soon forget it.

And so it was that, on his last day in India, President Eisenhower beheld two separate masses—as it were—a mass of marble and a mass of mankind. Out of the savage cruelty and oppression of a civilization now gone, rose a thing of beauty in the Taj Mahal; if the advertising boys had been around when it was built, they would have called it a personalized tribute to Queen Mumtaz. But the human hordes of those days, such as they were, did not count. Now they must and do count. Nothing could underline that urgent fact more vividly than the human structure of half a million Indians that stretched out in a kind of throbbing, disordered beauty of its own before the President at Ram Lila. Today, it is not monuments to the dead that count so much, whether in Agra, India, or Athens, Greece; it is the living edifice of people. We should know that without having to take trips. But maybe a journey such as this official one will impel us to apply the lesson with more and quicker purpose.

WITH SOCRATES
AT THE SUMMIT

Athens
December 16, 1959

THIS REPORTER hereby lays claim to the discovery of a plan for a do-it-yourself summit conference that can easily be adapted to individuals, family groups, and even, one hopes, governments. All it involves is a ticket to Athens and a hike to the Acropolis—one of the shining summits of history.

In fact, the name Acropolis, in Greek, means high city, or city of the summit. I cannot think of a more inspirational setting for a conference of statesmen than the glorious ruins of the Parthenon. You view it first from a western hill, not far from the spot where Socrates was condemned to drink the hemlock. Then, under a veil of gray clouds draped low in the sky, you cross the valley in the soft morning air and mount the rock itself.

As your feet touch the worn stone steps—worn by the striving, faltering steps of men for twenty-five centuries of history—you make a contact with the past that produces almost a physical sensation of shock, as if, for the moment, the current of history were being short-circuited through your own body.

Above you rise the massively graceful Doric columns of the entrance to the temple; to the right, the sheer elegance of the little temple of Athena Nike; and still farther above and beyond, that great marble hall that has defied reproduction or even restoration, the Parthenon itself—the sacred monument to the goddess Athena.

Once you have again caught your breath and the goose-pimples of excitement have subsided, you reflect with humility and wonder on the time of Pericles, and in your mind the inevitable question forms: What have we got that they did not have? Oh, it is possible, of course, that, if Socrates were forced to take his hemlock today, he might be given the poison in a sanitary paper cup. And, if the Athenians had had radar and other electronic marvels sported by the U.S. Navy in the Mediterranean, they might have

202

been able to give the Persians the old heave-ho from their city more quickly than they did. If Plato and Aristotle had had a radio network, they would have been able to broadcast their messages to somewhat larger audiences. The point is, they did so marvelously well with what they had that they are still communicating with us today—communicating lessons that we have not yet fully learned.

For example, the Parthenon was finished in 438 B.C., under the Golden Age of Pericles; but no architect has ever been able to duplicate its plan. There is not a straight line anywhere in the edifice. The floors are curved; the columns, irregularly spaced and not uniformly shaped. The sum total is a baffling harmony of perfect proportion, so much so that the modern Greeks have done a minimum of restoration, for fear of spoiling the original perfection. From a parapet of the Parthenon, you peek down at the amphitheater of Dionysus, where drama had its beginning, and you question whether Broadway has anything quite worthy of opening there. Then you walk around to the eastern front of the Parthenon, to a new, tidy little museum in which have been salvaged and restored a few sculptures by Pericles' friend Phidias and such works of his anonymous contemporaries as were not destroyed or carted away by foreigners. You gaze upon the sculptured body of a Greek maiden, its lines revealed in gossamer marble clothing, and you wonder what quality of this classic we have been able to approach, let alone match. Of course, the ancient Greeks were not very good at solving the riddles of war and peace, either. But some of the perfections they reached should remind us of the clean, vivid values that Western civilization rests on, and make us realize that our struggles with the problems of peace must be realistic ones, because we can afford war far less than they could—and look what happened to them.

LAFAYETTE, WE ARE—ER—HERE

Paris
May 31, 1961

IN THE POMP and ceremony of a big state visit, little things can mean so much. For his first speech on French soil, President Kennedy had prepared for delivery, upon his arrival at Orly Airport this morning, five graceful little paragraphs about the warm friendship that had long pervaded Franco-American relations. But, as he so often does, the President did not follow the text which had been distributed in advance; without notes, he improvised the same sentiments in his own words. Ordinarily this would have been quickly accepted for what it was: an effort to dispense with formalities and speak some simple sentences, sincerely, without props.

The trouble was, the speech had to be translated into French, not only for French radio and television, which carried the ceremonies live, but for a vast hook-up with Eurovision, the international TV network of Western Europe. The official State Department translator was caught somewhat unawares, with the prepared text in one hand, a note pad in the other, and a pencil fluttering somewhere in between. The change of pace ruffled him, and he faltered a little.

Although Ambassador Angier Biddle Duke, the U.S. Chief of Protocol, fussed and frowned silently, there was no major *gaffe,* but the incident illustrated, in its own way, the great difficulties of communication, even among friends. The diplomats regretted that President Kennedy left out a sentence which said, "Once again, France, under her great captain, is the central figure of the common effort." Reporters were more pleased with a sentence he injected into his actual remarks, in which he emphasized that he and President de Gaulle were meeting in the latest of many great causes in which France and the United States have been associated, the climactic moment in the defense of freedom. But reporters also were distressed because, ostensibly for security reasons to protect General de Gaulle and the U.S. President, even the public ceremonial festivities were almost impossible to cover, except through a limited pool of correspondents near enough to the heads of state to see, if not to hear, what was going on.

Ironically, the French could see Jacqueline Kennedy more easily on their TV sets or in the colored photograph of her with a shy smile on the cover of *Paris Match* (a sort of Gallic combination of *Life* and *Look*) than they could on the streets of Paris today. Although the two presidents rode in an open car, a shining black Simca Vedette, the sleek, slim, gorgeous, young Mrs. Kennedy and the older, plump, and pleasant Madame de Gaulle were all but invisible in the back seat of a sedan. This would have driven a Hollywood publicity man out of his mind, because, as far as the French who have been exposed to her are concerned, Jacqueline is *quelque chose*. She confirmed it last night in a program on French television, filmed in advance at the White House, in which she referred to her husband as *atient*—which is the way French women call their husbands a guy. These touches are valuable, even precious, because the false impressions and misinformation which abound are really staggering. A voluble French taxi driver shrugged his shoulders at me this noon and said, "Russia and the U.S. are going to partition Algeria. You will see, monsieur. Right now, the presidents are talking about that here, and Mr. Kennedy and Khrushchev will talk about it in Vienna. You will see."

BLUE REFLECTIONS
ON THE DANUBE

Vienna
June 6, 1961

SOME VIGNETTES from Vienna:

I witnessed the gruesome spectacle of what a pudgy young Austrian couple, in town no doubt for the music festival, were eating for breakfast at the next table—Coca-Cola and hot dogs. After such a sight at eight o'clock in the morning, the streets of the city, wet as they were in a downpour, provided a welcome escape.

It had been exactly fifteen years since my last visit to the Austrian capital, and the transition was almost unbelievable. In the spring of 1946, Vienna lay dead in the sun. Except for the four-power occupation troops and the human shadows which passed as Viennese, the streets were virtually empty—house after house was shuttered, store after store was locked—as if the former grand, gay Austro-Hungarian capital, which once had rung with Mozart's music, had been visited by the plague. There was not a single restaurant open, not even on the black market, because there was no food, except, of course, at the PX and in the military messes.

Today, Vienna is a seductive Lady Bountiful, plump with the world's most delectable delicatessens and pastry shops to sate the appetite of the greediest gormandizer; rich as silk with feminine finery, cashmere sweaters as bargains in the windows, and gleaming porcelain from Dresden and Hungary. At night, the city pulses with sin and culture—from the not too alluring smiles of the saucy streetwalkers to the State Opera House, where a vacant seat is a news item.

To paraphrase George Orwell badly: all neutrals are neutral, but Vienna is less neutral than others. Outwardly, the city's decorations for the private Summit meeting of K. and K. were neatly balanced between East and West by having nothing draped in the streets except the red and white stripes of the Austrian flag. A bookstore solved the problem by carefully featuring with equal prominence maps of America and Russia of the eighteenth century. Human feelings were a little less equal. It just could be that the Viennese welcome for the Kennedys was a bit warmer than the one for the Khrushchevs, not only because of the appeal of youth and glamor, but because the Red Army was in Austria for ten years after the war—the time it took to get the Communists to agree to a peace treaty.

Yet under the skin of Vienna's voluptuous serenity there is the internal bleeding of personal tragedy. In the smoky atmosphere of Fatty George's Jazz Club, a raven-haired beauty from Budapest insists that President Kennedy must help her. She was a freedom fighter in Hungary, and her eyes flash with a dark gypsy passion when she speaks of it. She escaped from Hungary four years ago, and for the last three years she has been a barmaid for Fatty George while trying futilely to emigrate to the United States.

She is more fortunate, however, than two or three teen-aged Hungarian boys who made it across the border last September. Just as they reached the boundary fence, one of them stepped on a mine. Two each had a leg blown off. The third dragged the others, torn and bleeding, across into Austria. They got their artificial limbs the other day, and are in the university, learning how to walk in addition to their other studies.

Beneath the capital's lightheartedness, the remainders of war are everywhere. A huge flak tower in the center of the city, where Nazi antiaircraft batteries once fired at Allied planes, has been converted into an aquarium. A medical student named Wilhelm is too young to remember World War II, but his reflexes have not forgotten the wail of the air-raid sirens, and every time he hears a factory whistle he still starts with fear.

Yesterday morning, as I was having coffee in the Vienna airport, waiting for Khrushchev to climb into his big Ilyushin jet-prop airliner and fly home, a newscast on Radio Austria came up with an item from the Eichmann trial in Jerusalem, about the death chambers at Auschwitz. Thereabouts lie the fragments of a history that nobody wants repeated. In Vienna, as in Berlin and elsewhere, move individual people caught between the memory of an indescribable past and the fear of an even more indescribable future.

These are the things and the beings, the human beings, which give a meaning of urgency to the problems dealt with so coldly, so distantly, and with the spongy vagueness of diplomatic language in the Vienna communiqué on the conclusion of the Kennedy-Khrushchev talks. On our side, we are supposed to be trying to protect and extend freedom, including the right of an Hungarian barmaid to a future she has helped protect for others, and the right of an Austrian countryman to have frankfurters and Coca-Cola for breakfast if he chooses.

International Affairs

HAPPY BIRTHDAY,
EVERYBODY!

San Francisco, Calif.
June 24, 1955

Maybe this reporter is getting old and crotchety, but I find myself losing patience with persons who expect the United Nations to do the impossible and then sound the crack of doom when it does not. The UN is no more perfect that the people, the nations, who make it up. With all the suggestions clogging the hopper as to how to secure peace, nobody has introduced a bill yet to change human nature.

That is why this marathon San Francisco birthday party has been quarrelsome as well as festive. With all the gadgets that we have invented, both lethal and lovely, people themselves remain the most fascinating mechanisms of all—contrary, petulant, nervous, and now and then afraid, but always hopeful and equipped with the basic instincts that make life valuable.

No one could cope very long with a jamboree like this UN celebration, unless he kept a little sense of humor handy in his purse, as Aunt Agnes used to keep smelling salts. It must be whiffed frequently, especially as one watches the diplomats, who are also people.

One of the traits of a diplomat is his ability to act; he is always playing a role. This can be both dismaying and delightful, and journalists, especially, can prove almost anything thereby. A diplomat likes this because it makes it easier to get off the hook with the home office. If, in one story, he is quoted unfortunately, he can point to another clipping as being nearer to what he meant to say. The trick is not to get too excited over either version.

This morning, I was talking to a particularly astute and agile middle eastern diplomat about Secretary Dulles' speech. He thought it a wee bit disappointing; he would have preferred to see it a little more pointed, or as he put it, a little more "red-blooded." At that moment, another reporter approached him and asked him for comment on the morning proceedings, including Dulles' address. "I enjoyed them all immensely," the diplomat said, not necessarily contradicting himself.

Early last evening, I went to a tea party at the Indian Consulate General. When the guests could take their eyes off the magnificent view of the Golden Gate through the bay window, they found the guest of honor, V. K. Krishna Menon, wreathed in smiles and wearing a well-tailored western suit. Less than three hours later, this shrewd, sensitive, and unpredictable scholar appeared at Secretary Dulles' teeming reception at the Mark Hopkins Hotel, wearing a studied scowl and the black-blouse-white-trouser garb of his native India.

At the same reception, incidentally, some minions of another network were complaining to our ambassador to Moscow, Charles Bohlen, of the vicissitudes involved in trying to get Molotov to commit himself to appear on a panel show. "Well," Ambassador Bohlen asked with a grin, "how do you like negotiating with the Russians?" (The panel show with Molotov was canceled shortly afterwards, because he would not agree to a "no holds barred" interview.)

Just to add another confusing color to the Russian spectrum, California's Governor Knight had a remarkable exchange with the Soviet Foreign Minister last night. "Relations between our countries," Knight told Molotov, "remind me of the story of two men standing on a corner talking about a man across the street. 'I don't like that guy over there,' the first man said, and the second man asked him why. 'I don't know him,' the first man replied."

To which Molotov remarked: "It's hard to hate somebody when you know him."

In reconstructing the encounter for this reporter, Governor Knight indicated it would take more than a Dale Carnegie course

210

for the Russians to win western friends, but he found the atmosphere inviting careful exploration.

I bring in these fragments of the UN birthday party because they are just as much a part of the mosaic of the meeting as a speech, a communiqué, or a headline in the afternoon paper screaming, "Tension mounts."

Tension will mount and tension will dismount many times before the United Nations or any other agency brings us the millennium, but I hazard the suggestion that we are learning that peace can be more fun than war, even though we have to work hard at it.

AN OILY ARABIAN KNIGHT

January 29, 1957

THERE IS a cartoon in the *New Yorker* showing a crowd of officials gathered at Washington National Airport to greet an obviously distinguished Arab visitor flying in from the Middle East. The visitor is seen in mid-air descending toward the deplaning ramp—riding on a magic carpet.

There was only a dock-bound red carpet, but a mixture of magic, mystery, misconceptions, and misgivings tinctured the atmosphere surrounding the arrival in the United States of bespectacled, berobed Saud ibn Abdul Aziz al Faisal Al Saud, his fifty-five-year-old majesty, king of Saudi Arabia. The public has already been inundated by a flood of feature stories about the royal household's riches, habits, heritage, and setting in a strange, romantic desert replete with its prize of black gold—oil. Saud is one of the few absolute monarchs still extant.

The picture emerges of crown princes rolling in a wealth of Cadillacs, concubines, and other comforts, in a feudal land where most of the six million * Koran-revering souls are impoverished, diseased, and illiterate; a country where thieves have their hands cut off and adulterers are beheaded; a country being rocketed

* 1962 population estimate: eight million.

from an archaic past through an explosive present into an uncertain future, because of its geography and its geology. It is directly in the path along which Moscow wants to expand politically and economically. Its sandy soil is saturated with fabulous oil reserves yielding the king nearly a million dollars a day. And so it is important to us.

How important? Saudi Arabia traffics in slavery and not only denies religious freedom to her own citizens, but also forbids Jews, for example, to enter, fly over, or even trade with the country. Government revenues, ninety per cent of which come from royalties from American oil companies, are being used to help prop up the anti-Western kingdom of Jordan.* Saudi money, by buying editors, has helped further the reckless cause of Nasser in the Middle East; yet King Saud wants and seems likely to get more money and arms from the U.S. government.** In proportion, Communist China would have to go some to come up with a more diabolical-looking record, but we do not even admit that Peking exists.

Many people who threaten to impeach the administration if it dares invite Tito to visit America seem to have few qualms about welcoming Saud. This points up one of our characteristic difficulties. Uncle Sam still is inclined to approach the outside world with the stern morals of a missionary zealot in one hand and a sales contract in the other. We pride ourselves on avoiding the now passé imperialism our European cousins clung to for so long in Africa and Asia, and we make a point of the contention that we do not intervene in the politics of another country. Then we cry with the anguish of a jilted lover if somebody violates our moral code—the shrillness of the cry depending upon the circumstances.

It is deplorable that the U.S. government and American companies operate in Saudi Arabia, where a royal edict bans Amer-

* Jordan's attitude toward the West has become consistently less brittle, softened in part, no doubt, because of handsome young King Hussein's recent marriage to a British girl, Antoinette Avril Gardiner, whose Arabic name is now Munaa Al-Hussein.

** The agreement under which the U.S. Air Force operated an air base at Dhahran expired in April, 1962, and was not renewed; the big base is now the Dhahran International Airport.

ican or other Jews from their missions. It is deplorable that the latest distinguished guest of the White House advocates, or did not long ago, the eradication of Israel as if it were a cancer. Do we have to tolerate these and other unpleasant facts merely because Saudi Arabia is important to us, politically and economically?

The answer is an unsatisfactory "Yes and no." We have to deal with things as they are. The trouble with our approach, carrying morals in one hand and expediency in the other, is that what we are actually delivering is hypocrisy. Persistently, the government *talks* as if it pursued foreign policy exclusively under the guiding star of some immutable moral law. Our record of relations with Saudi Arabia simply does not bear that out. No reasonable person would deny that compromise is sometimes necessary, but the record here cries out for more standing on principle and less moralizing about it—not a bad position, maybe, from which to approach the whole panorama of foreign policy.

LIGHT FOR THE DARK CONTINENT

Tunis
March 21, 1957

UP UNTIL NOW, world events have impressed themselves upon Africa. From now on, Africa is going to impress itself upon the world.

As if wearing blindfolds—so shortsighted were they to the sweep of history—some Americans, stirred by spiteful, narrow-minded politicians, charged and may still believe that a small group of men in Washington in the thirties and forties "lost" China to us. These strident critics failed to recognize that what was sweeping Asia, and China in particular, was a revolution demanding identity, recognition, and an end to the oppressive imperialism of the West—no matter that that imperialism in the end might be less bad than the imperialism of the Communists.

213

This is not to say that Americans did not make big mistakes regarding China which, if avoided, might have made our position there less untenable. But the ink for the pens of history flows from the receptacles of many events, from the decisions or indecisions, not merely of a few men, but of many countries. If, in hindsight, we have learned this lesson, we may be able to avoid oversimplification of our approach to Africa.

If we think that good-will tours, handsome propaganda brochures from the United States Information Agency, and the largess of financial and technical aid programs are going to "win" Africa and save the so-called Dark Continent from communism, we are insane and deserve to be committed to the confinement of bitter disappointment that will surely be our lot. Africa is, admittedly, a kind of ideological battleground between Communist and non-Communist forces.

But Africans who are emerging as leaders of this fascinating and potentially rich continent insist that they are going to decide the battle themselves, on their own terms. If we demand that they decide it on our terms, we will only alienate the respect they have for the revolutionary American tradition. Our revolution inspires them more than our Coca-Cola, our motorcars, and our ice cubes. When we appear to depart from that tradition, they are mystified and troubled. That is why, for example, the question of segregation in the United States is such a butcher knife in our foreign policy, cutting short the Africans' hope, their respect, their intense but dignified appeals to us for help and guidance as they emerge from the jungle. We may maintain that the race issue is a domestic matter—even a local community business—but it is not. Every time there is an incident, troubled questions and suspicions are raised from Accra to Addis Ababa, from Khartoum to Capetown.

That, among other large and obvious reasons, is why we need to assign to Africa the very best men and women available to the U.S. Foreign Service, why we need to spend more on that continent, but spend it with intelligence and care as an investment in a fuller future for us, as well as for them. That is why we need to impress the best talents, the best brains we can corral into the business of developing information services for, to, and

214

from Africa, and, above all, to formulate enlightened policy toward an awakening continent. But we are not even beginning to do these things today.*

IS THE FREE WORLD
A BARGAIN?

April 3, 1958

MAYBE IT IS time for the West to clean up its language. A term that has come to make me wince, so glibly and carelessly do we use it every day, is the "free world." Our statesmen talk so heroically and with such generalized inaccuracy of preserving the "free world" from communism. How much of the world *is* free? Automatically, we assume it includes everybody not under Communist domination or control. We are dangerously and needlessly deceiving ourselves. If we would be more discriminating in the application of the word "free" to a country or a people, it would give more meaning to that wonderful adjective and outline more clearly the vast dimensions of the struggle which lies before us.

As we know, but may be inclined to forget, almost a billion persons, or more than a third of the population of the planet, live under communism. But, the way we talk, you would think we assumed the other two-thirds were living up the free way of life and having a ball. The fact is—and Moscow Radio has not overlooked it—that in some respects a Muscovite is a freer citizen than a Monrovian or a resident of Johannesburg. The pacts and alliances and agreements which the State Department likes to refer to as the cornerstone of the defense of the free world embrace such partners—or did until Nasser started twisting his Arabian majesty's arm—as Saudi Arabia, whose seven million inhabitants

* This broadcast was based on impressions gathered in covering Vice-President Nixon's flying visit to eight African countries. Nearly six years later, the conclusions still don't seem outdated. We are paying that continent more intelligent attention, but the job of understanding has just begun.

215

include some slaves and wandering hosts of illiterates. Membership in the club is also claimed, with Washington's aggressive endorsement, by Chiang Kai-shek's somewhat theoretical Republic of China.

Again, such delinquent brothers as Franco of Spain, Trujillo of the Dominican Republic, and, lately, Batista of Cuba insist on active privileges and voting rights in the fraternity of freedom. Venezuela has divested itself of one dictatorship, but it is too soon to do more than hope that it can avoid another. Other governments, from Paraguay to Portugal and across to Turkey and Pakistan, are having trouble pursuing the code of basic civil rights that is the core of freedom.

There are countries outside the Soviet bloc which are free in a technical, political sense, but which are prisoners of poverty. The teeming dominion of India and the sparse kingdom of Iran are differing examples of these. There are other peoples on the waiting list, and some who are such neophytes in the lodge that they scarcely know the rituals and the responsibilities of a free society. How independent can a Tunisian, a Moroccan, an Indonesian feel? The Algerian is fighting, sometimes blindly, for a freedom that he has been denied too long. Not just a few, but most, of the more than thirteen million souls in the Union of South Africa are dominated by a tight little band of racist politicians who are incarcerated in a dead past. Although their doctrine of white supremacy is an anachronism, nobody knows how long it will take the vast body of South Africans to break the shackles that still hold them.

We must not be derisive or cynical toward the concept of a world that is free. The philosophy of democracy must nourish itself on this objective or wither. Nor should we take the pipe dreamer's position that all the world's ills and injustices can be set right overnight. What we have is not the best of all possible worlds, and we will do better to recognize the rough realities of it. There must be at least three-quarters of a billion persons in what we call the "free world" who do not have an inkling of what freedom means in any real sense. Unless it can be made to mean something on their terms, not just on ours, they may be persuaded that communism has more promise.

Perhaps the most overriding reason for us to use the term "free world" less recklessly is the telling fact that we have not yet given nearly eighteen million Negro citizens their freedom from second-class citizenship right here in the United States.*

BUT WHAT ECHOES
FROM THE SATELLITE?

August 19, 1960

ONE LONG-AGO summer when I was a boy in Idaho, we saw a total eclipse of the sun. It was a pretty impressive operation. The world got eerily dark in mid-afternoon; roosters crowed; and my grandfather studied the phenomenon intently through a piece of window glass, especially smoked up over a candle flame for the occasion. I remember the event was given added portent, at least in my tender mind, by a doleful religious cult in the community, which had been predicting the end of the world at about the same time.

Last night, I witnessed another wonder in the heavens. In the middle of peak evening television time, at 8:51 P.M., Echo I passed over my front yard in Washington, rising out of the southern horizon between the Lincoln Memorial and a one-time brewery, arcing brightly across a dark, clear sky and disappearing, after about nine minutes, in the direction of Baltimore. A lot of neighbors were out watching this shining aluminum star, too, the most easily visible man-made satellite so far. Some of them seemed to welcome it as another inspiration for togetherness; at least, it took no time at all for a man with a cocker spaniel to strike up a conversation with a girl with a poodle. But I could not get out of my mind the exciting changes represented by the span of time between the solar eclipse and the passage of Echo I over Georgetown.

Barring an occasional circus balloon, a barnstorming plane, buckshot, or a stone from a boy's slingshot, man wasn't hoisting

* The boundaries of freedom seem to stretch, then shrink. Trujillo and Batista are gone, but now the bearded one threatens the hemisphere from Havana. Eternal vigilance *is* the price of liberty. Grown to twenty million now, the American Negro population may know that lesson better than the rest of us.

217

anything of importance into the sky forty years ago; nothing, leastwise, to stay. Nature, in those days, had a corner on celestial phenomena. Now, suddenly, we are flinging all manner of objects into upper space—moons, stars, balloons, satellites, rockets, and nose-cones loaded with livestock. We are shooting the works, indeed, with everything except humility and perspective. They have been left behind on the launching pad.

I do not mean to belittle the conquest of space. As an eyewitness, I am thrilled and proud to see us regaining a favored place in the fray. There is, I believe, no turning back now. It is as unrealistic to expect the rocketeers and the spacemen to curb their appetites, as they taste initial success, as it is to expect African nationalists, with the heady wine of freedom on their tongues, to hold back until everybody is "ready."

But surely it is up to the rest of us to insist on as orderly and purposeful development as possible. Tall as a ten-story building, Echo I—launched one week ago today—is hurtling around the globe at more than 15,000 miles an hour, bouncing men's voices and picture images across oceans and continents from a thousand miles up. This presages a whole new concept in world-wide communications. The trouble is that these voices ring with the same provincial accent, these pictures reflect the same narrow lines of prejudice that existed before the wonderful metallic balloon named Echo I was invented. What is required, I think, is not a slowdown in its orbit, but a speedup in the quality and substance of man's communication with man.

We continue to hatch new and marvelous inventions, but we have hardly begun to understand the most fantastic invention of all, man himself. Why is it, I wonder, that other fields seem more exciting to explore? Where are the adequate crash programs to help send the world's illiterate into the orbit of even a minimal education? Where, indeed, is a dimensional American system to teach us to view the world more in perspective, to look at Echo I, for example, as something more than a guide for nuclear warheads, or a commercial cushion off which we can bounce "Lassie" and "The Lone Ranger" to Leopoldville and Lebanon? *

* Now Telstar has successfully and sensationally beamed the exchange of live television programs between the Old World and the New—giving even more urgent point to those questions.

The religious fanatics were wrong, of course, about the world's end, but, in the era we are now opening up, other fanatics can choose the final date with more accuracy unless we humans determine to discover ourselves, as well as the space around us.

WANTED: SOME NATIONAL SELF-RESPECT

September 26, 1961

THE COUNTRY, it seems to me, is in an agony of soul-searching uncertainty. The times call for toughness. Talk mounts that the United States may be forced increasingly to strike out on the rough international terrain alone. In disillusionment, it finds allies unwilling to go beyond narrow self-interest, and it finds neutrals unwilling or unable to go anywhere. Our image of the lone figure of Uncle Sam standing against a dark horizon, or on a brink, is inevitably accompanied, as if for reassurance against the troubling portent of the unknown, by heroic thoughts of great, daring deeds. Or, in simpler terms, it seems as if the suspense is killing us, and we long to bloody Khrushchev's nose and get it over with.

This is an understandable but dangerous posture. The frenzied feelings generated by the homecoming football game are not necessarily the most reliable support for the reason needed to address today, tomorrow, and the day after. Too often, we Americans insist on approaching our most serious problems as if they were athletic contests or the class play, in which the plot is always the good guys against the bad guys. We detest tie games, and the drama must always end happily, or at least the bad guys must get their just deserts.

I have a theory about some of our attitudes which is completely unscientific and could be monumentally wrong, but it fascinates and worries me. It is that, unable to engage the enemy in physical combat, we are engaging each other, and with mounting passion. This, I think, is reflected in the morbid multiplication in many

219

parts of the country of what are usually called anticommunist seminars. The strategy of these gatherings is based on the premise that communism's biggest threat to us is not from abroad but from inside the country.

For months, such meetings have been churning up sensational headlines in San Diego, Seattle, Salt Lake, San Antonio, and way points. Last Thursday's *St. Louis Globe-Democrat* reported that a Lions Club speaker urged a crash drive against communism, because, "If we are defeated, it will come from inside America." A week ago the Des Moines *Register* took note—an appropriately sour note—of the announced intentions of an Oklahoma preacher to found a secret fraternity of a number of unnamed groups to coordinate anti-Communist efforts.

Subversion is a stock tool of the Communists, and there is no logical reason to think that the U.S.A. is exempt from their subversive experiments. But the viciously vigilante aspect of so many of these seminars—adorned as they usually are with the bemedaled authority of some military figure, in or out of the National Guard, or, more alarmingly, an officer of the armed services on active duty—revives something very close to the witch hunt, cloaked in the respectability of civic approval. Under such circumstances, the Communists themselves could not ask for a more effective tool to stoke community dissension and distrust than the dogma of suspicions of the participants, preponderantly from the radical right. The patriotism of the participants is not at issue, but the quality of their intelligence and judgment should be.

I hasten to add that liberals should not object to having their intelligence and judgment questioned, too. Theirs is not infallible, either. Part of the country's current agony comes, I think, from the liberals' bitter, slowly dawning realization that it is a harsher world than they hoped it might be. But the heinous, unforgivable crime of the radical right is to leap on such misjudgments as evidence of disloyalty.

The times do indeed call for toughness, but for the toughness of reasoning, patient minds which have learned by experience, including the experience of mistakes. There is no room now for the toughness of a bully; that is not strength but the miserable hide of fear. What we do not need is a crash program to fight communism, for the first victims of the crash would be ourselves.

What we do not need to fight subversion is a subversive secret fraternity, whose very inspiration is anathema to the constitutional principles of an open society.

I doubt that we as a country are so alone as some might fear. It is very likely true that in the past we have been too worried over what others think of us, not realizing that if we did what we thought was right we would earn respect; and the company of the respectful is good company. It is hard to believe that, as the world absorbs President Kennedy's magnificent statement to the UN of our decent desires and the dangers to their fulfilment, respect will not grow. But it needs to grow from within the country, too, and I suppose that is called self-respect.

YES, VIRGINIA,
THERE IS A WORLD

January 23, 1962

ON THE FLOOR of the House one day last week, Congressman James B. Utt, a Republican from southern California, delivered a doleful speech. He started out by reminding his colleagues that on the first day of this session he had introduced a bill to "rescind and revoke membership of the United States in the United Nations and the specialized agencies thereof . . ."

It did not take him long to make his reasons plain. As he surveyed the brooding, beclouded horizons of the globe, he liked nothing of what he saw and blamed it all, in effect, on the UN as the root of all evil. "The power, the honor, and the prestige of America have fallen from their high point in 1945 to an absolute zero today," intoned the honorable Mr. Utt, as if he were reading the republic's epitaph. It is a wonder that he even bothered to deliver his funeral oration, because he clearly believes that the United States has already been dealt a mortal blow by entangling alliances with and through the UN. "This conversion of our limited republic to an unlimited democracy," he declared abruptly, "is a death blow to our nation."

Representative Utt's version of history and his vision of the

221

present danger, bizarre as they are, cannot be carelessly brushed aside. His logic is opaque, but his feelings are clearly genuine, and they are shared by a frustrated but vocal minority of citizens who will do their utmost to block Congressional authorization of the $100,000,000 subscription President Kennedy wants for the UN bond issue, to keep that organization a going concern.*

This school, or perhaps it should be called a kindergarten, of thought is also behind the charge that the Pentagon has been "muzzling" patriotic anti-Communist sentiments of the military brass, a charge brought under official public scrutiny today as a Senate subcommittee opened hearings on the subject. The reasoning of Congressman Utt and his friends is overwhelmingly simple. If something happens in the world which we do not like, we either ignore it completely, as if it did not exist, or we run up the flag, roll the drums, and rush out and change it. Our objective: total indifference or total victory. In other words, we play to win or we do not play.

In the good old days before Korea, this is the way we played, or, at least, this is the way we told ourselves we played. This handy, though outdated and dangerously oversimplified formula is being replaced by the realization that we may not necessarily win them all, that our will may now be opposed by forces of equal strength. It is this painful change which understandably infuriates generals, admirals, and amateur civilian dabblers in the

* This legislation met unexpectedly strong opposition on Capitol Hill, partly because of faulty liaison which left senators confused about the State Department's stand on the issue. The Senate authorized the President to *lend* the UN a maximum of $100,000,000: $25,000,000 outright and up to $75,000,000 more in matching other nations' contributions. As of August 1, 1962, other nations had pledged to buy $72,104,175 worth of bonds. The House struck the Senate's $25,000,000 "outright" proviso, insisted on a dollar-for-dollar matching for the full $100,000,000. The White House agreed, the Senate went along and the bill is now law. Meanwhile, in July, 1962, the World Court at the Hague ruled nine to five in an advisory opinion that emergency UN expenses in the Congo and the Middle East (the sources of the UN financial crisis) were undertaken in accordance with the principles of the UN charter and were therefore legitimate outlays, of which member nations must pay their share, or lose their votes in the General Assembly. All advisory opinions from the Court to the Assembly have been accepted in the past. In this case, the Soviet Union has said it won't accept the opinion. Thus, it remains for the General Assembly to accept it (a two-thirds vote is required) and take action.

risky game of international politics—especially when they are told that, partly due to the existence of a gadget known as a nuclear warhead, their own neatly packaged solutions are not adequate.

There are sincere citizens who cry that anything short of "total victory" is appeasement, surrender. Admittedly, there is a danger of being so benumbed by the threat of nuclear war that our foreign policy becomes impotent; but, taking the wagonload of fragile complexities into consideration, neither our allies nor our adversaries are reacting as if we were impotent.

Perhaps what we are in the process of surrendering is a narrowly nationalistic point of view. Even while Representative Utt was addressing Congress last week, the town of Redding, Connecticut, was in something of a turmoil over an editorial in the Joel Barlow High School paper attacking patriotism as "stupid." This was enough to mobilize almost instant protest from the American Legion, concern by the chairman of the school board, and criticism from the Republican town committee. Indeed, there was a public meeting in Redding on the issue tonight.

The editorial, entitled "A Higher Loyalty," was written by the paper's seventeen-year-old editor, Virginia Olsen. Her theme was that patriotism, in a narrow sense, had outlived its usefulness and needed to be replaced by a "loyalty to the world."

Principal Roy B. Briggs says he and the faculty believe the school paper should be a forum for opinion, where students have a right to say what they please and then, if necessary, answer to the consequences. Judging by the short-term consequences of bitter protest, Virginia may be a little before her time, and she may have expressed her hopes with the callow impatience of incautious youth. But the consequences in the long run will be far more disastrous if we do not realize that we do owe a loyalty to the human race. This does not mean disloyalty to our own country or to its foundation principles. It means recognizing the fact that we are a part, a large and influential part, of an international neighborhood, but not one in which what we say always goes.

Congressman Utt seems tired, discouraged, and irritated with the times and would like, in effect, to have us resign from the world. Virginia wants us to join it, risks, warts, and all. With or without a Santa Claus, Virginia, I am with you. Where else is there to go?

THE PEACE CORPS SCORES

March 16, 1962

IT IS DIFFICULT not to become excited about the potential of the Peace Corps. At first, skeptics regarded it as an operation on Cloud Nine, highly impracticable and loaded with dangers of international incidents involving soft, young American innocents equipped with rose-colored glasses and no experience. But the record is almost unblemished. With what must be called a touch of genius and a truckload of determination, Director Sargent Shriver and his small staff have recruited a Corps with such a blend of tender idealism and tough practicality that it fairly quivers with *esprit* and ingenuity. It is as if they had tapped some new source of energy, like the discovery of radium.

The Peace Corps is not some magic potion which will banish famine, fear, or war in a trice. But it could and may cause a fundamental change in American ideas about the world and the world's ideas about us. From this reorientation, great things could flow. What is happening is the harnessing of youth's boundless energies and hopes, which have been there all the time, and, before they are pressed into old, brittle patterns, letting their freshness play through the purposefulness of teaching and learning in genuine, earthy, people-to-people contacts. It is working so well that sixty countries have asked for volunteers; Nigeria wants 350 more teachers; U.S. communities with volunteers abroad are getting new ideas back in direct communications from them. Secretary of State Rusk is so impressed that he has indicated, unofficially, that here may be a tremendously valuable new source of manpower for future foreign-service officers.

Case histories read like fiction. A girl from Iowa went to the southern Philippines, built a hand loom, taught boys and girls to weave fibers of discarded sugar-cane stalks, made paintbrushes out of grass, produced colors from natural dyes of jungle plants, and now has a productive art class.

A boy from California invented a way to improve the processing of rice in Pakistan. Another volunteer in a Pakistani village so revolutionized its irrigation system that the government whisked him to an agricultural academy to teach the method.

In Colombia, a Peace Corpsman, short of steel, used bamboo to reinforce concrete. It worked so well that it is now an acceptable, and cheaper, building material.

A southern Negro agronomist in his thirties, a Korea veteran with Bronze Star and Purple Heart, is helping solve soil problems in Sierra Leone, in West Africa. So is a young Republican wheat farmer from Montana. With its nonpartisan appeal of purposefulness, the Corps has attracted a remarkable number of young Republicans, sometimes over the strenuous objections of their parents—who have since become converts, in spirit, themselves. Asked why he joined, the Montana farmer replied, "I was just sitting there watching the world go by and worrying, and this was the first time anybody had asked me to help."

In Ghana, while Washington officials and Nkrumah were arguing over money for the Volta River project, the all-Negro faculties of four secondary schools elected four white Peace Corpsmen as their headmasters.

Sometimes, whole concepts are uprooted and replaced. The son of a southern county sheriff is working side by side with his best friend in an engineering project in Africa. That new-found best friend is a Negro.

Gradually, painfully, U.S. community concepts are changing, growing. Letters from members of the Peace Corps, dispatches in the local paper about them, and homecoming visits by them to hundreds of communities eager to share their human experiences may nudge this process ahead.

But where this revolutionary technique of the simple approach may have its most direct effect is neither on Main Street nor in the jungles of Tanganyika, but in the State Department. Diplomats with Ivy League college degrees are not going to be displaced en masse by striplings from the Peace Corps, but there is something to be said for the ambassadorial qualifications of the latter when they include a knowledge of the language and the country based on a two-year hitch in the backlands, grappling with primitive but basic problems on ground a chief of mission probably never trod.

Measures are now being discussed by which men and women

of the Peace Corps may join the foreign service as a permanent career. If it works out, diplomacy may receive the greatest shot in the arm since the abolition of wigs and knee breeches.

AND HOW GUILTLESS ARE WE?

June 1, 1962

THE NUREMBERG war-crimes trials and those in Tokyo that followed were held not only to punish the Nazis and the Japanese militarists for their outrages, but also to serve as a precedent on which to fortify a flimsy body of international law against war as an instrument of aggression.

Historians themselves long will quarrel over the question of how much of a deterrent these proceedings have established. Now, there is the related issue of whether the hanging of Adolf Eichmann in Israel will stay the savage hands of would-be perpetrators of atrocities in the future. Society still demands vengeance more quickly than it prepares for the prevention of crime. Eichmann was doomed to die for his part in what was probably the most monstrous crime in the history of civilization. I, for one, am not fully prepared to say that that a more purposeful punishment might not have been to condemn him to live and watch the growth of a vibrantly viable, open, and civilized society built by the people who, by Hitlerian standards, were not even worthy of a decent death. What more fitting monument could there be to mock the monstrous pretensions of the so-called master race than the very existence of the state of Israel?

The extermination of six million Jews was an act of such utterly heinous dimensions that it is almost impossible for the rational human mind to grasp it. But will society's revulsion at the enormity of it prevent a repetition in some other part of the globe? Perhaps, though I am not so sure. Among Eichmann's defiant last words were these: "I had to obey the laws of war and my flag."

The laws of war are the laws of might alone, and the ghastly slaughters permitted under them are always justified by somebody in the name of some national flag. Our problem, the problem of men and women of good will everywhere, is to develop an allegiance to some higher moral code than narrow nationalism permits. We are not ready for this yet, but we are moving slowly toward the goal.

Maybe it will quicken our progress slightly if we manage to lower our self-righteous blinders a notch, to view the world in a manner a little more dispassionate and detached. We Americans tell ourselves that we would never be guilty of mass murder—yet that is what the next war would be. The power protagonists on both sides have even felt obliged to experiment with germ warfare and other exotic methods of liquidating or at least deactivating whole populations. And undoubtedly there are people who think that genocide would be a justifiable means of exterminating the Communists.

Sometimes the vastness of a problem can be better grasped by thinking of it, not in massive terms, but in terms of the individual. The Federal Radiation Council, after a long hassle within the government over both timing and content, has released a report stating that the fall-out hazards to Americans from all nuclear tests through last year are really not so bad. Only one in three hundred thousand risks developing bone cancer; one in a hundred thousand, leukemia; only one in a million of the next generation faces from radioactive-test dust the prospect of genetic mutations, that is to say, hereditary changes from which might develop blindness, mental incapacity, or a number of other malformations.

But what of that one? One in a million would mean two hundred unborn babies condemned in advance to feeble-mindedness or some other deformity. One in a hundred thousand would mean almost two thousand citizens now alive facing cancer of the blood from nuclear blasts since last New Year's Eve. Does society have the right to condemn them to such fates in advance? One answer is that this is the price we pay for the protection of the rest of us, and that it is a small price in comparison, say, to the forty thousand-odd traffic deaths in the United States every year.

This answer, however, does not satisfy me. It is not just that the protection itself is a highly questionable one. I am not sure, if the protection of a so-called nuclear-deterrent policy were foolproof and ironclad, that it would make the argument necessarily more justifiable. I am not rejecting the argument out of hand, be-

227

cause I do not have a better one to offer at the moment. But I do have my doubts about it. A society has to be pretty perfect and pretty arrogant in its perfection to declare that the projected condemnation of a certain number of the world's citizens to death or deformity in the future is the most satisfactory way of preserving civilization.

We Americans do not declare that, but now and then we seem resigned to it. If we reflect on these impending consequences, it may spur us to a nobler effort for a solution to the world's explosiveness. Without this effort, the nuclear powers are in a way condemning themselves as war criminals before the fact. My mind keeps returning to the American judge's answer, in the movie *Judgment at Nuremberg*, to the condemned Nazi jurist's plea that he was not guilty of the mass murders. "You were guilty," the American said, "when you condemned the first soul you knew to be innocent."

Strictly Personal

CHECK THE BAGGAGE,
OR CARRY IT?

New York City
March 30, 1955

THIS LITTLE ESSAY also might be entitled "Cleaning Out the Attic," or "Should You Throw Old Ideas and Rocking Chairs Away?"

A long time ago, when Westbrook Pegler was a writer and not a hater, he wrote a wonderfully cynical piece poking fun at people who accumulated things. He averred that sentimentality was a kind of a glue which stuck people to such extraneous matter as fly-specked dance programs, autographed convention photographs, and stuffed mooseheads. If I read Pegler correctly, he subscribed to the theory that "he travels fastest who travels alone and without excess baggage."

I had occasion to reflect on this message this morning, as I sat in a Manhattan apartment lost in a wilderness of cardboard cartons, wooden crates, a pile of soiled linen, a college annual which has come loose at the binding, and an old playbill from *Oklahoma*. As the man from the moving company said, "It beats me how people manage to collect so much junk!"

True, and yet where do you draw the line, and how? Take those sea shells, for instance, and especially that graceful little starfish. It was lying there on the beach on that gem of an island in the West Indies, and when it was transplanted to a table top in Manhattan, it recalled to me blue water and yellow sand and white sun, so disturbingly and without effort. Yet what do you put it in

229

to keep it from being crushed on the truck trip to Washington, and is it worth the trouble and the expense?

The workmen are as swift and careful as nurses in the maternity ward. Like those ministering sisters, they have sense enough to swallow their true opinions about the objects they handle. If you want a revealing look at the character of the American householder, ask the man on the moving van to describe the assorted bric-a-brac of his clients.

I cannot go the full distance with Pegler—the old non-carbolic acid Pegler—on this item of excess baggage. The man who travels alone may be going nowhere, and if so, what matters his speed or how light he travels? A man's accumulations are a part of his character, like the little marble chips that make a mosaic. The trick perhaps is to keep them sorted out sufficiently so that they do not weigh you down and leave you behind as a "stick-in-the-mud," but at the same time are substantial enough to provide ballast and keep you from being blown away by some whirlwind of irresponsibility.

It is probably a good exercise to sit in the wilderness of cartons and crates and old magazines and sort out your belongings, because, as you take inventory of the crockery and the assorted long-playing records and Pullman towels and other tangible things, it puts you in a mood to take inventory, too, of what baggage you are carrying in opinions and ideas. It is a good exercise to dust these off and discard the worn ones and make room for the new.

Closets, you reflect, can be cleaned out without too much difficulty, although it is work. But when a man's mind becomes a cluttered attic of junk, it sometimes becomes very hard to move it.

ODE TO A WATERMELON

August 19, 1955

ONE OF THE juiciest fruits known to man, an annual plant of the gourd family, the watermelon, or *citrullus vulgaris,* is not getting an even break, and neither am I. With the possible exception of pineapple sherbet, it is my favorite dessert, and I cannot get it in a restaurant.

This ovoid delicacy is native to Africa and dates back to prehistoric times; the Egyptians had taste enough to depict it in paintings when they were building the pyramids. And what modern mouth has not watered over the succulent canvas by Tamayo, the brilliant Mexican, demonstrating what the colors of tender green and juicy red were invented for? But I can't work off my appetite in an art gallery. I want to taste some of nature's sugary built-in goodness in a lightly salted morsel of melon on the end of a fork. Try and get it.

In Italy, in the summertime, roadside melon markets, under a little square of canvas for shade, are as numerous as hamburger stands in the U.S.A. I remember once driving through the Dolomites on my way from Venice to the Brenner Pass and coming upon a tiny *trattoria* beside a shaded spring at a curve in the road. Watermelons were cooling in the bubbling pool, their plump green skins wet and shining. I stopped and made an extra meal of crisp, crimson slices. Nothing *vulgaris* about that *citrullus;* it was delectable.

Last summer, I spent one entire steaming evening at a town in southern Illinois—which, out of deference to the chamber of commerce, I shall not name—trying to find a restaurant that had watermelon on the menu. I must have canvassed every eating place in the city, without avail. I was finally directed to a service station where, in disbelief, I found a supply of melons on ice. Splattering juice and seeds onto a newspaper, I ate mine in blissful bites next to a gas pump.

Admittedly, in season you can get melons at the crossroads of America almost as easily as in Italy. I can see their round green bottoms now, stacked in inviting pyramids. But what diabolical breed of dietitians do we have preparing the bill of fare of the nation's public dining rooms? Who wants baked Alaska, or crepes suzette, or even Jello, if he can get a wedge of what the *Encyclopaedia Britannica* describes as a fruit of berrylike structure filled nearly to the rind with red, pleasantly flavored pulp with abundant, sweet, watery juice? How's that for a commercial?

Some of the more exclusive rendezvous, like Manhattan's "Twenty-one" or Chicago's "Pump Room," reportedly do serve it,

231

but I feel this matchless product of the vine is basically a dem-ocratic delicacy and should not be left to trickle down to us common people from the top. Its very abundance should make it non-exclusive. The Department of Agriculture estimates this year's crop will total one hundred twenty-six million, four hundred sixty-one thousand watermelons. Assuming that a few people prefer a colorless hybrid called honeydew, that is a watermelon for nearly every man, woman, and child in the country.

I confess my crusade may be psychologically embedded in a childhood frustration: I was too scared of buckshot to go on many watermelon raids as a boy and consequently never got enough. In desperation the restaurateurs may try to twist this into proof that my call to watermelon fanciers of the world to unite simply stems from guilt feelings at not having defended the dessert I believed in at an earlier date.

Let them beware. Watermelons, my research shows, are particularly popular in south Russia. If coexistence continues, restaurants of America will be forced to add watermelon to the menu if they want to stay off the Attorney General's subversive list.

ON TULIPS AND TEST TUBES

October 20, 1955

I HAVE BEEN planting daffodil and tulip bulbs in my garden, six inches down and six inches apart, according to the seed man's instructions. Now all I have to do is wait for spring to come and for Nature to take her course. There is a certain nourishment that comes to man from this communion with the soil, something that seems to flow into the mind and the spirit when your fingers touch the moist, black dirt in the autumn coolness. Intrigued and exhilarated as we are by this mystery of growth, just to sense it is not enough, except maybe for a hermit. For the rest of us, it seems necessary to keep probing the mystery to see if we cannot discover a little better balance between man and the universe in general, between man and man in particular.

The science crowd is making new and monumental discoveries

232

nearly every day. Only last Tuesday, the University of California let it be known that the world's most powerful atom smasher, called the Berkeley bevatron, had come up with a little item named the anti-proton. This new atomic particle can annihilate matter as we know it, although the experts, paradoxically enough, hail it as a big step forward in man's effort to control his environment.

I will bet you a red tulip bulb against an old dandelion seed that not a single soul has bothered to denounce Dr. Ernest O. Lawrence, the boss of the bevatron, for tinkering with the affairs of the universe. The ghost of Galileo must smile at this. Three hundred and twenty-two years ago, he was punished as a heretic by the Inquisition for arguing that the earth did not stand still but rotated in a planetary system around the sun. A couple of thousand years before that, Pythagoras earned the scorn and suspicion of the Greeks by suggesting that the world was round.

The scientist, the expert on physical things, is not a witch any more. He is not pilloried for splitting the atom or for enslaving electrons to do the work of humans, even though the potential of each of those accomplishments may revolutionize, if not extinguish, civilization. It is right that he has earned—in the laboratory anyway—his freedom to operate, because his job is the work of discovery. There is a danger, of course, that we may become entranced by the magic of material progress, but we cannot blame the man with the test tubes and the atom smasher for that.

That danger will be easier to cope with, I think, if we realize we are still stunted in exploring the mysteries of the universe. We will take anything new off the assembly line of science in the production of things, as comfortably and as eagerly as trading in the old car on a new model. It is the production line of ideas from the workshop of the humanities which provokes scorn and suspicion today. It is the pioneers in the science of human behavior and thinking who are getting hit with the tomatoes and stones of prejudice now, as the Galileos and the Pythagorases did in their day.

These experts are not trying to sell us basic principles that are different from the basic principles of democracy and human decency that we are taught; they are simply trying to discover why we so often fail to function according to these principles. Yet we

233

are darkly dubious and ill-at-ease. It is almost as if we did not want to know why racial prejudice, say, exists, or why a mob will run down an individual because he wants to go in another direction or otherwise acts "different" from the pack, or why our first reactions to the threat of communism were emotional and physical instead of restrained and rational—the better to deal with the danger.

If we neglect the mysteries of human growth, the miracles of the physical world will not be worth much to us, tulip bulbs included.

MOTHER NATURE
DESERVES AN ITEM

April 10, 1956

DOWN AT the newsstand a while ago, I stared for some time at the cover of a fashion magazine before I realized I was looking at it upside down. What I thought I saw was a thin, tall clump of queer, exotic flowers, species unknown to me, sprouting from a wide tub encased in yellow straw. What I was supposed to see, it gradually developed, was Audrey Hepburn, the long stalk of her neck wrapped in a flowering print and her eyes peering out from under a huge, inverted wicker basket, which the editors of *Harper's Bazaar* insisted was a hat.

Women's hats are a subject for separate treatment, and I use the word treatment advisedly. The point I wish to dwell on now, with a mingling of wonder and downright awe, is the human proclivity to try to beat Nature at her own game. More than in any other season, our competitive yen seems to rise to its most foolish heights in the springtime. The flairs and furbelows of female fashion run a poor second to Mother Nature in any season. In the spring they simply haven't got a chance.

But let's be fair-minded about this thing. The compulsion to outdo the daffodils and the fruit blossoms may beat stronger in the female breast, but it smolders as well in the chest cavity of the male. The sportswear people must have realized this. It used

234

to be, and not long ago, that man's last sartorial sanctuary in Technicolor was his necktie. But, obviously mad with the power of their discovery of the neglected narcissism of us fellows, the clothing designers are rapidly cultivating our plumage with such garish items of apparel, from socks to evening wear, that the radiant ensemble of our garments almost rivals the splendor of a cock pheasant or some other princely bird of wood or field.

Almost, but not quite. This point was driven cruelly home to me only this morning, while I was admiring a few springtime acquisitions that had arrived from the haberdashery. I thought the smoldering silk four-in-hand and the pink-striped shirt looked rather fetching, until outside the window I happened to glimpse, in a blinding succession of colors, a bluejay, the saucy fellow with rakish crest and built-in cravat, and a cardinal, flaunting his feathers as a bullfighter does his cape. My own miserable purchases molted on the spot.

Psychologists might see in our hungry addiction to color for ourselves a desire to brighten the somber (and often man-made) walls of existence that we too frequently find ourselves living inside. But I think this capacity of Nature to give us our come-uppance now and then is a good thing. It makes us realize that there are still wonders of color beyond the dye vats of the industrial chemist, and mysteries of growth and change beyond the laboratories of the nuclear physicist.

Actually, I suppose we crave to satisfy an affinity with Nature, more than we are bent on trying to compete with her. The cherry blossom wasn't invented simply for the convenience of getting a pretty girl crowned queen of the festival. But we sometimes contrive these extracurricular activities in order to have an excuse for visiting the blossom, as if, much as it thrilled us, we would be uncomfortable in the presence of the blossom alone, embarrassed, maybe, by the sheer beauty of it.

All this suggestive analysis or analytical suggestion on the not exactly trifling subjects of man and nature may sound presumptuous and time-wasting to the men who must grapple with the immediate crises of the planet. It is a pity, though, that they can't manage to smuggle themselves out of their offices, as I did, and wheel around Washington's tidal basin, where the cherry trees are rioting in a foam of fragile pink. I might have kept my own sortie secret and attempted to pontificate on graver matters of moment, except that when I got there I found such a horde of fellow citizens on the same mission that I figured Mother Nature must be worth an item. Come to think of it, that is, in a way, good news in itself.

SAVOR THAT FLAVOR, MAN

May 25, 1956

UACCUSTOMED AS I am, I find myself in danger of being cast in the role of a one-man pressure group. If things keep on like this, I may be obliged to register as a lobbyist, but I am not sure whether it should be on behalf of people or pigs. I am caught in a cross fire of controversy over pork and beans; what is more serious, my loyalty seems to be in question. I am accused, in effect, of undermining that dish as a rich American tradition. Nothing could be further from my hungry mind. As a male domestic-science expert, I have spent many happy hours with a can opener and a tin of pork and beans.

Months ago I suggested, with tongue in cheek (I thought), that hog prices might be strengthened and the farm problem proportionately eased if somebody would take the trouble to put a piece of pork in a can of pork and beans. Whereas my other, graver pontifications on the state of the world had failed to cause any perceptible change in the policies of Washington, Moscow, or the then Miss Grace Kelly, this wisp of whimsy, to my astonishment, started a chain reaction from the kitchen to the highest reaches of the canning industry. Housewives besieged me with additional suggestions. A congressman from the Middle West called, in some alarm, to ask what it was all about, because he was being pressed to introduce a bill, and a lively local of the Packinghouse Workers of America actually proposed legislation calling for a minimum of two ounces of pork in every pound can of beans.

Whereupon the irate sales manager of a canning factory in Hoopeston, Illinois, wrote me to protest that unless such dam-

236

aging moves were checked they might drive a beloved and popular dish right off the American dinner table, injure the farmers, and wreck a market which amounts to about one billion pounds of beans and fifty million pounds of pork a year. I began to feel like a Benedict Arnold trapped in the pantry.

The reason you may not see any pork in the can, the Hoopeston man said, is that it is melted into the flavor.

"During the war," he wrote, "the armed services had our company pack beans with a larger than normal amount of fat pork because they were to be used in Alaska, and additional fat was needed in diets in the Arctic Circle to produce more body heat. The result was a very unappetizing-appearing can of beans with a layer of fat surrounding each bean. The writer," he went on, "sampled some beans packed that way, and the result was a coating of fat in my mouth which prevented my detecting any flavor in anything else eaten that day. No doubt the additional fat accomplished its purpose in the Arctic Circle."

Parenthetically, I am tempted to think it may have accomplished even more than its purpose: It may have saved the GIs on the frozen tundra from having to detect the flavor of some of the other items on their menu.

"Unfortunately," the cannery man's letter continued, "some of those beans were distributed in other areas also, and we received a number of complaints from people in the armed services because of the product those people thought to be inferior to our regular pack."

The factory saved the day by sending the complainants some samples from its regular recipe.

In acknowledging this letter, I fearlessly went on record as being uncompromisingly in favor of pork and beans, and conceded his point about the fat-pork content. I was emboldened to ask, though, what might happen if a little lean pork were added to the proper proportion of fat. He has not answered yet, but I can almost taste the scorching flavor of his reply.

That reminds me of the maxim that too many commentators cooking with gas can spoil the dinner. A bonus moral to the story is: If you want to be heard in this seemingly secure and opulent land, never treat a light subject like nuclear warfare seriously, and never treat a serious subject like pork and beans lightly.

THE "ANDREA DORIA"

A reporter, believe it or not, finds it awkward and embarrassing to be in the news himself. His training all points the other way. In one of those "It could never happen to me" quirks of fate, I became personally involved in one of the biggest news stories of a decade—the sinking of the "Andrea Doria." I broadcast two commentaries on the tragedy. They are reproduced here, but to put them in full perspective I have added a separate account of my own experiences and feelings stemming from that incredible accident.

PART I

It was going to be a full summer: the Democratic National Convention in Chicago, quickly followed by the GOP's certain renomination of Ike in San Francisco, and then the long Presidential campaign. But first I could look forward to a pleasant break in the routine—a week's holiday with friends on Martha's Vineyard, a spot whose delightful name alone had long lured me, but an island where I had never been. The happy prospect was heightened because my fourteen-year-old daughter, Linda, was going with me. She and her mother, her half-sister, Joan, and her stepfather, Camille Cianfarra, the New York Times correspondent in Madrid, were all coming home. Linda would stay and start high school in the autumn. It was Cian's home leave, and they had plenty of time, so they had taken a ship from Gibraltar. I flew up from Washington to New York on a Wednesday to meet them the following morning when their liner, the "Andrea Doria," was due to dock. . . .

About five o'clock on that Thursday morning, July 26, 1956, the phone rang in my New York hotel room. It was Francis Littlejohn, director of news at ABC. My first guilty reaction was that I had overslept. So it was almost with relief that I recognized Fritz's soft North Carolina drawl. "We didn't want to wake you before," he said, "because everything was so confused, but it's all right

238

now. The "Andrea Doria" and the "Stockholm" have collided off Nantucket in a fog, and the "Doria" is in a bad way, but the "Ile de France" has just radioed that everybody has been rescued. Nobody was lost."

I was dreaming. Ships with radar didn't collide on the high seas. But if they did, how could there be no casualties? Still I clung numbly to Littlejohn's reassurance, which, as he knew, was more tender than precise. "I'll call you back if we get anything more," he said.

I lay back on the bed a moment, trying to think. Then I called the Times. No, they hadn't heard from Cian yet, but they were sure they would soon. They had a radiophone call in for the "Ile," and they would relay me any information. That "no word from Cian" gnawed at me. I called colleagues at United Press and the AP and told them my problem. They, too, were frantically trying to contact the "Ile" and promised to try to find out what had happened to Linda and the Cianfarras. Knowing full well the effort would be swamped by higher priorities, I tried to call the "Ile" myself.

In mid-morning, I transferred my telephoning from the hotel to the ABC news room. First casualties had been landed by helicopter at Nantucket. (Linda and I had hoped to go to that neighboring island from Martha's Vineyard.) One victim was a girl. I called the Coast Guard station. It was not Linda or Joan. The "Ile de France" would be the first of several ships in with survivors. After hours of anguished haggling, I wangled a pass for the cutter assigned to meet the "Ile" down the bay and arranged with Littlejohn for somebody else to do my broadcast if I did not return in time.

I had never missed a broadcast, and I was determined to make this one if I could. But it was already well past noon before the cutter, a rolling chaos of reporters, photographers, and officials, even began to move out of the East River, and the 7:00 P.M. deadline added a smaller agony of suspense to the growing uncertainty about Linda and the Cianfarras. The chaos aboard the "Ile de France" seemed even greater. Survivor lists were incomplete. Someone had heard that Mrs. Cianfarra was aboard, gravely injured. I found her in the sick bay, swathed in bandages. "Cian is dead," Jane murmured. "I heard him die. Where are the children?" I told her she couldn't be certain about Cian, that the children undoubtedly were aboard one of the other rescue ships. Then I went to the purser's office to recheck the lists. No familiar names. I trudged the decks. No familiar faces. The answer was obvious now: The "Stockholm" had hit the very staterooms of the Cianfarras. Still, if Jane had survived . . .

The longest, hardest time seemed to be while maneuvering her on a stretcher through the narrow companionways, down the narrow gangplank, onto the pier. At the bottom was an ABC News colleague with a "live" TV camera. Couldn't I give him a few details? Breaking, no doubt, some journalistic code of ethics, I declined and hurried on with Linda's mother into an ambulance. My thought was to get her to Roosevelt Hospital, the only one I knew in Manhattan. But a nurse on the pier peremptorily said the ambulance was going to St. Claire's, nearer the waterfront. By the time we had gotten Jane into a hospital bed, it was after 6:00 P.M. I phoned the office and told Fritz Littlejohn that I would be there in time to do my whole broadcast, ad-libbing from notes. Kindly but firmly, he said it was not necessary and not possible.

He was right. One doesn't do a fifteen-minute network newscast without a script. But when I arrived, twenty minutes later, he crossed his fingers and yielded to my entreaties. The sponsor had already called and said they would eliminate the commercial which traditionally separated the news report from my own commentary. This made the timing easier for me, and I could mention the headlines and then concentrate on trying to reconstruct what I had seen on the "Ile de France."

About ten minutes before air time, as I was shuffling through my notes, the Times called me.

Did I have a photograph of Linda?

Yes, a snapshot—but why?

A pause. Then, with an apology in its brusqueness, the voice said, "Of course, you know she and Joan and Cian are dead."

"Who the hell said so?" I shouted. "I've just come off of the 'Ile de France,' and I couldn't find anybody to confirm anything."

"Well," said the voice, "Harrison Salisbury found the doctor who rescued your ex-wife, and he saw the bodies."

I said they could send a messenger for the snapshot, and then I hung up, feeling more angry than anything else. Now it was *time, and I went into the studio not knowing quite what I was going to say. But, according to the tape recording, it went as follows:*

GOOD EVENING. Here is the shape of the news: Tonight, it is the shape of disaster.

There are other headlines: Stassen meets with Republican Chairman Hall and says afterwards he is going to make a new poll to see whether his Vice-Presidential candidate, Herter, or Vice-President Nixon, pulls ahead. Mr. Nasser of Egypt announces the intention of nationalizing the Suez Canal.

But the main story—the story around the world tonight—is the story of the sinking of the Italian liner "Andrea Doria," after a somewhat miraculous rescue at sea—some four hundred miles northeast of New York City and some forty-odd miles off the island of Nantucket, Massachusetts.

About seventeen hundred persons were picked up from the "Andrea Doria" in the fog of the early morning. Conflicting reports say that about five or six people were killed, and hundreds injured. There is no conclusive count yet. The French liner "Ile de France" has just arrived in New York with the first group of survivors—some 756. Other survivors are due on other rescue ships tonight and tomorrow. The other ship in the collision, the "Stockholm," was not so badly damaged and is proceeding to New York under her own power. She is due tomorrow with 425 survivors of the "Andrea Doria" aboard.

The vessel "Cape Anne," with some 421 persons aboard, is due in New York City this evening. The military transport "Private Thomas," with some 155 persons aboard, is due in Brooklyn tomorrow morning. The "Stockholm" itself, limping slowly under her own power with a bashed-in bow, is due in New York about midday tomorrow. A vessel called the "Alecto" has picked up some sixty-three, according to the Italian consulate here, and an American military vessel, the "DE 551," has several more. Both of those vessels are due tomorrow.

This reporter has just returned from a trip down New York

241

Harbor to board the liner "Ile de France," and has come back after interviewing a number of the first survivors to reach New York City. This is a jumbled story—a story told in the faces of the persons that you see on the ship. Perhaps the best way to tell it, from notes and from memory, is just to jog down through the notes informally as I go.

Take, for instance, a particular case: the case of a person who had persons, relatives, aboard the "Andrea Doria," and was notified this morning about five o'clock that the two ships—the "Andrea Doria" and the "Stockholm"—had collided in the fog last night. There is the numbing . . . the wait, the confusion, the conflicting reports. And then, in the afternoon, the news that correspondents would be picked up by the Coast Guard and taken down the harbor to board the ship—to board the "Ile de France," which, as I have said, picked up most of the survivors. The afternoon in New York Ctiy was warm and humid, with a gauze of cotton cloud on the sky, and as the Coast Guard tugboat, which was ironically named "Nevasink" (not a pun, but the name, one was told, of an Indian chief), as the "Nevasink" went down New York Harbor toward Gravesend Bay, the afternoon was alive with activity. There were Army helicopters; there were helicopters of the Coast Guard; and the New York Port Authority hovered over the harbor. It was warm and humid, and the sea gulls sought shelter from the sun.

One approached the end of the harbor, passing the incoming traffic, looking for the ship. Then, after about forty or fifty minutes, some six miles from the lower end of Manhattan Island with the tall, thin buildings of Wall Street vaulting to the sky, one saw out of a sort of muggy smudge of fog, a huge body materialize. This—coming bigger and bigger—was the "Ile de France," her two stacks sticking up in the sky, and, in the still air, her smoke rising almost vertically.

A lump comes in one's throat as one sees this vessel, a vessel of mercy, and the vessel bearing the people home—some 756, more than two-thirds, more than three-fourths, perhaps, of the total passenger list of the "Andrea Doria," which was due in New York regularly scheduled from Europe this morning. The tugboat comes alongside the "Ile de France." The Customs and Immigration officials were put aboard from another tug, appropriately, first. The band of reporters, the television crews, the radio tape-recording crews, the correspondents hovered around the rail of the "Nevasink." As we push under the starboard side of the "Ile de France," one looks up and sees a line—a necklace of faces—looking down from the rail. Somebody wants to know who are the passengers and who are the survivors. Soon, one is able to tell. Here a shirt tail sticking out. Here a nightshirt. Here a bandaged head.

You are directly under the "Ile de France," which is under way now, hurrying into New York Harbor, in order to bring the hospitalized cases in, and it's tricky to get aboard. You get aboard and then the story comes—told in little fragments. Fragments of people who were there. One, for instance, a radio and TV consultant of the American Federation of Labor and Congress of Industrial Organizations, Morris Novik, and his wife, who are just coming back from a trip on vacation to Europe. You find Novik, you fling your arms around him and find that he is well. And you say, "What happened?"

And he says, sobbing a little: "It was eleven fifteen last night by the ship's clock, the worst fog you could think of, and then there was a hideous crash. And there was the longest time . . . the longest time . . . And women and children were put into the boats . . . and Richardson Dilworth, the mayor of Philadelphia, and I," Novik said, "helped them to get in, and I suppose we were among those of the last to get off. We got on the 'Ile de France.' I don't know how long it took. We were there in the boats . . . in the 'Andrea Doria's' boats." This conflicts with the report earlier that the "Andrea Doria" was not able to lower her boats. Then Novik said, "There was the 'Ile' . . . there was the 'Ile de France.' There was God . . . and that was the end of it."

But there were other people. There was Camille Cianfarra, the Madrid correspondent of the *New York Times*, his wife Jane, and his stepchild, and another child. Where were they?—I asked. I was told that Mrs. Cianfarra was badly hurt and was in the sick bay of the "Ile de France." One finds her. She is badly hurt, but she is not on the critical list. She has multiple fractures and cuts. She asks about her husband. It is reported, but it is not confirmed, that Camille Cianfarra of the *New York Times* is among the dead. The children may be aboard another ship. It is not proved. It is not certain. It could be this that I am reporting now—the same

243

kind of tenuous feeling of anticipation and fear for all the other people aboard whose relatives had not yet been able to determine their safety. Most of them, of course, were saved with heroism and calmness. There was no panic, apparently, but there was confusion.

Mrs. Cianfarra tells her story: She and her husband were in the stateroom—perhaps—which suffered the direct hit of the prow, the bow of the "Stockholm." She was trapped. Her husband was trapped in another part of the room. She tried to call to him. She tried to get to him and could not. And he did not answer. She thought that the door to the children's stateroom was open. She did not know. She was not sure. She did not hear their cries. But a crewman of the Italian Line, whose name she cannot remember, and a Dr. Peterson from New Jersey, whose name she hopes she will always remember, helped her out. She stood there stunned ... and bleeding ... and broken.

This, her stateroom, was on the starboard side of the ship, which is where the prow of the "Stockholm" knifed in. Nobody knows the exact reason for the crash. It has been said that there was a fault of the radar of the "Stockholm" or the "Andrea Doria," or both. The Minister Counselor of the embassy of the Italian government flew up to board the "Ile de France" with the rest of the reporters, to facilitate the sorting out and identity of the survivors as much as possible. Signore Ortona.

There was a story of another person aboard the vessel, a friend of Mrs. Cianfarra from shipboard, the wife of the movie actor Cary Grant—Betsy Drake—a blonde and lovely-looking girl, who had just undressed and was ready to go to bed on the port side of the ship. She was on the boat deck; the Cianfarras were on "A" deck. She felt the crash. She felt intuitively there had been an accident, and she quickly put her clothes back on. She was calm and collected.

But she told a story that perhaps portrays the feelings and reactions of a person in danger. You are calm, but you do foolish things. "I went up topside," she said, "on the highest part of the ship that was tilting high. It was the starboard side that was sinking. I was fully dressed, and the first thing I knew (I thought about it afterwards) I took off my shoes; I put them in my pocketbook, and I hung the pocketbook on the peg." The "Andrea Doria" was sunk, and Betsy Drake's shoes and pocketbook presumably have sunk with it.

This afternoon, she was lively aboard the "Ile de France," waiting for friends to meet her here, and telegraph and if possible telephone her husband, Cary Grant, who is making a picture in Spain, that she is all right. She was wearing cotton socks.

And that is the story of one of the greatest accidents in the history of maritime commerce. A miracle that none of the persons who were taken off the ship were lost at sea—apparently.

Slowly, little by little . . . torturously for the persons who don't know—happily for the persons who do . . . the whole pieces of the disaster will be fitted together. It is a horrible thing—but an inspiring thing—to see the way people react under duress and under accident.

The people on the "Ile de France" gave shoes and clothing and more than a thousand dollars for the relief of the victims.

PART II

When I returned from the studio to the news room, three friends were standing there waiting for me. We went back to my hotel room, and I had to begin the grisly business of calling Jane's and my relatives on the west coast. But first I thought I must try to reach Dr. Thure Peterson, the chiropractor from Upper Montclair, New Jersey, who had helped rescue Jane and whose wife had died—trapped in the wreckage.

"Doctor," I said, when I got him on the telephone, "I apologize for bothering you now, but I need your confirmation that Linda and Joan are dead."

"There is no doubt of it," he said, in the tense, even voice that shock sometimes brings. "I saw their bodies."

There was a certain comfort in an end to doubt. Yet the stunning news seemed to push me outside myself. My mind worked, my body moved, but I was not there. Later, somebody asked me, rather accusingly, why I had not identified Linda in the broadcast. I don't really know how much thought I gave it; it just seemed improper, as if I would be soliciting condolences in a public place. What bothered me most that evening, even after I went back to the hospital and told Jane what Dr. Peterson had

245

said, was that I had no feeling. My eyes were dry, even after Betsy Grant had said so tenderly outside Jane's room, "The girls had such an utterly happy time on the voyage—you can remember that." Finally, walking the muggy midnight streets back to the hotel with a friend, I was able to break down and cry.

The next morning, I got started somewhat late. But I resolved to keep working. Just as I was leaving my room, the telephone rang. It was Littlejohn. "I hate to do this to you," he said, "but the Times just phoned. They have a list of survivors coming in on the 'Stockholm,' and the name Linda Morgan is on it. Probably a mistake, but the ship is docking now, and you'd better go down and find out."

This was too much. Who would play such a cruel joke? If there was a Linda Morgan aboard, she was sure to be an elderly schoolteacher from Detroit. But I grabbed a taxi and raced to the pier. With the whole of her bow torn jaggedly away, leaving a hideous wound of tangled steel, the "Stockholm" was already tying up. Despite my press passes and urgent explanations, I could not get aboard. Finally, as they were beginning to wheel away the injured to ambulances, a company official took me onto the ship. By this time, I had seen the survivor list, and the name Linda Morgan loomed out boldly. But I would not let it mean anything to me. It had to be the schoolteacher.

Then the purser was talking. "You ought to know where we found your daughter," he said. "In the wreckage on the bow."

Never mind where! Suddenly, she was alive. I wasn't old enough to have an elderly schoolteacher for a daughter. But where was she now?

While a crewman went to check, the ship's doctor told me she had a badly broken arm and probably fractures of both knees. "She did a rather unusual thing," he added, "after she realized she was not aboard the 'Andrea Doria.' She insisted on writing a radiogram to her mother to tell her she was safe aboard the 'Stockholm.' " (The message, of course, never got through—but her presence of mind thrilled me.)

The crewman came back to report that Linda had already been taken off the ship and was on her way to Roosevelt Hospital. I thanked the officers, sprinted to the street, and hailed a cab.

The nurses at Roosevelt were wonderful, but they couldn't find

Linda. Presently, after a phone call, one of them said, "They rerouted her to St. Vincent's. She's there now."

The drive downtown to Greenwich Village seemed like a trip across the continent. I found her just as they were wheeling her into the X-ray room. "Oh, Daddy," her first words were, "where is Joan?" (Later, when Linda's bones had mended, a psychoanalyst suggested that the only vestige of a wound she would carry from her nightmare would be a feeling of guilt that she was saved while her half-sister was killed. A college girl now, she rarely speaks of the accident.)

As the doctors took over, I hurried to telephone Jane. "Linda is alive," I heard myself saying, with my own ears listening in disbelief. "I am with her now." Then I mumbled something about its being what people would describe as a miracle. Through her own pain, Jane uttered a crying sigh of joy which I have never forgotten.

Other bits of this fantastic story were to fall into place later—including the appearance of a shy, fragile, wonderful little man named Bernabe Polanco Garcia, the only Spanish-speaking crewman on the "Stockholm," who pulled Linda tenderly from the wreckage after he had been astonished to hear her cries of "Donde está mi mamá?" in the darkness. (Linda was born in Mexico, and her first language was Spanish.)

But now, what was I to do with my own story, or rather Linda's, which the newspapers already were beginning to headline? My first impulse was to play it straight, without personal overtones. But, as my own doctor and I rode back uptown after he had seen Linda, he said I could not possibly get away with that. "After last night," he said, "you've simply got to finish the story."

This time, out of a winelike delirium, the script came easily and seemed to write itself. . . .

New York City
July 27, 1956

How DOES a reporter cover a story in which he himself is partly involved? Especially, a story that touches emotions springing from the very roots of being, the emotions that are now the lovely flower of life, now the hard, piercing cactus of death.

If you say, "No comment," you are joining the fraternity of human clams which you have spent your professional life trying to pry open with the pincers of probing questions. If you try to steel yourself and treat it routinely, you are open to the accusation that you are crass and callous and have no feeling, just an infusion of printer's ink or electrons, instead of red cells and white cells flowing in your veins.

If you overplay the assignment, you commit, I think, the most unforgivable sin of all: exploiting the secret privacy of individual human feeling for the fleeting sensation of the moment. So, in the end, you have to let your instinct and an inclination that you hope is tilted in the direction of good taste be your guide. Above all, you try to frame your story in the humble realization that this is not your story alone, but belongs to all people with human feelings, that what happened to you could happen to others, even though there is the diamond twinkle of miracle in the facts.

Within the space of twenty-four hours, this reporter has been pushed down the elevator shaft of the sub-basement of despair and raised again to the heights of incredible joy, washed, one suspects, with a slightly extravagant rivulet of some heavenly champagne.

Last night, as far as the world at large was concerned, a girl—age, fourteen, nationality, American, named Linda Morgan—was dead. She happens to be this reporter's daughter. She had been killed, according to the incontrovertible evidence of an eyewitness, by the crash of the liner "Stockholm" into the very stateroom on the "Andrea Doria" which her stepfather, *New York Times* correspondent Camille Cianfarra, and her mother, Jane Cianfarra, occupied. Linda and her half-sister, Joan, were sleeping in their cabin, just forward of the Cianfarras'.

But Linda is *not* dead. One can only deduce that the impact hurled her from her bunk into the wreckage of the bow of the "Stockholm," where she was found, alive, painfully but not critically hurt. Her mother was seriously injured, but rescued. Cianfarra and Joan are missing and presumed lost, but now—who knows?

How do you feel, sir? a fellow reporter asks.

Not "No comment," but a simple, "I don't know." Webster neglected to invent the words to describe the feeling.

There is something sacred about the mystery of life which, in

248

the alchemy of the unknown, ennobles people as they face the supposed tragedy of death, their own or that of another. It makes other things seem so petty and unimportant.

The meanness and the pettiness of people are there, and they must be dealt with, just as surely as death and the Bureau of Internal Revenue. Yet let them be measured for what they are. Waiting to board the tug to go out to the "Ile de France" yesterday afternoon, I saw a reporter elbow and curse a harried Italian diplomat trying to get aboard, too, in line of duty. This morning, I unforgivably insulted a taxi driver who would not drive fast enough to Linda's hospital. But one must remember that nothing ever happens until it happens to you.

Through all this incredible blackness and sunshine, I kept remembering what a wonderful human being from Philadelphia named C. Jared Ingersoll once told me, in recounting how he kept right on going after the death of his wife, and then of his son. "I try to live fully," he said, "so that when my luck changes, there will be little room for regret or recrimination over time lost or misspent."

This reporter hopes tonight that he has learned that lesson well enough to teach it with tenderness to a girl young enough to grow with it into a full blossom, who will give joy to others for her very living. Perhaps, perhaps, she has learned it already herself.

DON'T SMILE, DAMN YOU

June 27, 1958

I CONSIDER MYSELF a long-suffering fellow, but I have finally decided to rebel against the photographic grin. The air is throbbing with international crises; the headlines quiver with alleged malfeasance; and in television, the newsreel, and the spread on page one invariably looms the beaming countenance of some key figure in the case. It is time either to let the public in on the joke or to replace the camouflage with an appropriate frown.

249

With this public service in mind, I hereby declare the establishment of the benevolent and protective order of SWOSPPIPP, a handy contraction of the organization's full and official name, which is, of course, the Society to Wipe Out the Smiles on Pictures of People in Public Places. Membership is open to anybody who can certify that he has experienced schizoid sensations similar to my own after trying to relate the daily shambles of news to the accompanying columns' pictures of the cherubic, chuckling faces who are said to make it. As an earnest of active membership, lodge brothers and sisters must equip themselves with a black crayon, the better to obscure the latest leering countenance in a news picture with a false mustache or to convert the smile into the anxious scowl that really lurks underneath. The motto of SWOSPPIPP will be, naturally, "Why Cheer Up When the Worst Is Yet to Come?" Its insignia will be a jaundiced eye on a field of stuffed shirts.

The founding of SWOSPPIPP, I confess, comes too late to penetrate the petrified photo-studio smiles of most of the current crop of June brides and get to the tortures of their real feelings, but surely its appearance on the scene could not be more timely as far as the coming off-year election campaigns are concerned. Think of the balm to public nerves—to be spared the jack-o'-lantern-like spectacle of the grinning faces of candidates ill concealing their lack of confidence!

To move off page one for a moment, I have often fancied that some manufacturer would make a killing if he would only once people the ad for his product with a slattern and a lout, instead of the radiant brace of lovebirds you see greeting each other for breakfast in a Technicolor nook spread across a double-page display in *Life*. Indeed, if my movement develops with the lighthearted vengeance I anticipate, we may eventually be obliged to establish an auxiliary to SWOSPPIPP, probably to be known as OWPHIM, or Out with Phony Happiness in the Media.

It is not that I am allergic to happiness. A lark's song lifts me as high as the next fellow. What I am after is perspective induced by a more realistic set of values. I can brood right along with you on the black seriousness of the middle eastern crisis, and then I open the paper and find Nasser greeting Dag Hammarskjöld with a grin wide enough to make Groucho Marx in his palmiest days look like a pallbearer.

Come to think of it, Groucho Marx looks like a pallbearer anyway, in a gleeful kind of way, but that is beside the point. The point is, what is the gag?

Of course, some psychologists maintain that laughter can be an expression of nervousness, and on that theory I suppose we should expect the world's statesmen, in this thermonuclear age, not just to contract a case of girlish giggles, but to break up completely and, as it were, whoop themselves to death.

I held off forming SWOSPPIPP for a long time. I didn't want to be accused of lacking a sense of humor. I sort of got used to the smiling beak of Secretary Dulles in the public prints. I was a little shaken when I thought I caught a flicker of amusement on the granite visage of Sherman Adams in a current news-magazine photo, but the last straw came this morning when I picked up the *Herald Tribune* and there, almost laughing out loud, was General Charles de Gaulle.

I fell on the photo with a fury, divided de Gaulle into three parts to wipe off his smile, and there, without further ado, SWOSPPIPP was born.

A TOAST TO ANGER

November 26, 1959

I CAN NEVER travel across even a part of this broad, bountiful land without being lifted by the sweep of it, stimulated by the strength of it, dormant, wasted, or misused as this power may sometimes be. Perhaps the anxious wish was father to the thought, but on a trip across the country and back last fortnight, I somehow got the impression that people already had begun to test some values and that their curiosity about political figures reflected a measure of their preoccupation with the state of the nation.

Can the national morality, or lack of it, be translated into a meaningful political issue? Can a critical examination of what some speech writers love to call—a little too smugly, perhaps—the American Way of Life, be conducted on the campaign platform? Why not? Better an examination of the living, if overstuffed, pattern now than an autopsy later. We are not rotten to the core, Maud, as Bea Lillie's song went, but we are suffering something more serious than a skin rash. The spreading eczema of juvenile defiance, the boils of greed, the goose pimples of insecurity are all manifestations of varying degrees of inner torment.

I wonder if some of this conflict does not stem from a growing inability or disinclination to display an old-fashioned emotion called anger. I am not talking about the terrifying, vengeful lust of a mob. I am talking about public outrage, or, as some of the crusaders of the past called and understood it, righteous wrath. Like any force, this one is replete with dangers; it can be misdirected or detonated by accident. But, if our scientists can conduct controlled experiments with megaton bombs, surely it is high time that we were able to explode indignation where it will do the most good—particularly if we are as enlightened and informed a body politic as we take such persistent pride in calling ourselves.

That brings up a vital point. Despite—or in some cases because of—all the marvels of the mass media, I submit that we are a superficially informed public, that that is a dangerous weakness, and that much of the blame for it must be laid on the doorsteps of the publishers, broadcasters, and other purveyors of what passes for information. One hundred and seventy-eight million Americans cannot automatically become aroused about something. They have to be alerted. They have to be informed. And they have to be stimulated by responsible controversy.

Controversy is what advertisers are allergic to; their theory seems to be that it somehow shrinks the buying appetite of the consuming public. And advertisers, with their theories—not always, but too often—are, or seem to be, more important to the media men than the audiences they are supposed to inform.

WE HAVEN'T COME FAR
FROM THE FISH

February 29, 1960

DURING A considerable portion of the week just past, I found myself staring at fish. While Premier Khrushchev was angling for additional catches in Southeast Asia and the President was casting the Eisenhower allure around South America, I had my gaze fixed through a snorkeling mask on tropical marine fauna in the blue-green island waters of the Caribbean. I wish those two distinguished travelers could have been with me. There is something about looking a fish in the eye in his own habitat which makes you realize the human world is only one little bubble in the vast, mysterious caldron of the universe.

In many respects, the fish has adapted himself better to his world than we have to ours. Of course, he has been at it a little longer. Fishes, the ichthyologists remind us, have inhabited the earth for some four hundred million years, longer than any other backboned animal, and they show greater diversity in their way of life than even Americans do. This contrast should shame us because fish are, in fact, our ancestors. Looking at some of the man-made messiness around us, it is obvious that we descendants of that daring snout which emerged from the primeval ooze onto dry land after the Devonian period, some three hundred fifty million years back, we failed to improve the stock as we should. Indeed, our shame sometimes should burn in us with double intensity because the fishes keep adapting and changing.

In a marvelously moving book about creation called *The Immense Journey*, anthropologist Loren Eiseley indicates we should be humbled but not frightened by the flexibility displayed by the denizens of the deep. "It gives one a feeling of confidence," he writes, "to see nature still busy with experiments, still dynamic, and not through nor satisfied because a Devonian fish managed to end as a two-legged character with a straw hat. There are other things brewing and growing in the oceanic vat. It pays to

253

know this. It pays to know there is just as much future as there is past. The only thing that doesn't pay," the Nebraska-born naturalist continues, "is to be sure of man's own part in it.

"There are things down there still coming ashore. Never make the mistake of thinking life is now adjusted for eternity. It gets into your head—the certainty . . . the human certainty—and then you miss it all; the things on the tide flats and what they mean. . . ."

As I goggled at a sunfish wandering through a watery Caribbean valley, past a coral tree and a wavering shrub of seaweed, I was not equipped to know the meaning of this strange, beautiful, exotic, and, yes, forbidding world. I hope the southern filibusterers will pardon me if I remark on the fact that there did not seem to be any segregation on the basis of color in that segment of the marine universe I saw; smartly striped little blueheads of the wrasse family flitted unconcernedly past rainbow parrot fish. Black angelfish shared the same feeding grounds with red snapper and white and silvery types which I could not immediately identify. Of course, they were not sitting down to their meals. This analogy, I concede, could lead to the reckless conclusion that the fishes have organized their civilization into a kind of aquatic Utopia, whereas even a landlubber knows something of the ferocity of the barracuda and the shark.

One basic question, I guess, is whether man is as durable and as adaptable and as capable of growth as the fish. Studying that marvelous machine called the human brain, I am tempted to vote in man's favor. Then, from the detached distance of a wave-washed Caribbean beach, I follow the monstrous arrogance of men attempting to classify other men as a lower species because they were born—figuratively speaking—pompano instead of pickerel. With equal anger and sadness, I regard the larger spectacle of the human species bickering over social systems and brandishing weapons which threaten to end them all, and I duck back under the surface of the sea to take another, more respectful look at the fish.

THE CAUSE OF THE
HUMAN SPIRIT

December 30, 1960

ONE OF mankind's tragic wonders is the inability of people to approach the heights of human effort except from the pit of crisis into which their own folly has tumbled them. War is savagery, but out of it have come some of the most ennobling of experiences. What a pity that we seem almost to need such a ghastly extravagance before we can bring ourselves to make the supreme sacrifices we might not need to make if we were a little wiser, a little more self-disciplined and purposeful in pursuit of our daily lives.

Last night, for an hour and a half, I watched with grief and pride and disbelief a version of one of the most incredible television film documentaries ever put together, a moving masterpiece of World War II called "Victory at Sea." It had everything: the blind swaggering pompousness of Hitler and Mussolini; the lovely, courageous stubbornness of London's limeys in the blitz; the icy battles of the Atlantic; the awful, murderous majesty of air-sea combat in the Pacific; the little human flashes of kindness and cruelty at the front; the triumph of victory over tyranny; and the stark revelation of civilization's blackest obscenities, the concentration camps.

Here was a document to prove that man is capable of anything, the best and the worst. I looked and remembered and was moved to vow that it should never happen again. Yet, what New Year's resolution has history recorded as having been so piously promised and so faithlessly kept?

Buffeted by the intimate crises of the family circle and the palpable urgency of year-end bills, befuddled by the galaxy of weapons systems that now describe a nightmarish arc from outer space to his own back yard, dizzied by the complexities of this explosive age, and a little drunk, maybe, from the deceptive wine of its creature comforts, the lowly layman is baffled by events and

255

portents. What in the world can you and I do to keep the faith of men and women who died in the name of freedom for a peaceable world? I can only think of a simple thing. It carries no built-in promise of the millennium, yet it is a cause which has kept man struggling upward since his beginnings. Let us call it the cause of the human spirit. What it needs is belief and dedication and the realization that wars and revolutions are not the only ways it can be fought for, or even the best.

In the far past there was a certain pageantry to war, and the so-called heroics of it served as a kind of inspiration. For inspiration in the richly human cause of dignity and equal opportunity for every individual, I suggest we need go no farther than our own American South. A hundred years late perhaps, a revolution is under way there, a rebellion against the cruel inequalities of the past which have bled the American democratic ideal. Yesterday I received a holiday greeting card from that strong, brave, talented Georgian, author Lillian Smith. She had written: "It is an exciting time to live in the South—just dangerous enough to be fun. Everything is breaking open: minds, hearts, imaginations. . . . Words are popping out of mouths unused to phrasing them: human dignity, compassion, a child's right to grow. . . . People are thinking, creating. It is our rebirth and God knows it is late, but it is on its way now."

Every day something happens to give substance to those hopeful observations. Today, a high federal court indicated that Negro sharecroppers could not be evicted from their land because they had registered to vote. Yesterday, a grand dragon of the Ku Klux Klan resigned because he saw no legal way of stopping racial desegregation.

I find inspiration in the relentless struggle of the human spirit to be free, a struggle that is as eloquent and important in its way as the courage and sacrifice that contributed to "Victory at Sea."

SOMETHING KEEPS
BOTHERING ME

January 2, 1961

ON A RADIO PROGRAM the other night, a lady was asked what New Year's resolutions she planned to make. "Oh," she replied, "I don't make resolutions. I'm retired." Seeming to confuse pledges with wishes, another woman allowed that her resolution would be to have more fun in '61.

I am sorely tempted to moralize on those answers as reflecting all too vividly a national state of mind, a dangerous demand for even more self-indulgence, and a detachment from the harsh realities of life, instead of a desire to face up to them with high resolve. But I have been privately warned by persons whose wisdom I profoundly respect that I have been doing too much moralizing and humanizing in this corner lately, that I ought to get on with more illuminating analysis, if not caustic comment, on specific events and circumstances.

My constructive critics have, of course, pierced my Achilles heel. It is a commentator's weakness, indeed his occupational disease, to pompously point the moral on the one hand and on the other to Pollyanna-ize, to bestir beliefs in basic human goodness to such a degree as to verify the illusion that everybody is going to live happily ever after. It is easier that way; besides, it gives the pontificator a vague sense of well-being to denounce sin and extol man's virtues at the same time, or at least on alternative evenings. He begins to appreciate some of the enjoyments of the self-righteous preacher, without being aware of the pitfalls of prejudice and pretense he may be digging for himself.

Although I plead guilty to the indictment, I respectfully refuse to reform completely. I believe that the conscience, national and personal, has a valuable goading function, the more effective when it is allowed to operate in public view and is not locked in a closet, where the fuss it makes is more easily muffled. And I also stubbornly believe that, whereas man is his own worst enemy,

257

he may be induced to become a little less cussed, even though I concede on the basis of his record that it may take a frontal lobotomy to make him his own best friend.

CALL THE DOCTOR, ROLL OUT THE COUCH

October 2, 1961

SOMETIMES I AM inclined to think that what this sick and worried old world needs is more doctors and fewer statesmen. My hunch is that neurologists, psychologists, psychoanalysts, and others with some expert knowledge of the human mind and nervous system may have a better understanding of the causes and possible cures of international tensions than politicians do.

Surely, some of the blindly passionate fervor called nationalism, the arrogant and dangerously aggressive pride of Communist zealots, the almost pathological fear felt by some of our own superpatriots toward anybody who doesn't think or act exactly as they do, and the heaving, vengeful prejudices of the racists and the bigots are manifestations of deep emotional distress in nations and groups. Countries can be sick just as people can. Hitler's Germany suffered a vast neurosis. I see no reason why it is not logical and appropriate to suppose—and even hope—that doctors of the mind can be as useful as diplomats in dealing with a world crisis. I would like to think that the time will come—though I confess that it does not seem to be approaching with much speed —when experts in human behavior will be named as invariably to disarmament bodies, peace conferences, treaty conclaves, and other meetings aimed to calm international friction as economists, parliamentarians, bankers, bureaucrats, and demagogues are named to them now.*

These reflections have been stimulated by growing concern

* The almost pathetically enthusiastic response to this broadcast from psychologists, psychotherapists, and related experts made it clear that they are eager to tackle the job. It turns out that a few of them have been tapped by the State Department and the Pentagon on a consultative basis.

258

over the condition of our own national morale and spirit. America seems to be spinning in a turmoil of doubt and frustration and fear. The threat of nuclear holocaust is, I admit, not exactly conducive to serenity. But there seem to be other sources of our sickness, too. In a thoughtful but disturbing article in the *Manchester Guardian*, one of our best and most understanding friends, Professor D. W. Brogan of Cambridge University, finds that "something has gone wrong" with us. ". . . I think the irritation and malaise that I encounter," he writes, after his most recent visit of several months in the U.S., "have deeper roots than apprehension at the state of the national defenses. It is more a matter of the whole moral tone of the American way of life. . . . The American people," Brogan concludes, "are looking in the mirror at the moment, and are not, I fear, very pleased with what they see."

It strikes me that many of our value judgments are in the process of being kicked into a cocked hat. Instead of being exhorted to love they neighbor, thou art supposed to kill him, or at least it is O.K. to do so if he tries to climb into thine air-raid shelter to escape a nuclear attack. A member of the clergy has stated publicly that he finds this, in effect, justifiable homicide. To me, this is an interesting rationalization of the survival of the fittest, the application of the law of the jungle to preserve civilization, which is supposed to have risen from the jungle's swamps. Interestingly and terrifyingly enough, I have heard of at least two people, a man in Texas and a friend of a friend in New York City, who have already bought machine guns to guard the entrances to their private bunkers. Assuming that an H-bomb hits us and that these foresighted citizens survive, after having murdered half the neighborhood to keep their shelters down to the most efficient occupancy levels, what shape will they be in to reinstate the ethical values of a shattered civilization?

As I started to say in the beginning, is there a doctor in the house?

TYRANNY STARTS SMALL

May 8, 1962

I WISH THAT every citizen in the land could arrange to see the Oscar-winning film *Judgment at Nuremberg*. We need to be reminded anew of the wild fanaticism and pervasive power of Hitler's dictatorship, of the ghastly, unbelievable savagery of the concentration camps, which comprised the most monstrous crime ever committed against the human race—at least, I hope future history will record none worse. Stanley Kramer's remarkable, courageous picture recalls these things with moving but carefully unsensationalized drama. The scene showing Spencer Tracy as the strong New England judge listening to the echoes of *"Sieg Heil!"* in an empty Nuremberg stadium brings back the Nazi horrors more strongly than could a newsreel of *der Führer* whipping a party rally to a frenzy.

But *Judgment at Nuremberg* does something more than revive these bitter, significant memories, and it is this above all that I wish we could grasp in today's observances of the seventeenth anniversary of Nazi Germany's surrender. Growing through the film like a sturdy oak is something called principle. It is reflected in the gnarled, troubled, kindly face of that old American judge presiding over the trial of the key men who administered justice, so-called, in Nazi courtrooms. I could trace this tree of principle, root and branch, in Tracy's pursuit of the truth. It reminded me that free men, whose lives are full of compromise and expediency, will fight for an ideal. Its most penetrating admonition is that tryranny is built on little corruptions of justice and on the bit-by-bit erosion of freedom, that, once this decay sets in, ideals are rotted—and then what is there left to fight for?

Near the end of the picture, the principal German defendant, once an internationally renowned jurist, begs the American judge to believe that his self-confessed guilt was minimal because he had had nothing to do with the concentration camps or the extermination chambers. Your guilt, the weathered New Englander

260

replies, echoing the stern conscience of the Puritans, began when you condemned the first man you knew to be innocent.

Ah, what crimes we all commit in the name of Machiavelli. The ends justify the means, we say. We went along with Hitler, one Nuremberg defendant reasons in the film, because that way we could eventually control him. Hitler, another argues, was a lesser evil than communism; therefore, the Germans were justified in condoning his crimes in order to stem a larger menace.

Even as the trial reveals the treacherous emptiness of all these rationalizations, the threat arises that America herself will succumb to a fresh crime of expediency. The court is under heavy pressure to let the Nazi judges off lightly, because the Berlin blockade is on and, a U.S. Army general warns, we need all the support we can get from the German people—support which will change to hostility if the defendants are harshly punished. But they are convicted and sentenced to life imprisonment.

Then comes the cutting irony of the drama. The brilliant young German defense lawyer, a role which won Maximilian Schell his Academy award, predicts to the departing American jurist that the sentences will not stick. As the movie ends, this footnote is flashed on the screen: "The Nuremberg trials held in the American zone ended July 14, 1949. There were ninety-nine defendants sentenced to prison terms. Not one is still serving his sentence."

What purpose, then, did principle serve here? Rudolf Hess and a handful of Hitler's topflight henchmen are still behind bars in Spandau Prison in Berlin, but the ninety-nine smaller fry were freed, and there are even some ex-Nazis in the West German government. The point is not whether the war-crimes trials were effective. The point is that they were held at all, as part of a feeble but stubbornly continuing effort to improve the codes under which human society operates.

The more ruthless the dictatorship, the more fully it embraces the code that anything goes. This is a powerful weapon to use against the code of individual freedom, because the freedom of the individual is a tender, fragile thing, so easily violated that a man does not know—or necessarily care—that his neighbor's liberty has been reduced, until the encroachment reaches into his own life. We need to be aware in advance. We need to be re-

261

minded that unlimited expediency is the enemy of principle; if we were so reminded by more inspirations in real life reflecting the character of the hero in *Judgment at Nuremberg*, we might be surprised at the strength that faithfully held principles can impart. We might find it easier to avoid a worse carnage than the one whose end seventeen years ago we note today.

NEVER MIND HOW
MY GARDEN GROWS

May 18, 1962

I AM AFRAID I cannot give Agriculture Secretary Orville Freeman much guidance on the Billie Sol Estes case, but I may be able to ease his mind a trifle on another matter: The government will not have to lease extra facilities to store the surplus from the Morgan vegetable garden. The fact is, it is no garden in the normal sense of the word. What I have is a small piece of the Sahara Desert, spotted with little oases of weeds.

Last March, dutifully and hopefully, I planted some modest rows of radishes, carrots, onions, and lettuce in a clearing which my wife had abandoned as a flower garden. "Planted" may not be precisely the appropriate verb. I peppered the furrowed ground with seeds in the manner of a sheepherder seasoning his breakfast. This may well have been my original mistake. Perhaps I was acting on an unarticulated suspicion that my wife had abandoned the plot in the unshared knowledge that nothing would grow there, and, therefore, I stubbornly reasoned that a saturation bombing of seeds might miraculously produce something.

Well, at first it did. Nature worked her magic; in due course, tiny green tendrils in the radish rows were pushing up through the brown earth to the sunlight, and all that jazz. Even then, I began to assume postures of smugness as I passed the vegetable troughs in the supermarket. Even then, I was projecting my potential tax deductions as a truck farmer, writing off the cost of a hand cultivator, a section of hose with brass nozzle, and, if Secretary Freeman will pardon the expression, fertilizer. I became the Walter Mitty of the kitchen-garden set. I saw myself in a trim aquamarine pickup truck rolling, pocketa, pocketa, pocketa, down Pennsylvania Avenue to get the first crop of choice Bolting Bibb lettuce and Evergreen Bunching onions to the White House in time for the Kennedy's cultural cookout for André Malraux.

But I had forgotten the chore of thinning. My saturation seeding had induced incipiently choking lines of green among the Sparkler White Top and the Early Scarlet Globe radishes. There were interesting signs of a population explosion by the Bolting Bibb, though no vestige of life on carrot row and only a few green toothpicks of promise from the onions. So, shivering slightly under the early-morning Potomac mists, I fell to thinning the radishes.

Now I know why government storage bins are bursting. Farmers simply cannot bear not to let things grow. I felt like a baby-killer as I wrenched up the helpless surplus radish roots. But the plants left to live, instead of burgeoning with gratitude, began to languish all by themselves, their leaves turning a bilious yellow. The thinned lettuce waned, too.

A miasma of crisis hung over the garden, and I desperately rose to meet it with copious irrigation and gouges between the rows with my cultivator. Mostly, I stood disenchanted at the bottom of my garden and glared at my potential dust bowl. With nature failing me, I thought, perhaps I could simply order the vegetables up from their beds, like new recruits at Fort Dix. Needless to say, this silent reveille did not work, though, in the process of fuming, I did succeed in cultivating a handsome cluster of ulcers.

Impatience is one of my many weaknesses, and I realized I might be trying to hurry my harvest prematurely. So I retrieved the envelopes from the stakes I had thoughtfully put at the top of the rows and read the propaganda the snickering seed merchants had printed there. "One of the most easily grown home-garden vegetables," I read of the radishes, "reaching full maturity in from twenty to thirty days."

It was now more than sixty days since my March planting. It suddenly dawned on me that the crop might have subversively fooled me below its sickly foliage and was bursting to merchandisable succulence underground. I eagerly plucked a sample radish. Dangling between my fingers was, not a plump vegetable, but what seemed to be the wizened appendix of a pygmy, remotely resembling a radish only in its unhealthy, high-blood-pressure blush of red. If this was maturity, it had suffered an unhappy childhood and was already overdue for old-age medical care.

There is still no trace of the carrots, and the onion sprouts are withering with fatigue, one by one. I do not know what went wrong. Maybe they sold me last year's seeds. Even the batches the Department of Agriculture used to mail on request did better than that.

I am investigating my eligibility for participation in the soil bank, and I am having a battery of attorneys examine the possibility that, if I promise not to fail next year by not planting a garden, I may be in line for some compensation from the government.

I was determined to salvage something from my horticultural disaster. By using a pair of tweezers, I was able to assemble enough Bibb lettuce leaves to fill the saucer of a demitasse. I have put the exhibit under glass. When Billie Sol Estes comes up for the Congressional hearings, I am going to ask him what kind of fertilizer he would recommend.

HAVE WE REALLY GOT RHYTHM?

May 25, 1962

EXCEPT FOR AN occasional limerick, a banal greeting-card couplet, or a quotation out of *Bartlett's* to make an article sound erudite, the information media have largely given verse the fishy eye.

Man hungers for harmony, and poetry is the bread of it. Tragedy and beauty move him, and poetry is the vessel that carries their expression. Yesterday, feverishly occupied as he was with keeping his space ship in orbit, Scott Carpenter had time to report that the sunrises and sunsets he glimpsed from his window were "out of this world."

"My heart leaps," Wordsworth wrote, "when I behold a rainbow in the sky."

It seems to me there hasn't been enough of this kind of heart-leaping lately. Either we are too busy looking for the gold at the bottom of the rainbow, too fearful of the fall-out from the sky, or too angrily engaged in elbowing our neighbors to pause and oil our senses with the lovely, soothing lubricant of, not only the metrical, but the broken, rhythms of the bards.

On the ladder of these thoughts, I climbed out of the mare's nest of urgent and unfinished business heaped on my desk this morning, and fled to the countryside for inspiration. The day itself was a poem. The sky was a great blue dome burnished by a bright but freshly air-conditioned sun. Dazzling light and dark shadow played back and forth like tides over the brown fields and green trees.

Washington was awash with an early gush of summer and was humming with the noises at noon. Viewed from between the corpulent white columns of the Custis-Lee mansion on Arlington Cemetery Hill overlooking the Potomac, the Lincoln Memorial, the Washington Monument, and the Capitol gleamed like alabaster on a wide horizon.

Farther down the river, Mount Vernon drowsed impeccably. In a field of high grass, just beyond the old red-brick arch fronting Washington's tomb, a quail whistled. Aloft on a high branch, a thrush broadcast a message of his own. On an iron bench nearby, an elderly couple refreshed themselves in the shade. A plump, self-conscious Girl Scout, wearing glasses and a green jumper, snapped a picture of the tomb with a box camera and then scurried away to join her squealing, scouting sisters. Dangling from her arm was a white handbag; to it was fastened a huge plastic button which said in red, white, and blue letters, "I Like Boys."

It was a soothing scene, caught in flight between reverie and reality, sweet as honeysuckle, fully enriching as a bottle of vitamin pills. Then, suddenly, something snapped, and this brimming cup of May-day poetry began to spill. Perhaps it was the wail of turbojet planes homing toward Washington National

Airport that did it. As the shrieking noise drowned the hot, comfortable, midday drone of the flies, ugly probabilities pounded back into my mind. Item: Somebody wants to erect a sewage-disposal plant smack across the Potomac from Mount Vernon. Item: The national capital, like most other major cities, is caught up in a quarrel about how and where inner loops and outer loops will connect with the thruways thrusting through our city blocks like asphalt juggernauts. Item: Urbanization of the land, the White House Conference on Conservation was told yesterday, is chewing up a million acres a year.

As I drove back to the office through the Virginia countryside, my eyes burned with dust from bulldozers gouging superhighways through the green pastures. Do we know where we are going? May we not end up in a strangling traffic jam between the supermarket and apartmentalized suburbia? Grow we must, but are uncoordinated, profiteering real-estate promotions and barreling billion-dollar highways the poetry we want in our lives?

An eight-year-old girl I know wrote a poem in school recently to a tulip. "Little tulip," it ran, "why do you always carry a cup of wine? Now I see, you want to toast everybody that comes along the path."

I hope we can plan our growth sensibly enough and rhythmically enough so that she has a path to come along when she grows up.

THINK—WITH SUPPLE MINDS

March 1, 1955

Now, as the roots begin to stir and the sap begins to run, is probably as good a time as any to dust off the observation that things not only grow, they change. Nature seems a little more sedate with her changes, a little more dependable. If winter comes, spring cannot be far behind, give or take a few days, and making allowances for what, in Florida and California, they usually call "unusual weather."

But somehow men contrive to revolve in more violent orbits

than planets do, and as we spin we never quite know what's going to happen, or what we are going to cause to happen, next. This can dispel boredom, but it also can induce a twitch as we struggle to adjust to the change or, more likely, rebel against it.

We become adjusted, aesthetically if not financially, to the diamonds Woolworth's doesn't sell, only to learn that General Electric has invented a diamond which may eventually drive the real one down to the dime-store level. No sooner is the country's circulatory system enlarged with bulging arteries pumping oil and gas from border to border, than this industry, like a man in his prime after a lunch of spareribs, feels a little tightening around the heart. Not that arteriosclerosis is about to set in, but atomic power is on the way, and atomic power will not need pipelines.

And we are not yet fully adjusted to "ground-control approach," or even the wonderful but more orthodox clear-weather glides and climbs of airplanes as they make their ports of call. Now we are told to fasten our seat-belts and prepare to take off straight up. Of course, what goes up will come straight down, fluttering gently, one hopes.

The moral, I suppose, is as vivid as a vapor trail: If we are going to survive and enjoy it, we will have to keep our minds and thinking flexible. How else can the swain of the future learn to pick the right assembly-line diamond, catch the perpendicular flight to Niagara Falls, and have his biscuits burned on a nuclear pile?